Lecture Notes in Computer Science   5913

Commenced Publication in 1973
Founding and Former Series Editors:
Gerhard Goos, Juris Hartmanis, and Jan var

Anupam Datta (Ed.)

Advances in Computer Science – ASIAN 2009

Information Security and Privacy

13th Asian Computing Science Conference
Seoul, Korea, December 14-16, 2009
Proceedings

 Springer

Volume Editor

Anupam Datta
Carnegie Mellon University
5000 Forbes Ave
Pittsburgh, PA 15213, USA
E-mail: danupam@cmu.edu

Library of Congress Control Number: 2009939838

CR Subject Classification (1998): F.3, E.3, D.4.6, K.6.5, C.2, D.2.4, J.2

LNCS Sublibrary: SL 1 – Theoretical Computer Science and General Issues

ISSN   0302-9743
ISBN-10   3-642-10621-8 Springer Berlin Heidelberg New York
ISBN-13   978-3-642-10621-7 Springer Berlin Heidelberg New York

springer.com

© Springer-Verlag Berlin Heidelberg 2009
Printed in Germany

Typesetting: Camera-ready by author, data conversion by Scientific Publishing Services, Chennai, India
Printed on acid-free paper   SPIN: 12801756   06/3180   5 4 3 2 1 0

Preface

This volume contains the papers presented at the 13th Annual Asian Computing Science Conference (ASIAN 2009) held in Seoul, South Korea, December 14-16, 2009. The theme of this year's conference was "Information Security and Privacy: Theory and Practice." The series of annual Asian Computing Science Conferences (ASIAN) was initiated in 1995 by AIT, INRIA and UNU/IIST to provide a forum for researchers in computer science from the Asian continent and to promote interaction with researchers in other regions. Accordingly, the conference moves every year to a different center of research throughout Asia. This year ASIAN was co-located with the 7th Asian Symposium on Programming Languages and Systems (APLAS 2009).

We received 45 submissions. Each submission was carefully reviewed by the Program Committee. The committee decided to accept seven regular papers and three short papers, which are included in the proceedings. The program also included two invited talks by Jean Goubault-Larrecq (LSV, ENS Cachan, CNRS, INRIA Saclay) and Naoki Kobayashi (Tohoku University); the corresponding papers are also included in this volume. I would like thank the Program Committee members and external reviewers for their work in selecting the contributed papers. I would also like to thank the Steering Committee for their timely advice, in particular, Kazunori Ueda and Iliano Cervesato. Finally, I would like to thank the Local Arrangements Chair, Gyesik Lee, for ensuring that the conference proceeded smoothly.

September 2009   Anupam Datta

Conference Organization

Steering Committee

Iliano Cervesato
Philippe Codognet
Joxan Jaffar

Mitsu Okada
R.K. Shyamasundar
Kazunori Ueda

Program Chair

Anupam Datta

Program Committee

Michael Backes
Adam Barth
Lujo Bauer
Bruno Blanchet
Iliano Cervesato
Stephen Chong
Hubert Comon-Lundh
Veronique Cortier
Yuxi Fu
Vinod Ganapathy
Masami Hagiya

Dilsun Kaynar
Steve Kremer
Ralf Kuesters
Sanjiva Prasad
R. Ramanujam
Andre Scedrov
Vitaly Shmatikov
Kazunori UEDA
Bogdan Warinschi
Yuqing Zhang
Liang Zhenkai

Local Arrangements Chair

Gyesik Lee

External Reviewers

Attrapadung, Nuttapong
Bursztein, Elie
Cai, Xiaojuan
Chadha, Rohit
Fuchsbauer, Georg
Hanaoka, Goichiro
Jayadeva, Jayadeva
Kalra, Prem
Long, Yu

Mitra, Niloy
O'Neal, Adam
Ota, Kazuo
Pereira, Olivier
Qi, Zhengwei
Rial, Alfredo
Sans, Thierry
Sarkar, Palash
Shi, Elaine

Shin, SeongHan
Suresh, S.P.
Truderung, Tomasz
Tschantz, Michael Carl
Tsukada, Yasuyuki
Tuengerthal, Max
Umeno, Shinya

Vergnaud, Damien
Vogt, Andreas
Yang, Liu
Ying, Mingsheng
Zhang, Rui
Zhao, Jianjun

Table of Contents

"Logic Wins!"

Jean Goubault-Larrecq[*]

LSV, ENS Cachan, CNRS, INRIA Saclay
ENS Cachan, 61, avenue du président Wilson, 94230 Cachan, France
goubault@lsv.ens-cachan.fr

Abstract. Clever algorithm design is sometimes superseded by simple encodings into logic. We apply this motto to a few case studies in the formal verification of security properties. In particular, we examine confidentiality objectives in hardware circuit descriptions written in VHDL.

1 Introduction

As a computer scientist, I tend to be fond of clever, efficient algorithmic solutions to any particular problem I may have. Probably like many computer scientists, I have long thought that the key to success was *clever algorithm design*, together with well-crafted data structures, clever implementation techniques and some hack power. I certainly did not believe seriously that elegant semantic foundations, nice encodings into logic, or similar mathematically enjoyable concerns could actually help *in practice*, although I took some delight in these as well. Over the years, I came to realize I was wrong[1], and I will illustrate this on a few examples. In all these examples, my concern will be to find algorithms to verify security properties of protocols, and logic will be instrumental in finding elegant and efficient solutions.

Now, in this paper, by logic I will mean fragments of first-order logic expressible as finite sets of Horn clauses. I will also concentrate on security properties, and in fact on abstract interpretation frameworks for security properties. One sometimes loses precision in abstract interpretation, and I will take this for granted: I won't use logic to solve

---

[*] Partially funded by RNTL project Prouvé.

[1] An anecdote to explain the title. In 1996, I realized that binary decision diagrams (BDDs), an extremely efficient way of handling Boolean functions [4], could be used to provide a basis for tableaux-style proof search in *non-classical* (modal, intuitionistic) logics, only orders of magnitude faster than previous implementations [13]. I needed to compare my algorithm to other implementations. Since there were not too many non-classical provers available at that time, I compared my clever implementation, specialized to the case of the run-of-the-mill system **LJ** for intuitionistic propositional logic, to a quick, naive implementation of proof-search in Roy Dyckhoff's contraction-free sequent calculus **LJT** for intuitionistic logic [10]. Now **LJT** is only meant to avoid a rather painful check for loops during proof search that is inherent to **LJ**, but is otherwise not intended to be a basis for efficient implementations. Despite this, my naive implementation of **LJT** beat my sophisticated, state-of-the-art BDD-based implementation of **LJ** flat-handed. This has taught me a lesson, which I have been meditating over ever since. When I told this to Roy Dyckhoff at the Tableaux conference in 1996, his reaction was simply "Logic wins!", in a deep voice, and with clear pleasure in his eyes.

A. Datta (Ed.): ASIAN 2009, LNCS 5913, pp. 1–16, 2009.

security problems exactly but to obtain reasonably precise, terminating algorithms. One may say that my motto is the infamous 80-20 rule: do 80% of the work with only 20% of the effort. Logic will be crucial to reach this goal.

After some preliminaries, I'll show how this motto helps us analyze weak secrecy and correspondence assertions in the spi-calculus, expanding on work by Nielson, Nielson and Seidl [19] (Section 2). I'll then comment on generic abstraction algorithms in Section 3, and proceed to something new in Section 4: verifying confidentiality objectives in hardware circuit descriptions written in VHDL. I'll conclude by proposing some open problems in Section 5.

Preliminaries. We shall consider terms s, t, u, v, ..., over a fixed, usually implicit, finite signature. We assume finitely many predicate symbols p, q, ..., and countably many variables $X, Y, Z, \ldots$ *Atoms* are expressions of the form $p(t)$. Notice that all our predicates are unary. This incurs no loss of generality, as e.g., $p(t, u)$ is easily encoded as $p(c(t, u))$ for some fresh binary function symbol c.

Substitutions σ are finite maps from variables to terms, e.g., $[X_1 := t_1, \ldots, X_n := t_n]$, and substitution application $t\sigma$ works in parallel, i.e., $X_i\sigma = t_i$, $X\sigma = X$ if $X \notin \{X_1, \ldots, X_n\}$, $f(t_1, \ldots, t_n)\sigma = f(t_1\sigma, \ldots, t_n\sigma)$.

Horn clauses C are of the form $H \Leftarrow B$ where the *head* H is either an atom $p(t)$ or $\perp$, and the *body* B is a finite set $A_1, \ldots, A_n$ of atoms. The meaning is that C is true iff H is true whenever all of $A_1, \ldots, A_n$ are. If B is empty ($n = 0$), then $C = H$ is a *fact*.

We always assume that there is at least one constant, i.e., one function symbol of arity 0, so that the set of ground atoms is non-empty. An atom or a term is *ground* iff it contains no variable. A *Herbrand model* I of a set of clauses is a set of ground atoms; intuitively, those that we want to consider as true. Any satisfiable set S of Horn clauses has a least Herbrand model, in the sense that it is a Herbrand model, and is contained in every other Herbrand model of S. This can be defined as the least fixpoint lfp T_S of the monotone operator $T_S(I) = \{A\sigma \mid A \Leftarrow A_1, \ldots, A_n \in S, A\sigma \text{ ground}, A_1\sigma \in I, \ldots, A_n\sigma \in I\}$. If $\perp \in \text{lfp } T_S$, then S is unsatisfiable. Otherwise, S is satisfiable, and lfp T_S is a set of ground atoms, which happens to be the least Herbrand model of S. Note that $A \in \text{lfp } T_S$ iff A is *deducible* by finitely many applications of clauses of S, seen as rules allowing one to deduce heads from the corresponding bodies.

Given a finite set S of Horn clauses, it is undecidable whether S is satisfiable, i.e., whether $\perp \notin \text{lfp } T_S$, even in very constrained cases [8]. However, some specific formats of Horn clauses *are* decidable. One that I find most remarkable is the $\mathcal{H}_1$ class, which was identified as such by Nielson, Nielson and Seidl [19], but had been introduced with a different name by Weidenbach [21]. Using the presentation of [15], $\mathcal{H}_1$ clauses are Horn clauses whose head is restricted to be of the form $\perp$, $p(X)$ for some variable X, or $p(f(X_1, \ldots, X_n))$ for pairwise distinct variables $X_1, \ldots, X_n$ ($f(X_1, \ldots, X_n)$ is then called a *flat* term). Note that bodies of $\mathcal{H}_1$ clauses are not restricted in any way. Deciding $\mathcal{H}_1$ clause sets is decidable, and EXPTIME-complete [19,15]. The h1 tool in the h1 tool suite [14] is an efficient implementation of the resolution algorithm of [15].

We shall exert considerable freedom in writing formulae. For example, we shall use predicates of the form $P \vdash e \simeq \_$, where the hole $\_$ is meant to denote the missing argument, and we shall write $[P \vdash e \simeq t]$ instead of $P \vdash e \simeq \_(t)$.

Let us quickly turn to abstract interpretation. All extensional and non-trivial properties of programs are undecidable, by Rice's theorem. The reachability problem in the more constrained world of cryptographic protocols is also undecidable [9]. In verifying such properties, one must therefore choose between correct and complete procedures that will fail to terminate on some inputs, or correct, terminating algorithms that cannot be complete. The latter strand is the tradition in the so-called *abstract interpretation* community. We also speak of *over-approximation*, because the set of inputs that are accepted by an abstract interpretation algorithm is only guaranteed to be a superset of those satisfying the intended property.

2   Reachability and Correspondence Assertions in the Spi-Calculus

Nielson *et al.* [19] introduced $\mathcal{H}_1$ as a convenient tool in deciding reachability in (an over-approximated semantics of) the spi-calculus [1]. As such, they literally applied the "Logic wins!" motto, going through logic instead of defining an ad hoc algorithm.

Reachability questions include so-called *weak secrecy* questions, since the message M remains secret in the protocol P iff $P|DY(I_0, c)$ does not rewrite in any finite number of steps to a process where M is sent over channel c, where $DY(I_0, c)$ is a *Dolev-Yao observer*, see below. We shall provide a slightly more precise over-approximation, and also deal with authentication properties, inter alia.

The main trick is to express a few relatively trivial facts about spi-calculus processes, in the guise of Horn clauses. Then, we pay special attention to the form of these clauses, so that they fall into the $\mathcal{H}_1$ class.

$$
\begin{array}{lll}
P, Q, R, \ldots ::= & \texttt{stop} & \text{stop} \\
\mid & !_x P & \text{replication} \\
\mid & P \mid Q & \text{parallel composition} \\
\mid & \nu x; P & \text{fresh name creation} \\
\mid & \texttt{out}(e_1, e_2); P & \text{writing to a channel} \\
\mid & \texttt{in}(e_1, x); P & \text{reading from a channel} \\
\mid & \texttt{let } x = e \texttt{ in } P & \text{local definition} \\
\mid & \texttt{case } e_1 \texttt{ of } f(x_1, \ldots, x_n) \Rightarrow P \texttt{ else } Q & \text{constructor pattern-matching} \\
\mid & \texttt{case } e_1 \texttt{ of } \{x\}_{e_2} \Rightarrow P \texttt{ else } Q & \text{symmetric decryption} \\
\mid & \texttt{case } e_1 \texttt{ of } [x]_{e_2^{-1}} \Rightarrow P \texttt{ else } Q & \text{asymmetric decryption} \\
\mid & \texttt{if } e_1 = e_2 \texttt{ then } P \texttt{ else } Q & \text{equality test} \\
\mid & \texttt{event } f\langle e_1 \rangle; P & \text{event}
\end{array}
$$

Fig. 1. The spi-calculus

Expressions e in the spi-calculus are defined as variables x (distinct from the logical variables X), constructor applications $f(e_1, \ldots, e_n)$, symmetric encryptions $\{e_1\}_{e_2}$ and asymmetric encryptions $[e_1]_{e_2}$, where e_2 serves as key in the latter two forms. *Processes* are described in Figure 1. Note that decryption is handled through pattern-matching. In the case of constructor pattern-matching, $x_1, \ldots, x_n$ are pairwise distinct. Replication $!_x P$ launches several copies of P in parallel, keeping a unique integer id of each in variable x; we write $!P$ when x is irrelevant. We also write $\mathsf{out}(e_1, e_2)$ instead of $\mathsf{out}(e_1, e_2); \mathsf{stop}$ and similarly for other actions. Finally, events $\mathsf{event}\ f\langle e_1\rangle$ are meant to express correspondence assertions, i.e., certain forms of authentication.

The semantics of this language is standard: see [1]. The essential rules are the communication rule $\mathsf{out}(e_1, e_2); P \mid \mathsf{in}(e_1, x); Q \rightarrow (P \mid Q[x := e_2])$, the fact that $P \equiv\rightarrow\equiv Q$ implies $P \rightarrow Q$, where structural congruence $\equiv$ obeys some obvious laws, plus the extrusion law $(\nu x; P) \mid Q \equiv \nu x; (P \mid Q)$ if x is not free in Q.

The Dolev-Yao observer $DY(I_0, c)$ mentioned above, for example, is $\nu id; !A$, where A is the parallel composition of $\mathsf{out}(c, I_0)$ (the Dolev-Yao attacker can emit the *initial knowledge* expression I_0 on channel c), $\mathsf{out}(c, id)$ (it can emit its own identity), $\mathsf{in}(c, x); \mathsf{out}(c, x); \mathsf{out}(c, x)$ (it can duplicate messages), $\nu N; \mathsf{out}(c, N)$ (emit fresh names), $\mathsf{in}(c, x_1); \mathsf{in}(c, x_2); \mathsf{out}(c, \{x_1\}_{x_2})$ and $\mathsf{in}(c, x_1); \mathsf{in}(c, x_2); \mathsf{out}(c, [x_1]_{x_2})$ (encrypt), $\mathsf{in}(c, x); \mathsf{in}(c, x_2); \mathsf{case}\ x\ \mathsf{of}\ \{x_1\}_{x_2} \Rightarrow \mathsf{out}(c, x_1)\ \mathsf{else}\ \mathsf{stop}$ and $\mathsf{in}(c, x); \mathsf{in}(c, x_2); \mathsf{case}\ x\ \mathsf{of}\ [x_1]_{x_2^{-1}} \Rightarrow \mathsf{out}(c, x_1)\ \mathsf{else}\ \mathsf{stop}$ (decrypt), and various processes of the form $\mathsf{in}(c, x_1); \ldots; \mathsf{in}(c, x_n); \mathsf{out}(c, f(x_1, \ldots, x_n))$ or $\mathsf{in}(c, x); \mathsf{case}\ x\ \mathsf{of}\ f(x_1, \ldots, x_n) \Rightarrow (\mathsf{out}(c, x_1) \mid \ldots \mid \mathsf{out}(c, x_n))\ \mathsf{else}\ \mathsf{stop}$, depending whether f is a constructor or a function, and whether it is private or public in the terminology of ProVerif [3].

Fix a spi-calculus process P_0. We define an approximate semantics, specialized to P_0, as follows. First, for every subprocess P of P_0, and every list of variables Ξ, meant to denote the list of variables bound above P in P_0 (except by ν, which will be dealt with differently), we collect all pairs $(Q; \Xi')$ where Q is a subprocess of P, and Ξ' is the list of variables bound above Q in P, in a set $Sub_\Xi(P)$. Formally, let $Sub_\Xi(P) = \{(P; \Xi)\} \cup Sub_\Xi^\pm(P)$, where $Sub_\Xi^\pm(\mathsf{stop}) = \emptyset$, $Sub_\Xi^\pm(!_x P) = Sub_{x, \Xi}(P)$, $Sub_\Xi^\pm(\mathsf{out}(e_1, e_2); P) = Sub_\Xi^\pm(\mathsf{event}\ f\langle e_1\rangle; P) = Sub_\Xi^\pm(P)$, $Sub_\Xi^\pm(\mathsf{in}(e_1, x); P) = Sub_{x, \Xi}(P)$, $Sub_\Xi^\pm(P|Q) = Sub_\Xi^\pm(\mathsf{if}\ e_1 = e_2\ \mathsf{then}\ P\ \mathsf{else}\ Q) = Sub_\Xi(P) \cup Sub_\Xi(Q)$, $Sub_\Xi^\pm(\mathsf{let}\ x = e\ \mathsf{in}\ P) = Sub_{x, \Xi}(P)$, $Sub_\Xi^\pm(\mathsf{case}\ e_1\ \mathsf{of}\ pat \Rightarrow P\ \mathsf{else}\ Q) = Sub_{\Xi', \Xi}(P) \cup Sub_\Xi(Q)$ (where Ξ' is $x_1, \ldots, x_n$ in constructor pattern-matching, and x in the cases of decryption); finally, if $\Xi = x_1, \ldots, x_k$, we let $Sub_\Xi^\pm(\nu x; P) = Sub_\Xi(P[x := \ulcorner \nu x; P \urcorner(x_1, \ldots, x_k)])$, where $\ulcorner \nu x; P \urcorner$ is a (fresh) function symbol, one for each process starting with a name creation action. This is Blanchet's fresh name creation as skolemization trick [3].

We shall also need to represent *contexts* ρ, i.e., finite mappings $[x_1 \mapsto t_1, \ldots, x_k \rightarrow t_k]$ from variables to terms, as terms. We choose to represent such mappings as $c_\Xi(t_1, \ldots, t_k)$, where $\Xi = x_1, \ldots, x_k$ and c_Ξ is a fresh function symbol of arity k.

Without loss of generality, we shall assume that P_0 is *well-formed*, in the intuitive sense that the only expressions e that occur in P_0 are either spi-calculus variables x bound by $!$, in, let, or case (but not by ν), or are to the right of an equals sign $=$ in a let-expression. This is easily achieved by adding extra let constructs in P_0. Formally, we require that whenever $(Q; \Xi') \in Sub_\emptyset(P_0)$, then Q is given by the grammar obtained from Figure 1 by requiring e_1 and e_2, wherever they appear, to be variables x, y; moreover, x and y must be in Ξ' and $x \neq y$. We also require that whenever $(\mathsf{let}\ x = e\ \mathsf{in}\ Q; \Xi') \in Sub_\emptyset(P_0)$, then all the variables in e must occur in Ξ'.

Our approximate semantics will use the following predicate symbols. First, $\rightarrow^* P\langle\!\langle \_\rangle\!\rangle$, for each $(P; \Xi) \in Sub_\emptyset(P_0)$: $[\rightarrow^* P\langle\!\langle \rho\rangle\!\rangle]$ states that execution may reach

P, with values of variables given by context ρ; second, $\_ \triangleright \_$: $[t \triangleright u]$ means that message u was sent on channel t; event $f\langle \_ \rangle$: event $f\langle t \rangle$ says that we have passed the corresponding event in P_0; and auxiliary predicates $\_ \in \mathbb{N}$ ($[t \in \mathbb{N}]$ means that t denotes an integer process id), and for each expression e in P_0, a predicate symbol $P \vdash e \simeq \_$ ($[P \vdash e \simeq t]$ means that expression e may have value t when we reach P in P_0).

We now compile P_0 to a set $S(P_0)$ of $\mathcal{H}_1$ clauses. First, execution starts at P_0: write the fact $[\rightarrow^*\text{main}\langle\!\langle c_\epsilon() \rangle\!\rangle]$, where ϵ is the empty sequence, so that $c_\epsilon()$ is the empty context. Then, for each $(P; \Xi) \in Sub_\emptyset(P_0)$, do a case analysis on P. If P is a replication $!_x P_1$, then create a fresh process identifier X and proceed to P_1:

$$[\rightarrow^* P_1 \langle\!\langle c_{x,\Xi}(X, X_1, \ldots, X_k) \rangle\!\rangle] \Leftarrow [\rightarrow^* P \langle\!\langle c_\Xi(X_1, \ldots, X_k) \rangle\!\rangle], [X \in \mathbb{N}] \qquad (1)$$

$$[0 \in \mathbb{N}] \qquad [\mathsf{s}(X) \in \mathbb{N}] \Leftarrow [X \in \mathbb{N}] \qquad (2)$$

If P is a parallel composition $P_1 \mid Q_1$, then state that from P, execution may proceed to P_1 or to Q_1, as in [19], while the context, denoted by Z, does not change:

$$[\rightarrow^* P_1 \langle\!\langle Z \rangle\!\rangle] \Leftarrow [\rightarrow^* P \langle\!\langle Z \rangle\!\rangle] \qquad [\rightarrow^* Q_1 \langle\!\langle Z \rangle\!\rangle] \Leftarrow [\rightarrow^* P \langle\!\langle Z \rangle\!\rangle] \qquad (3)$$

If $P = \nu x; P_1$, then use Blanchet's skolemization trick. Write $\Xi = x_1, \ldots, x_k$, and output the clause:

$$[\rightarrow^* P_1[x := \ulcorner \nu x; P_1 \urcorner (x_1, \ldots, x_k)] \langle\!\langle Z \rangle\!\rangle] \Leftarrow [\rightarrow^* P \langle\!\langle Z \rangle\!\rangle] \qquad (4)$$

At this point, it is probably good to realize why these are $\mathcal{H}_1$ clauses. The head of (4) is just one big predicate symbol $\rightarrow^* P_1[x := \ulcorner \nu x; P_1 \urcorner (x_1, \ldots, x_k)] \langle\!\langle \_ \rangle\!\rangle$ applied to the logical variable Z, for instance. The spi-calculus variables $x_1, \ldots, x_k$ do not serve as logical variables, and are only part of the *name* of the predicate. Similarly, the head of (1) is the predicate $\rightarrow^* P_1 \langle\!\langle \_ \rangle\!\rangle$ applied to the flat term $c_{x,\Xi}(X, X_1, \ldots, X_k)$.

Let us return to the subprocesses P of P_0. When P is an out command, remember that P_0 is well-formed, so P must be of the form $\text{out}(x_i, x_j); P_1$, where $\Xi = x_1, \ldots, x_k$ and $1 \leq i \neq j \leq k$. We then write one clause (5) to state that the value X_j of x_j has now been sent on (the value X_i of) the channel x_i, and another one (6) to state that execution should proceed to P_1:

$$[X_i \triangleright X_j] \Leftarrow [\rightarrow^* P \langle\!\langle c_\Xi(X_1, \ldots, X_k) \rangle\!\rangle] \qquad (5)$$

$$[\rightarrow^* P_1 \langle\!\langle c_\Xi(X_1, \ldots, X_k) \rangle\!\rangle] \Leftarrow [\rightarrow^* P \langle\!\langle c_\Xi(X_1, \ldots, X_k) \rangle\!\rangle] \qquad (6)$$

The case of events, i.e., when $P = \text{event } f\langle x_i \rangle; P_1$, is very similar:

$$\text{event } f\langle X_i \rangle \Leftarrow [\rightarrow^* P \langle\!\langle c_\Xi(X_1, \ldots, X_k) \rangle\!\rangle] \qquad (7)$$

When $P = \text{in}(x_i, x); P_1$, where again $\Xi = x_1, \ldots, x_k$ and $1 \leq i \leq k$, we write one clause stating that one may proceed to P_1 after binding x to any value X found on (the value X_i of) the channel x_i:

$$[\rightarrow^* P_1 \langle\!\langle c_{x,\Xi}(X, X_1, \ldots, X_k) \rangle\!\rangle] \Leftarrow [\rightarrow^* P \langle\!\langle c_\Xi(X_1, \ldots, X_k) \rangle\!\rangle], [X_i \triangleright X] \qquad (8)$$

When $P = \text{let } x = e \text{ in } P_1$, we produce:

$$[\rightarrow^* P_1 \langle\!\langle c_{x,\Xi}(X, X_1, \ldots, X_k) \rangle\!\rangle] \Leftarrow [\rightarrow^* P \langle\!\langle c_\Xi(X_1, \ldots, X_k) \rangle\!\rangle], [P \vdash e \simeq X] \qquad (9)$$

where we define the evaluation of expressions e, given a list of bound variables $\Xi = x_1, \ldots, x_k$, as follows. Clause (10) below states that x_i equals X_i in any context $[x_1 \mapsto X_1, \ldots, x_k \mapsto X_k]$ (represented as the term $c_\Xi(X_1, \ldots, X_k)$). Names are evaluated in clause (11), where we observe that the arguments to $\ulcorner \nu x; Q \urcorner$ must be a suffix $x_i, \ldots, x_k$ of Ξ. Clause (12) deals with subexpressions where a function symbol is applied to pairwise distinct variables (a special case where we can still write an $\mathcal{H}_1$ clause). Finally, clause (13) deals with the remaining cases.

$$[P \vdash x_i \simeq X_i] \Leftarrow [\rightarrow^* P \langle\!\langle c_\Xi(X_1, \ldots, X_k) \rangle\!\rangle] \tag{10}$$

$$[P \vdash \ulcorner \nu x; Q \urcorner (x_i, \ldots, x_k) \tag{11}$$
$$\simeq \ulcorner \nu x; Q \urcorner (X_i, \ldots, X_k)] \Leftarrow [\rightarrow^* P \langle\!\langle c_\Xi(X_1, \ldots, X_k) \rangle\!\rangle]$$

$$[P \vdash f(x_{i_1}, \ldots, x_{i_n}) \simeq f(X_{i_1}, \ldots, X_{i_n})] \Leftarrow [\rightarrow^* P \langle\!\langle c_\Xi(X_1, \ldots, X_k) \rangle\!\rangle] \tag{12}$$
$$(i_1, \ldots, i_j \text{ pairwise distinct})$$

$$[P \vdash f(e_1, \ldots, e_n) \simeq f(X_1, \ldots, X_n)] \Leftarrow [P \vdash e_1 \simeq X_1], \ldots, [P \vdash e_n \simeq X_n] \tag{13}$$
$$(e_1, \ldots, e_n \text{ not pairwise distinct variables})$$

When $P = \texttt{case } x_i \texttt{ of } f(y_1, \ldots, y_n) \Rightarrow P_1 \texttt{ else } Q_1$, with $\Xi = x_1, \ldots, x_k$ and $1 \le i \le k$, we write:

$$[\rightarrow^* P_1 \langle\!\langle c_{y_1, \ldots, y_n, \Xi}(Y_1, \ldots, Y_n, X_1, \ldots, X_k) \rangle\!\rangle] \Leftarrow \tag{14}$$
$$[\rightarrow^* P \langle\!\langle c_\Xi(X_1, \ldots, X_i, \ldots X_k) \rangle\!\rangle], [\rightarrow^* P \langle\!\langle c_\Xi(X_1, \ldots, \underbrace{f(Y_1, \ldots, Y_n)}_{i}, \ldots X_k) \rangle\!\rangle]$$

to handle the case of a match. In the second premise, the argument $f(Y_1, \ldots, Y_n)$ occurs at argument position i, in lieu of X_i; we have made this explicit with an underbrace. Our intent was really to write the clause:

$$[\rightarrow^* P_1 \langle\!\langle c_{y_1, \ldots, y_n, \Xi}(Y_1, \ldots, Y_n, X_1, \ldots, f(Y_1, \ldots, Y_n), \ldots, X_k) \rangle\!\rangle] \Leftarrow$$
$$[\rightarrow^* P \langle\!\langle c_\Xi(X_1, \ldots, f(Y_1, \ldots, Y_n), \ldots X_k) \rangle\!\rangle] \tag{15}$$

however (15) falls outside $\mathcal{H}_1$. But (14) is a safe over-approximation of the latter, in the sense that if $[\rightarrow^* P \langle\!\langle c_\Xi(X_1, \ldots, f(Y_1, \ldots, Y_n), \ldots X_k) \rangle\!\rangle]$ holds, then certainly both premises of (14) hold, with $X_i = f(Y_1, \ldots, Y_n)$, and assuming this equality, the head of (14) implies that of (15). So (14) includes at least all the behaviors intended in (15).

The cases of a failed match are handled by the following clauses, where g ranges over all function symbols other than f:

$$[\rightarrow^* Q_1 \langle\!\langle c_\Xi(X_1, \ldots, X_k) \rangle\!\rangle] \Leftarrow [\rightarrow^* P \langle\!\langle c_\Xi(X_1, \ldots, X_i, \ldots X_k) \rangle\!\rangle], \tag{16}$$
$$[\rightarrow^* P \langle\!\langle c_\Xi(X_1, \ldots, g(Y_1, \ldots, Y_n), \ldots X_k) \rangle\!\rangle]$$

When $P = \texttt{case } x_i \texttt{ of } [x]_{x_j}^{-1} \Rightarrow P_1 \texttt{ else } Q_1$ (with $i \ne j$), we produce the following, where we assume that the only keys that can be used are of the form $\mathrm{pub}(X)$ or $\mathrm{prv}(X)$, and that each form is the inverse of the other:

$$[\rightarrow^* P_1 \langle\!\langle c_{x, \Xi}(X, X_1, \ldots, X_k) \rangle\!\rangle] \Leftarrow [\rightarrow^* P \langle\!\langle c_\Xi(X_1, \ldots, X_k) \rangle\!\rangle], $$
$$[\rightarrow^* P \langle\!\langle c_\Xi(X_1, \ldots, [X]_{\mathrm{prv}(Y)}, \ldots, \mathrm{pub}(Y), \ldots, X_k) \rangle\!\rangle] \tag{17}$$

$$[\rightarrow^* P_1 \langle\!\langle c_{x,\Xi}(X, X_1, \ldots, X_k) \rangle\!\rangle] \Leftarrow [\rightarrow^* P \langle\!\langle c_\Xi(X_1, \ldots, X_k) \rangle\!\rangle],$$
$$[\rightarrow^* P \langle\!\langle c_\Xi(X_1, \ldots, \underbrace{[X]_{\mathrm{pub}(Y)}}_{i}, \ldots, \underbrace{\mathrm{prv}(Y)}_{j}, \ldots, X_k) \rangle\!\rangle] \qquad (18)$$

Finally, we over-approximate the failed match case bluntly, by estimating that one can always go from P to Q_1; this is benign, as in most protocols $Q_1 = \texttt{stop}$:

$$[\rightarrow^* Q_1 \langle\!\langle Z \rangle\!\rangle] \Leftarrow [\rightarrow^* P \langle\!\langle Z \rangle\!\rangle] \qquad (19)$$

We leave symmetric decryption, $P = \texttt{case } x_i \texttt{ of } \{x\}_{x_j} \Rightarrow P_1 \texttt{ else } Q_1$, as an exercise to the reader. Tests $P = \texttt{if } x_i = x_j \texttt{ then } P_1 \texttt{ else } Q_1$ are handled similarly:

$$[\rightarrow^* P_1 \langle\!\langle c_\Xi(X_1, \ldots, X_k) \rangle\!\rangle] \Leftarrow [\rightarrow^* P \langle\!\langle c_\Xi(X_1, \ldots, X_k) \rangle\!\rangle], \qquad (20)$$
$$[\rightarrow^* P \langle\!\langle c_\Xi(X_1, \ldots, \underbrace{X_i}_{i}, \ldots, \underbrace{X_i}_{j}, \ldots, X_k) \rangle\!\rangle]$$
$$[\rightarrow^* Q_1 \langle\!\langle Z \rangle\!\rangle] \Leftarrow [\rightarrow^* P \langle\!\langle Z \rangle\!\rangle] \qquad (21)$$

This terminates our description of the set $S(P_0)$ of clauses.

Assume we wish to prove that some message M remains secret to the Dolev-Yao attacker throughout the execution of some system, represented as a process P. This is equivalent to saying that $P|DY(I_0, c)$ cannot ever send M over the public channel c. (We assume that all public communications of P goes through channel c, which is shared with the attacker.) In turn, this is implied by the fact that $[c \triangleright M]$ is not a logical consequence of $S(P|DY(I_0, c))$, because the latter is an over-approximation of the behavior of $P|DY(I_0, c)$. But $[c \triangleright M]$ is not a logical consequence of $S(P|DY(I_0, c))$ if and only if $S(P|DY(I_0, c))$ plus the single clause $\bot \Leftarrow [c \triangleright M]$ is *satisfiable*.

All these clauses are in $\mathcal{H}_1$, and satisfiability in $\mathcal{H}_1$ is decidable, so we have it: a terminating, sound algorithm for weak secrecy in the spi-calculus, in an abstract interpretation setting. In practice, just use h1 [14], for example, to decide $S(P|DY(I_0, c))$ plus $\bot \Leftarrow [c \triangleright M]$. One may formalize this thus:

Theorem 1. *Let Spi_1 be the spi-calculus of Figure 1, with semantics of processes P_0 given by predicates defined through the clause set $S(P_0)$. Then weak secrecy is decidable in Spi_1, in exponential time.*

One can do much more with $\mathcal{H}_1$. Nielson, Nielson and Seidl observed [19] that $\mathcal{H}_1$ defined *strongly regular relations*, and this makes a deep connection to automata theory. The set $S(P_0)$ is a collection of *definite* clauses, i.e., no clause in $S(P_0)$ has head $\bot$. Sets of definite clauses are always satisfiable: take the Herbrand model containing *all* ground atoms. So $S = S(P_0)$ has a least Herbrand model $\mathrm{lfp}\, T_S$. Now, for each predicate symbol p, let the *language* $L_p(S)$ be the set of ground terms t such that $p(t) \in \mathrm{lfp}\, T_S$; we also say that t is *recognized* at p in S. This generalizes the corresponding notions for tree automata to arbitrary satisfiable sets S of Horn clauses. In particular, we retrieve tree automata [6] by encoding the transition $f(q_1, \ldots, q_n) \rightarrow q$ (whose effect is that whenever t_1 is recognized at q_1, ..., t_n is recognized at q_n, then $f(t_1, \ldots, t_n)$ should be recognized at state q) as the clause $q(f(X_1, \ldots, X_n)) \Leftarrow q_1(X_1), \ldots, q_n(X_n)$.

Nielson, Nielson and Seidl observed that, whenever S was a set of definite $\mathcal{H}_1$ clauses, $L_p(S)$ was always a regular language, i.e., one of the form $L_p(\mathcal{A})$ for some tree automaton $\mathcal{A}$, and that one could compute $\mathcal{A}$ from S in exponential time. In fact, one can compute a tree automaton $\mathcal{A}$ that is *equivalent* to S in exponential time, meaning that $L_p(S) = L_p(\mathcal{A})$ for all predicate symbols p at once. This was refined, following the "Logic wins!" motto, in [15], where I showed that no new algorithm was needed for this: good old, well-known variants of the resolution proof-search rule [2] achieve this already. This is in fact what I implemented in h1 [14].

We use this to decide correspondence assertions as follows. A *correspondence assertion* is a (non-Horn) clause of the form $A \Rightarrow A_1 \vee \ldots \vee A_k$, for some atoms A, $A_1, \ldots$, A_k, and our goal will be to check whether such a clause holds in lfp $T_{S(P_0)}$. Typically, one checks authentication of Alice by Bob, in the form of (non-injective) agreement, following Woo and Lam [22], by writing an event $begin\langle e_1 \rangle$ at the end of a subprocess describing Alice's role, where she sent message e_1, and event $end\langle e_2 \rangle$ in Bob's role, where Bob just received message e_2. We now check that $end\langle X \rangle \Rightarrow begin\langle X \rangle$ holds in lfp $T_{S(P_0)}$, i.e., that there is no term t such that $end\langle t \rangle$ holds in lfp $T_{S(P_0)}$ (Bob received t) but $begin\langle t \rangle$ does not (i.e., Alice never actually sent t).

Although my purpose was different then, I have shown that the model-checking problem for clauses C (in particular, of the form $A \Rightarrow A_1 \vee \ldots \vee A_k$) against models lfp T_S described in the form of $\mathcal{H}_1$ clause sets S, was decidable in [16]: convert S to an equivalent so-called alternating tree automaton $\mathcal{A}$, using the resolution algorithm of [15] for instance, then check whether C holds in the least Herbrand model of $\mathcal{A}$. The latter takes exponential time in the number of predicate symbols of $\mathcal{A}$, equivalently of S, so that the whole process still only takes exponential time. This was implemented in the h1mc model-checker, another part of the h1 tool suite [14]. A bonus is that it also generates a Coq proof of the fact that C indeed holds in lfp T_S, which was the main topic of [16]. Anyway, these logical considerations immediately entail:

Theorem 2. *Non-injective agreement is decidable in Spi$_1$, in exponential time. This is also true of any correspondence assertion $A \Rightarrow A_1 \vee \ldots \vee A_k$, or in fact of any property expressed as a finite set of (not necessarily Horn) clauses.*

3 Logic Programs as Types for Logic Programs

However, we have not gone as far as we could in Section 2. In particular, we have been careful so as to define clauses in the decidable class $\mathcal{H}_1$. But logic allows us not to care, or at least to care less. The idea is to write general Horn clauses, and to let a generic algorithm do the abstraction work for us. I.e., this algorithm must take any set S of clauses, and return a new set S' satisfying: (a) if S' is satisfiable, then so is S, and (b) S' is in some fixed decidable class, e.g., $\mathcal{H}_1$.

That such generic abstraction algorithms (for different decidable classes) exist was discovered by Frühwirth *et al.* [12] in a remarkable piece of work. In the case of $\mathcal{H}_1$, the generic abstraction algorithm is simple, and for the main part consists in introducing fresh predicate symbols to name terms t in heads that are too deep [15]. Formally, let a one-hole context $C[]$ be a term with a distinguished occurrence of the *hole* $[]$. $C[u]$ is $C[]$ with u in place of the hole. $C[]$ is *non-trivial* iff $C[] \neq []$. Then define the rewrite relation $\rightsquigarrow$ on clause sets by:

$$p(C[t]) \Leftarrow \mathcal{B} \quad \rightsquigarrow \quad \begin{cases} p(C[Z]) \Leftarrow \mathcal{B}, q(Z) & (Z \text{ fresh}) \\ q(t) \Leftarrow \mathcal{B} \end{cases} \qquad (22)$$

where t is not a variable, q is fresh, and $C[]$ is a non-trivial one-hole context, and:

$$p(C[X]) \Leftarrow \mathcal{B} \quad \rightsquigarrow \quad p(C[Y]) \Leftarrow \mathcal{B}, \mathcal{B}[X := Y] \qquad (23)$$

where X occurs at least twice in $C[X]$, and Y is a fresh variable. The relation $\rightsquigarrow$ terminates, and any normal form S' of a clause set S satisfies (a) and (b) [15].

So instead of writing clauses, carefully crafted to be in $\mathcal{H}_1$, one may be sloppier and rely on the generic abstraction algorithm. (The h1 tool does this automatically in case the clause set given to it as input is not in $\mathcal{H}_1$.) For example, we *can* write clause (15) as we intended. While replacing it by clause (14) looked like a hack, one can instead use rule (22) in the definition of $\rightsquigarrow$: take $p = \rightarrow^* P_1 \langle\langle \_ \rangle\rangle$, $C[] = c_{y_1,\dots,y_n,\Xi}(Y_1,\dots,Y_n,X_1,\dots,[],\dots,X_k)$, $t = f(Y_1,\dots,Y_n)$, then (15) rewrites to clauses that are about as over-approximated as (14). (We let the reader do the exercise.)

Generic abstraction algorithms give us considerable freedom. I have long been interested in static analysis frameworks for the security of various actual languages, and an early example is a piece of work I did with F. Parrennes in 2003–2005 [17]. Our csur static analyzer takes a C program and security objectives as input, and outputs sets of Horn clauses that over-approximate the system. However, these clauses are in general not Horn, and we rely on the above generic abstraction algorithm to produce $\mathcal{H}_1$ clauses that h1 can work on.

4 Analyzing Hardware Circuits in VHDL

Until now, I have only stated principles that I have been using in the past. What about tackling a new problem? Over the past few years, several people from industrial and military milieus have asked me whether one could design algorithms to verify cryptographic hardware automatically. These are circuits, described in languages such as VHDL [20], with modules implementing pseudo-random number generation, encryption, decryption, hashing, and signatures. One needs to check whether no sensitive datum inside the circuit ever gets leaked out, and this is done by hand to this date.

However, it seems like techniques such as those that we have used above, or in [17], should apply. The following is a first attempt, on a cryptographic variant of a small subset of VHDL, and should be considered as a proof of concept.

Consider the following variant of behavioral VHDL, obtained by enriching the core language used by Hymans [18] with additional cryptographic primitives. We assume a finite set of *signals* x, y, z, ...; "signal" is the VHDL name for a program variable. These will take values from a domain we leave implicit, but which should include cryptographic terms. Expressions e are built from signals as in Section 2. *Processes* are now described by the following grammar:

$P, Q, R, \ldots ::=$	$\texttt{stop}$	stop
	$\mid \texttt{proc}; P$	loop
	$\mid x <= e; P$	signal assignment
	$\mid \texttt{wait on } W \texttt{ for } m; P$	suspension
	$\mid \texttt{if } e_1 = e_2 \texttt{ then } P \texttt{ else } Q$	equality test
	$\mid x <= \nu; P$	fresh name creation
	$\mid f(x_1, \ldots, x_n) <= e_1 \texttt{ in } P \texttt{ else } Q$	constructor pattern-matching
	$\mid \{x\}_{e_2} <= e_1 \texttt{ in } P \texttt{ else } Q$	symmetric decryption
	$\mid [x]_{e_2^{-1}} <= e_1 \texttt{ in } P \texttt{ else } Q$	asymmetric decryption

Constructs above the line are from [18], while constructs below the line are extra cryptographic constructs. (Encryption, hashing, etc., are handled in expressions e, e_1, e_2 as in Section 2, through specific function symbols.) E.g., $f(x_1, \ldots, x_n) <= e_1 \texttt{ in } P \texttt{ else } Q$ is similar to $\texttt{case } e_1 \texttt{ of } f(x_1, \ldots, x_n) \Rightarrow P \texttt{ else } Q$ in the spi-calculus, binding the signals x_1, ..., x_n, except with a signal assignment semantics (see below). In $\texttt{wait on } W \texttt{ for } m; P$, W is a finite set of signals, and $m \in \mathbb{N} \cup \{\infty\}$: this process waits until some signal in W changes, or until m units of time have elapsed, and then proceeds to P. (For complexity purposes, we assume m is written in unary.) A VHDL *program* is a parallel composition of a fixed number of processes $P_1, \ldots, P_n$.

We assume that VHDL programs are well-formed. The critical point is that no two processes in parallel are allowed to write to the same signal. We shall therefore assume that we are given pairwise disjoint sets of signals A_1, ..., A_n, such that any signal assignment $x <= e; P$ in P_i satisfies $x \in A_i$ ($1 \leq i \leq n$). A_i will be called the *domain* of P_i; Hymans [18] uses a slightly more general definition.

Again, we won't give a formal definition of the semantics, the non-cryptographic part of which can be found in Hymans (op. cit.). The loop $\texttt{proc}; P$ executes P in an infinite loop, i.e., it behaves just like $P; \texttt{proc}; P$, where $P; Q$ denotes sequential composition of P and Q, obtained by replacing $\texttt{stop}$ by Q everywhere in P. We need to explain the peculiar semantics of signal assignment, and how suspension is achieved. One should first realize that execution proceeds in successions of *simulation cycles*, where each process P_i runs sequentially until it stops, i.e., until it reaches $\texttt{stop}$ or a suspension $\texttt{wait on } W_i \texttt{ for } m_i; Q_i$; in this case we say that P_i is *waiting* on W_i for m_i units of time, and Q_i is its *continuation*.

Signal assignment $x <= e$ is peculiar in that it does not assign the value of e to x, but instead *schedules* this change of values to happen at the next simulation cycle. Several assignments to the same signal x are allowed in each process P_i, and the value scheduled for the next simulation cycle is the last one to be assigned to x during the simulation cycle. Say that x *has changed* during a simulation cycle if its scheduled new value is different from its current value.

A simulation cycle terminates once every P_i has reached $\texttt{stop}$ or a suspension; simulation cycles may fail to terminate, but this will be irrelevant. Let E be the set of signals that have changed during the simulation cycle. At the end of the simulation cycle, execution proceeds to the next one. First, all signals are updated to their scheduled new values. Then, say that P_i is *resumable* if it is waiting on a set W_i of signals that meets E, i.e., such that $W_i \cap E \neq \emptyset$, or it is waiting for $m_i = 0$ unit of time. (The latter case is not considered in [18], since $m_i \neq 0$ there; allowing for $m_i = 0$ will simplify our clauses below.) If at least one process is resumable, then resume all resumable processes, by executing their continuation. Otherwise, let *time pass*, and resume the first processes whose timeout m_i expires. Time passes in this case only.

We define an abstract semantics of a fixed VHDL program by writing clauses defining some predicates indexed by the simulation cycle number k, ranging from 0 to K. It is indeed important not to abstract away this timing information. Practically, this means that we shall write one clause set per simulation cycle, and we shall therefore be limited to a fixed number K of simulation cycles, a situation not uncommon in model-checking. (We shall lift this restriction later.)

Assume our fixed VHDL program P^0 is the parallel composition of $P^0_1, \ldots, P^0_n$, and write the clause set $S_{\text{VHDL}}(P^0, K)$ defining our abstract semantics for P^0 during K cycles. The process P_i starts at P^0_i in simulation cycle 0. It is customary to assume that VHDL signals must be assigned before they are used, so that the initial context ρ is irrelevant. We shall therefore start in a context mapping each signal in A_i to a dummy value $\perp$. Let Ξ_i be the *domain list* obtained by sorting A_i in some fixed way, and let a_i be the length of Ξ, i.e., the cardinality of A_i. We write:

$$[\rightarrow^*_0 P^0_i \langle\!\langle c_{\Xi_i} (\underbrace{\perp, \ldots, \perp}_{a_i \text{ times}}) \rangle\!\rangle] \tag{24}$$

where the subscript (0 here) to $\rightarrow^*$ is the simulation cycle number. We shall need another predicate $\bigcirc_{ki} \langle\!\langle \_ \rangle\!\rangle$ ("next cycle") recognizing the scheduled environments for simulation cycle k, $1 \leq k \leq K$, and process i, $1 \leq i \leq n$. Initially:

$$\bigcirc_{ki} \langle\!\langle c_{\Xi_i} (\perp, \ldots, \perp) \rangle\!\rangle \tag{25}$$

Now consider the various forms that a process P among $P_1, \ldots, P_n$ may assume at simulation cycle k, $0 \leq k \leq K - 1$. We shall enumerate clauses, one for each $P \in \bigcup^n_{i=1} Sub(P_i)$, where $Sub(P)$ is the set of *subprocesses* of P. We require wait on W for $m'; Q$ to be a subprocess of wait on W for $m; Q$ for all $m' \leq m$, and $Sub(\text{proc}; Q)$ to contain $Q; \text{proc}; Q$ and all its subprocesses. A definition such as $Sub(\text{proc}; Q) = \{\text{proc}; Q\} \cup Sub(Q; \text{proc}; Q)$ would be ill-formed, so use the Fischer-Ladner closure trick [11]. Let $Sub(Q) = Sub_{\text{stop}}(Q)$ where $Sub_P(\text{stop}) = \{P\}$, $Sub_P(\text{proc}; Q) = \{\text{proc}; Q; P\} \cup Sub_{\text{proc};Q;P}(Q)$, $Sub_P(\text{wait on } W \text{ for } m; Q) = \{\text{wait on } W \text{ for } m'; Q; P \mid m' \leq m\} \cup Sub_P(Q)$, $Sub_P(x <= e; Q) = \{x <= e; Q; P\} \cup Sub_P(Q)$ (and similarly for $x <= \nu$), $Sub_P(\text{if } e_1 = e_2 \text{ then } P_1 \text{ else } Q_1) = \{\text{if } e_1 = e_2 \text{ then } P_1; P \text{ else } Q_1; P\} \cup Sub_P(P_1) \cup Sub_P(Q_1)$, and similarly for constructor pattern-matching and decryption. Clearly, $Sub_P(Q)$ is finite. Moreover, an easy induction on Q shows that $Sub_P(Q) = Sub(Q; P)$, so that indeed $Sub(\text{proc}; Q) = \{\text{proc}; Q\} \cup Sub(Q; \text{proc}; Q)$.

Now enumerate i and k, $1 \leq i \leq n$, $0 \leq k \leq K - 1$, and then enumerate $P \in Sub(P_i)$. If $P = \text{proc}; Q$, we just write:

$$[\rightarrow^*_k Q; \text{proc}; Q \langle\!\langle Z \rangle\!\rangle] \Leftarrow [\rightarrow^*_k \text{proc}; Q \langle\!\langle Z \rangle\!\rangle] \tag{26}$$

Assignment is subtler, as we have said. In general, let x_{ij} be the jth signal in Ξ_i. The assignment $P = x_{ij} <= e; Q$ will proceed to Q with its current context Z *unchanged* (clause (27)); only the scheduled value of x_{ij} will change (clause (28)). Clause (29) defines $\text{changed}_{kij}\langle\langle\rho\rangle\rangle$ to over-approximate the cases where x_{ij} has changed during simulation cycle k, with context ρ: we estimate that x_{ij} may have changed if some value has been assigned to it, even when this is x_{ij}'s old value.

$$[\rightarrow_k^* Q\langle\langle Z\rangle\rangle] \Leftarrow [\rightarrow_k^* x_{ij} <= e; Q\langle\langle Z\rangle\rangle] \tag{27}$$

$$\bigcirc_{(k+1)i}\langle\langle c_{\Xi_i}(Y_1, \ldots, \underbrace{X}_{j}, \ldots, Y_{a_i})\rangle\rangle \Leftarrow \bigcirc_{(k+1)i}\langle\langle c_{\Xi_i}(Y_1, \ldots, Y_{a_i})\rangle\rangle, \tag{28}$$
$$[\rightarrow_k^* x_{ij} <= e; Q\langle\langle Z\rangle\rangle],$$
$$[x_{ij} <= e; Q \vdash_k e \simeq X]$$

$$\text{changed}_{kij}\langle\langle Z\rangle\rangle \Leftarrow [\rightarrow_k^* x_{ij} <= e; Q\langle\langle Z\rangle\rangle] \tag{29}$$

In (28), we need to make sense of the predicate $P \vdash_k e \simeq \_$, and this is done by clauses similar to (10), (12) and (13), only with the subscript k added to $\vdash$ and $\rightarrow^*$.

The clauses for $x <= \nu$, if and case constructs are obtained from the corresponding clauses in the spi-calculus by adding k subscripts, and replacing updates of signals by scheduling of new values. E.g., when $P = x_{ij} <= \nu; Q$, we produce the clauses:

$$[\rightarrow_k^* Q\langle\langle Z\rangle\rangle] \Leftarrow [\rightarrow_k^* x_{ij} <= \nu; Q\langle\langle Z\rangle\rangle] \tag{30}$$

$$\bigcirc_{(k+1)i}\langle\langle c_{\Xi_i}(Y_1, \ldots, \underbrace{\ulcorner P \urcorner(Z)}_{j}, \ldots, Y_{a_i})\rangle\rangle \Leftarrow [\rightarrow_k^* x_{ij} <= \nu; Q\langle\langle Z\rangle\rangle], \tag{31}$$
$$\bigcirc_{(k+1)i}\langle\langle c_{\Xi_i}(Y_1, \ldots, Y_{a_i})\rangle\rangle$$

$$\text{changed}_{kij}\langle\langle Z\rangle\rangle \Leftarrow [\rightarrow_k^* x_{ij} <= \nu; Q\langle\langle Z\rangle\rangle] \tag{32}$$

where $\ulcorner P \urcorner = \ulcorner x_{ij} <= \nu; Q \urcorner$ is a fresh function symbol. Note that (31) is not in $\mathcal{H}_1$ as we have defined it. However it is in Nielson *et al.*'s version of $\mathcal{H}_1$, and in this case the generic abstraction algorithm of [15] is exact; i.e., although we could have given an equivalent set of clauses in (our definition of) $\mathcal{H}_1$, we could afford to be lazy.

The case of resumptions is more interesting. Clause (33) handles the case where P (which we recall is in $Sub(P_i)$) is of the form wait on W for $m; Q$, and some signal $x_{i'j}$ in W, for some i', $1 \leq i' \leq n$ and j, $1 \leq j \leq a_{i'}$, has changed during simulation cycle k. We write one such clause for each value of i' and j with $x_{i'j} \in W$. Clause (34) handles the case of a timeout.

$$[\rightarrow_{k+1}^* Q\langle\langle Z'\rangle\rangle] \Leftarrow [\rightarrow_k^* \text{wait on } W \text{ for } m; Q\langle\langle Z\rangle\rangle], \tag{33}$$
$$\text{changed}_{ki'j}\langle\langle Z\rangle\rangle, \bigcirc_{(k+1)i}\langle\langle Z'\rangle\rangle$$

$$[\rightarrow_{k+1}^* Q\langle\langle Z'\rangle\rangle] \Leftarrow [\rightarrow_k^* \text{wait on } W \text{ for } 0; Q\langle\langle Z\rangle\rangle], \bigcirc_{(k+1)i}\langle\langle Z'\rangle\rangle \tag{34}$$

Finally, we must write clauses to handle the cases where time passes. We use our right to over-approximate, and estimate that time may pass even when some subprocess was resumable. Let $P = \text{wait on } W \text{ for } m'; Q \in Sub(P_i)$, where $m' = m + 1$ is a non-zero timeout, different from ∞, in (35):

$$[\rightarrow_{k+1}^* \text{wait on } W \text{ for } m; Q\langle\langle Z'\rangle\rangle] \Leftarrow \bigcirc_{(k+1)i}\langle\langle Z'\rangle\rangle, \tag{35}$$
$$[\rightarrow_k^* \text{wait on } W \text{ for } m + 1; Q\langle\langle Z\rangle\rangle]$$

For each P of the form `wait on` W `for` $m; Q \in Sub(P_i)$ $(m \in \mathbb{N} \cup \{\infty\})$, we also add a clause (36) that states that, when execution is resumed at Q with context Z', the context of scheduled values for the next simulation cycle starts out being just Z':

$$\bigcirc_{(k+1)i} \langle\!\langle Z' \rangle\!\rangle \Leftarrow [\rightarrow_k^* Q \langle\!\langle Z' \rangle\!\rangle] \tag{36}$$

This completes the description of the clause set $S_{\text{VHDL}}(P^0, K)$.

We still need to model interaction with an attacker, which we shall again take to be a Dolev-Yao attacker. To this end, we use a predicate att_k so that $\text{att}_k(t)$ holds whenever the attacker is able to infer the value of t during simulation cycle k. Letting I_0 denote a predicate recognizing the messages initial known to the attacker, we write:

$$\text{att}_0(X) \Leftarrow I_0(X) \tag{37}$$

$$\text{att}_{k+1}(X) \Leftarrow \text{att}_k(X) \tag{38}$$

$$\text{att}_k(\{X\}_Y) \Leftarrow \text{att}_k(X), \text{att}_k(Y) \quad \text{(sym. encryption)} \tag{39}$$

$$\text{att}_k(X) \Leftarrow \text{att}_k(\{X\}_Y), \text{att}_k(Y) \quad \text{(sym. decryption)} \tag{40}$$

$$\text{att}_k([X]_Y) \Leftarrow \text{att}_k(X), \text{att}_k(Y) \quad \text{(asym. encryption)} \tag{41}$$

$$\text{att}_k(X) \Leftarrow \text{att}_k([X]_{\text{pub}(Y)}), \text{att}_k(\text{prv}(Y)) \quad \text{(asymmetric} \tag{42}$$

$$\text{att}_k(X) \Leftarrow \text{att}_k([X]_{\text{prv}(Y)}), \text{att}_k(\text{pub}(Y)) \quad \text{decryption)} \tag{43}$$

$$\text{att}_k(f(X_1, \ldots, X_k)) \Leftarrow \text{att}_k(X_1), \ldots, \text{att}_k(X_k) \tag{44}$$

$$\text{att}_k(X_j) \Leftarrow \text{att}_k(f(X_1, \ldots, X_n)) \tag{45}$$

where $0 \leq k \leq K$ (except $k \leq K - 1$ in (38)), $1 \leq j \leq n$ in (45), and f is usually restricted to sets of so-called public functions in (44), and public constructors in (45), in ProVerif parlance [3]. Note that clause (38) states that the attacker remembers from one simulation cycle to the next one. Call this set of clauses S_{DY}.

Next, we model which signals the attacker can read from and write to, yielding a clause set S_{pub}. For any signal x_{ij} that the attacker can read from, write the following clause (46), and for any signal x_{ij} the attacker can write to, write (47), $1 \leq k \leq K$:

$$\text{att}_k(X_j) \Leftarrow \bigcirc_{ki} \langle\!\langle c_{\Xi_i}(X_1, \ldots, X_{a_i}) \rangle\!\rangle \tag{46}$$

$$\bigcirc_{ki} \langle\!\langle c_{\Xi_i}(X_1, \ldots, \underbrace{X}_{j}, \ldots, X_{a_i}) \rangle\!\rangle \Leftarrow \text{att}_k(X), \bigcirc_{ki} \langle\!\langle c_{\Xi_i}(X_1, \ldots, X_{a_i}) \rangle\!\rangle \tag{47}$$

This is the *interface* of the circuit to the attacker.

We finally write clauses stating which signals are *sensitive*, i.e., which signals hold data that the attacker should never learn, and at which simulation cycles. Let $Sens$ be a set of triples (k, i, j): our goal is to ensure that the contents of signal x_{ij} at simulation cycle k is secret for each $(k, i, j) \in Sens$. Then write the collection $S_{\text{sec}}(Sens)$ of all clauses of the following form, $(k, i, j) \in Sens$:

$$\bot \Leftarrow \text{att}_K(X_j), \bigcirc_{ki} \langle\!\langle c_{\Xi_i}(X_1, \ldots, X_{a_i}) \rangle\!\rangle \tag{48}$$

$S = S_{\text{VHDL}}(P^0, K) \cup S_{\text{DY}} \cup S_{\text{pub}} \cup S_{\text{sec}}(Sens)$ is a collection of $\mathcal{H}_1$ clauses, modulo our remark about (31). Moreover, if S is satisfiable, then no Dolev-Yao attacker can ever obtain the values of sensitive signals at the designated simulation cycles.

Taking the approximate semantics defined by $S_{\text{VHDL}}(P^0, K)$ as a reference semantics for a language that we shall call $\text{VHDL}_1(K)$, we say that the *confidentiality objective* $Sens$ is met by P_0 in VHDL_1, with given interface, iff the Dolev-Yao attacker cannot obtain the value of any signal x_{ij} at any simulation time k for any $(k, i, j) \in Sens$.

Theorem 3. *For any $K \in \mathbb{N}$, for any $VHDL_1(K)$ program P^0, any interface, and any finite set $Sens$, it is decidable in exponential time whether the confidentiality objective $Sens$ is met by P^0 with the given interface.*

This only deals with the case of at most K simulation cycles. One way want to overcome this limitation. The standard cures in abstract interpretation are called *widenings*. Here, there is a trivial, *logic-based* widening: fix k_0 with $0 \leq k_0 < K$, and decide to equate all simulation cycles $k \geq k_0$ that are equal modulo $K - k_0$. This is easy to achieve: realizing that all our predicate symbols have a k subscript, say p_k, just add the clauses $p_{k_0}(X) \Leftarrow p_K(X)$ for all p, in effect adding a loop in time. Call $\text{VHDL}_2(k_0, K)$ the language whose semantics is defined by these clauses in addition to $S_{\text{VHDL}}(P^0)$, for each VHDL program P_0. Since these clauses are again in $\mathcal{H}_1$, we obtain:

Theorem 4. *For any $k_0 < K$, for every $VHDL_2(k_0, K)$ program P^0, for any interface, and any finite set $Sens$, it is decidable in exponential time whether the confidentiality objective $Sens$ is met by P^0 with the given interface.*

5   Conclusion

We hope to have shown how logical encodings afforded us easy terminating abstract interpretation algorithms for security. Doing so, we have made the first forays into the design of algorithms that verify cryptographic circuits. Much still has to be done, though.

For one, we have not considered *equational theories*; e.g., if one ever uses the bitwise exclusive-or $\oplus$, a common practice in hardware circuits, one should really reason modulo the fact that $\oplus$ is associative, commutative, idempotent, and has a unit. One promising avenue stems from [16], where I showed that all that h1 did was essentially looking for finite models. If one replaces h1 by a finite model-finder such as Paradox [5], and applies the latter to the various clause sets described in this paper, with additional equality clauses that axiomatize the ambient equational theory, one may hopefully obtain proofs of security as finite models, with few states [16, Section 8].

Second, one should really consider computational proofs of security instead of the useful, but unsatisfactory, Dolev-Yao model. Approximating a Hoare logic such as [7] through Horn clauses is probably a good starting point for this.

Finally, when one comes to hardware circuits, one is led to evaluate the impact of timing attacks (which we cannot yet, since time was left implicit in our model—only simulation cycles, not time, were handled), but also of fault injections, of differential power analysis, of electromagnetic leaks... this opens a whole can of worms.

Acknowledgments. We thank David Lubicz, Nicolas Guillermin, and Riccardo Bresciani for fruitful interaction on the question of static analysis of VHDL for security.

References

1. Abadi, M., Gordon, A.D.: A calculus for cryptographic protocols. Information and Computation 148(1), 1–70 (1999)
2. Bachmair, L., Ganzinger, H.: Resolution theorem proving. In: Robinson, J.A., Voronkov, A. (eds.) Handbook of Automated Reasoning, ch. 2, vol. I, pp. 19–99. North-Holland, Amsterdam (2001)
3. Blanchet, B.: An efficient cryptographic protocol verifier based on Prolog rules. In: Proc. 14th Computer Security Foundations Workshop, pp. 82–96. IEEE, Los Alamitos (2001)
4. Bryant, R.E.: Graph-based algorithms for boolean functions manipulation. IEEE Trans. Comp. C35(8), 677–692 (1986)
5. Claessen, K., Sörensson, N.: New techniques that improve MACE-style finite model building. In: Baumgartner, P. (ed.) Proc. CADE-19 Workshop W4, Miami, Florida (July 2003)
6. Comon, H., Dauchet, M., Gilleron, R., Jacquemard, F., Lugiez, D., Tison, S., Tommasi, M.: Tree automata techniques and applications (1997), http://www.grappa.univ-lille3.fr/tata (Version of September 6 2005)
7. Courant, J., Daubignard, M., Ene, C., Lafourcade, P., Lakhnech, Y.: Towards automated proofs for asymmetric encryption schemes in the random oracle model. In: Proc. 15th ACM Conf. Computer and Communications Security, pp. 371–380. ACM Press, New York (2008)
8. Devienne, P., Lebègue, P., Parrain, A., Routier, J.-C., Würtz, J.: Smallest Horn clause programs. Journal of Logic Programming 27(3), 227–267 (1994)
9. Durgin, N.A., Lincoln, P.D., Mitchell, J.C., Scedrov, A.: Undecidability of bounded security protocols. In: Workshop on Formal Methods and Security Protocols (July 1999)
10. Dyckhoff, R.: Contraction-free sequent calculi for intuitionistic logic. Journal of Symbolic Logic 57(3), 795–807 (1992)
11. Fischer, M.J., Ladner, R.E.: Propositional dynamic logic of regular programs. Journal of Computer and System Sciences 18, 194–211 (1979)
12. Frühwirth, T., Shapiro, E., Vardi, M.Y., Yardeni, E.: Logic programs as types for logic programs. In: Proc. 6th Symp. Logic in Computer Science, pp. 300–309. IEEE, Los Alamitos (1991)
13. Goubault-Larrecq, J.: Implementing tableaux by decision diagrams. Interner Bericht 1996-32, Institut für Logik, Komplexität und Deduktionssysteme, Universität Karlsruhe (1996)
14. Goubault-Larrecq, J.: The h1 Tool Suite. LSV, ENS Cachan, CNRS, INRIA projet SECSI (2003), http://www.lsv.ens-cachan.fr/~goubault/H1.dist/dh1index.html
15. Goubault-Larrecq, J.: Deciding $\mathcal{H}_1$ by resolution. Inf. Proc. Letters 95(3), 401–408 (2005)
16. Goubault-Larrecq, J.: Finite models for formal security proofs. Journal of Computer Security (to appear 2009); Long version of Towards producing formally checkable security proofs, automatically. In: Proc. 21st Computer Security Foundations Symposium, pp. 224–238. IEEE, Los Alamitos (2008)
17. Goubault-Larrecq, J., Parrennes, F.: Cryptographic protocol analysis on real C code. In: Cousot, R. (ed.) VMCAI 2005. LNCS, vol. 3385, pp. 363–379. Springer, Heidelberg (2005); Long version, with mistakes corrected, submitted to a journal (June 2005); available as LSV Research Report 2009-18 (July 2009)
18. Hymans, C.: Checking safety properties of behavioral VHDL descriptions by abstract interpretation. In: Hermenegildo, M.V., Puebla, G. (eds.) SAS 2002. LNCS, vol. 2477, pp. 444–460. Springer, Heidelberg (2002)
19. Nielson, F., Nielson, H.R., Seidl, H.: Normalizable Horn clauses, strongly recognizable relations and Spi. In: Hermenegildo, M.V., Puebla, G. (eds.) SAS 2002. LNCS, vol. 2477, pp. 20–35. Springer, Heidelberg (2002)

20. VHDL synthesis interoperability working group (April 1998),
    `http://www.eda.org/siwg/`
21. Weidenbach, C.: Towards an automatic analysis of security protocols in first-order logic. In:
    Ganzinger, H. (ed.) CADE 1999. LNCS (LNAI), vol. 1632, pp. 314–328. Springer,
    Heidelberg (1999)
22. Woo, T.Y.C., Lam, S.S.: A semantic model for authentication protocols. In: IEEE Symposium
    on Security and Privacy, pp. 178–194. IEEE, Los Alamitos (1993)

Higher-Order Program Verification and Language-Based Security
(Extended Abstract)

Naoki Kobayashi

Tohoku University

Abstract. Language-based security has been a hot research area of computer security in the last decade. It addresses various concerns about software security by using programming language techniques such as type systems and program analysis/transformation. Thus, advance in programming language research can also benefit language-based security. This paper reports some recent advance in verification techniques for higher-order programs, and discusses its applications to language-based security. More specifically, we summarize the recent result on model-checking of *higher-order recursion schemes*, and show how it may be applied to language-based security such as secure information flow and stack-based access control.

1 Recursion Schemes and Program Verification

A higher-order recursion scheme (recursion scheme, for short) is a grammar for describing an infinite tree. Unlike regular tree grammars, non-terminal symbols can take trees or higher-order functions on trees as parameters. For example, the following is an order-1 recursion scheme, where the non-terminal F takes a tree as a parameter.

$$S \rightarrow F\,\mathsf{c}$$
$$F\,x \rightarrow \mathsf{a}\,x\,(F\,(\mathsf{b}\,x))$$

The start symbol S is reduced as follows:

$$S \longrightarrow F\,\mathsf{c} \longrightarrow \mathsf{a}\,\mathsf{c}\,(F\,(\mathsf{b}\,\mathsf{c})) \longrightarrow \mathsf{a}\,\mathsf{c}\,(\mathsf{a}\,(\mathsf{b}\,\mathsf{c})\,(F\,(\mathsf{b}(\mathsf{b}\,\mathsf{c}))))) \longrightarrow \cdots,$$

and the following infinite tree is generated.

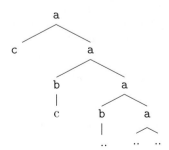

A. Datta (Ed.): ASIAN 2009, LNCS 5913, pp. 17–23, 2009.

From a programming language point of view, a higher-order recursion scheme is a simply-typed call-by-name functional program with recursion and tree constructors (but without destructors).

A major breakthrough was brought by Ong [1], who showed that the modal μ-calculus model checking of recursion schemes ("Given a recursion scheme $\mathcal{G}$ and a modal μ-calculus formula φ, does the tree generated by $\mathcal{G}$ satisfy φ?") is decidable.[1] The model-checking of recursion schemes subsumes finite-state model checking and pushdown model checking, as recursion schemes are at least as expressive as higher-order pushdown systems (for describing trees) [2]. We have recently applied the model checking of recursion schemes to various verification problems of higher-order programs, including reachability, flow analysis, resource usage verification [3], and exact type checking of XML-processing programs [4,5,6]. The idea behind those pieces of work is that, given a simply-typed functional program with recursion, one can transform it into a recursion scheme that generates a tree containing all information about interesting event sequences or program output. For example, consider the following program that accesses file "foo" [4]:

```
let rec f x = if * then close(x) else read(x); f x in
let fp = open_in "foo" in f(fp)
```

It can be translated into the following recursion scheme $\mathcal{G}$:

$$S \rightarrow F\,\mathsf{fp}\,\mathsf{end} \qquad F\,x\,k \rightarrow \mathsf{br}\,(\mathsf{close}\,k)\,(\mathsf{read}\,(F\,x\,k))$$

It generates the following tree:

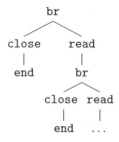

Note that the tree above represents all the access sequences to file "foo", so that, by model-checking the recursion scheme, one can verify that the file is accessed in a valid manner.

The worst-case time complexity of model-checking recursion schemes is n-EXPTIME (where n is the largest order of the type of a non-terminal: see [1,7]). Thus, one may think that the model-checking of recursion schemes is only of theoretical interest. A type-based model checking algorithm, however, has recently been developed that actually runs reasonably fast for recursion schemes obtained from various program verification problems [5,6].

---

[1] In prior to Ong's result, Knapik et al. [2] showed the decidability for a subclass of recursion schemes called *safe* recursion schemes. From the viewpoint of application to program verification, however, the safety restriction is rather restrictive.

2   Applications to Language-Based Security

Based on the results summarized above, it is natural to expect that one can also apply model-checking of recursion schemes to language-based security. We consider a simply-typed, call-by-value λ-calculus with recursion and booleans below, and sketch that non-interference and stack-based access control are decidable for that language.[2]

The syntax of the language is:

$$e ::= \mathbf{true} \mid \mathbf{false} \mid x \mid e_0 e_1 \mid \lambda x.e \mid \mathbf{fun}(f, x, e) \mid \mathbf{if} \ e_1 \ \mathbf{then} \ e_2 \ \mathbf{else} \ e_3$$

Here, $\mathbf{fun}(f, x, e)$ denotes a recursive function. The type system and the call-by-value operational semantics are defined as usual.

2.1   Non-interference

The non-interference property defined below is a formal criterion for secure information flow. It states that information about an input value does not flow to the output; see [8] for a nice survey of secure information flow.

Definition 1 (non-interference). *Let e be a term of type $\mathbf{bool} \to \mathbf{bool}$. The term e satisfies* non-interference *if, for every $b \in \{\mathbf{true}, \mathbf{false}\}$, $e(\mathbf{true})$ evaluates to b if and only if $e(\mathbf{false})$ evaluates to b.*

Given a term e' of type $\mathbf{bool}$, one can easily transform it into a recursion scheme that generates a tree consisting of a single node b just if e' evaluates to b. For example, consider the following program:

```
let g x = if x then false else true in
let f x = if x then g x else false in
  f true
```

As usual, $\mathbf{let} \ f(x) = e_0 \ \mathbf{in} \ e_1$ is an abbreviated form of $(\lambda f.e_1)\mathbf{fun}(f, x, e_0)$. It can be transformed into the following recursion scheme:

$$\begin{aligned}
S &\to F \ \mathit{True} \ \mathbf{true} \ \mathbf{false} \\
G \ x \ t \ f &\to x \ \mathit{False} \ \mathit{True} \ t \ f \\
F \ x \ t \ f &\to x \ (G \ x) \ \mathit{False} \ t \ f \\
\mathit{True} \ t \ f &\to t \\
\mathit{False} \ t \ f &\to f
\end{aligned}$$

Here, S corresponds to the main body of the program, and G and F correspond to functions g and f respectively. (The reason why G and F take additional parameters is that both sides of each rule of a recursion scheme must have a tree type.) Booleans $\mathbf{true}$ and $\mathbf{false}$ have been encoded into $\lambda t.\lambda f.t$ and $\lambda t.\lambda f.f$ respectively. The conditional $\mathbf{if} * e_0 \ e_1 e_2$ has been encoded into $e_0 \ e_1 \ e_2$ as usual.

---

[2] Formal proofs of the decidability are however deferred to a longer version of this paper.

It is easy to see that the recursion scheme generates a tree consisting of a single node `false`, which is the same output as the original program.

Given a term e of type **bool** $\rightarrow$ **bool**, one can transform $e(\textbf{true})$ and $e(\textbf{false})$ into recursion schemes, and then apply the model checking to decide whether $e(\textbf{true})$ and $e(\textbf{false})$ output b for each $b \in \{\textbf{true}, \textbf{false}\}$. Thus, we have:

Theorem 1. *The non-interference property is decidable (for the language above).*

Note that although e does not take a higher-order function, arbitrary higher-order functions may be used inside e. The same result holds for the call-by-name language.

The above decidability result does not extend to the higher-order case. Let us write $\approx_\tau$ for the standard observational equivalence at type τ.

Definition 2 (higher-order non-interference). *Let e be a term of type* **bool** $\rightarrow \tau$. *The term e satisfies* non-interference *if $e(\textbf{true}) \approx_\tau e(\textbf{false})$.*

From Loader's result [9], it follows that $\approx_\tau$ is undecidable in general,[3] hence so is the higher-order non-interference.

2.2 Stack-Based Access Control

Stack inspection [10,11,12] is a mechanism for controlling resource accesses based on call sequences of functions or methods. Following Pottier et al. [11],[4] we extend the language as follows:

$$e ::= \cdots \mid R[e] \mid \textbf{enable } R \textbf{ in } e \mid \textbf{check } R \textbf{ in } e$$

Here, R represents a set of access permissions. The expression $R[e]$ updates the current permissions (say, R_0) with $R \cap R_0$, and executes e; after evaluating e, the permissions R_0 is restored. The expression **enable** R **in** e adds R to the current permissions, and executes e, and **check** R **in** e checks whether R is a subset of the current permissions, and if so, executes e; otherwise the program is aborted. Please consult [11,12] for the formal semantics of those primitives.

Consider the following program.

```
let f x = Trusted[check Trusted then x else fail] in
let g x = Untrusted[f x] in
  g true
```

Here, `Trusted` (`Untrusted`, resp.) is a set of permissions given to trusted principals. The program first invokes `g` (which is untrusted), which in turn invokes

---

[3] Loader's undecidability is for call-by-name, finitary PCF, but one can modify it to derive the undecidability of the observational equivalence for call-by-value, finitary PCF.

[4] Pottier et al. also allows permission testing **test** e_0 **then** e_1 **else** e_2. We conjecture that the decidability result below holds also with permission testing.

trusted code f. The permission test in f fails, since it has been invoked through g, so that the current permission is the intersection of Untrusted and Trusted.

On the other hand, the permission test in the following program succeeds, since f is invoked only after the call of h has returned.

```
let f x = Trusted[check Trusted in x] in
let h x = Untrusted[x] in
  f(h true)
```

We consider the following stack-based access control problem (SBAC, for short):

> "Given a term e of type **bool**, will e be aborted (due to the failure of a check opertion)?"

We show that SBAC can be encoded into a model-checking problem for a recursion scheme.

The idea of the encoding is to transform a term e into a recursion scheme that generates a tree consisting of sequences of framing ($R[\cdot]$), enable, and check operations.

For example, the first program above is transformed into the following recursion scheme:

$$S \rightarrow G \ True \ (\lambda t.\lambda x.t)$$
$$F \ x \ k \rightarrow k \ (\texttt{frameTrusted} \ (\texttt{checkTrusted end})) \ x$$
$$G \ x \ k \rightarrow F \ x \ (\lambda t.\lambda x.k \ (\texttt{frameUntrusted} \ t) \ x)$$

Here, we have used λ-abstractions for the sake of readability. The idea is similar to that of the CPS (continuation-passing-style) transformation. The function F takes an additional parameter k, which takes a tree representing the event sequences and a return value of F. The recursion scheme above generates the following tree:

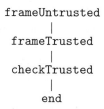

```
frameUntrusted
      |
 frameTrusted
      |
 checkTrusted
      |
     end
```

To check whether the program is aborted, it suffices to check whether checkTrusted occurs below frameUntrusted.

The second program is transformed into the following recursion scheme.

$$S \rightarrow H \ True \ (\lambda t_1.\lambda x_1.(F \ x_1 \ (\lambda t_2.\lambda x_2.\textsf{seq} \ t_1 \ t_2)))$$
$$F \ x \ k \rightarrow k \ (\texttt{frameTrusted} \ (\texttt{checkTrusted end})) \ x$$
$$H \ x \ k \rightarrow k \ (\texttt{frameUntrusted end}) \ x$$

The tree generated by the recursion scheme is:

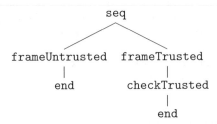

Since `checkTrusted` does not occur below `frameUntrusted`, the second program is safe.

As sketched above, one can always transform a term of type **bool** into a recursion scheme that generates a tree representing sequences of framing, enabling, and checking of permissions. SBAC is therefore decidable. (Note that the actual transformation is a little more complicated than sketched above, because of the need to handle non-termination. More details will be described in a longer version.)

Remark 1. Another way for encoding SBAC into a model chekcing problem for a recursion scheme is to transform a program into a recursion scheme (extended with finite data domains [6]) that computes the current permission eagerly and passes it as an extra argument of each function, so that the recursion scheme generates a tree consisting of a single node `fail` if and only if the original program is aborted. This encoding is probably simpler, although the above encoding may be more intuitive.

2.3   Further Directions

In this paper, we discussed two applications of higher-order model checking to language-based security: secure information flow and stack-based access control. We think higher-order model checking is applicable to many other problems in language-based security. For example, we expect that our technique for SBAC is also applicable to history-based access control [13,14].

At this moment, it is not clear how much our verification method scales in practice. Even if automated verification does not scale, however, our method may be useful in the context of proof-carrying code [15]. Our model-checking algorithm for recursion schemes [5] is based on type inference. Therefore, if type information is given as a certificate of the correctness of a program, then the correctness can be checked efficiently by a type checking (instead of inference) algorithm.

We have considered a simply-typed language having only booleans as base values. For infinite data domains such as integers, predicate abstractions can be used to obtain a sound (but incomplete) verification method. For a language with more advanced types (such as recursive types), it is unclear whether a similar approach is applicable (even if we give up the completeness of a verification algorithm).

Acknowledgments

We would like to thank Luke Ong for pointing us to Loader's work on the undecidability of finitary PCF.

References

1. Ong, C.H.L.: On model-checking trees generated by higher-order recursion schemes. In: LICS 2006, pp. 81–90. IEEE Computer Society Press, Los Alamitos (2006)
2. Knapik, T., Niwinski, D., Urzyczyn, P.: Higher-order pushdown trees are easy. In: Nielsen, M., Engberg, U. (eds.) FOSSACS 2002. LNCS, vol. 2303, pp. 205–222. Springer, Heidelberg (2002)
3. Igarashi, A., Kobayashi, N.: Resource usage analysis. ACM Transactions on Programming Languages and Systems 27(2), 264–313 (2005)
4. Kobayashi, N.: Types and higher-order recursion schemes for verification of higher-order programs. In: Proceedings of ACM SIGPLAN/SIGACT Symposium on Principles of Programming Languages, pp. 416–428 (2009)
5. Kobayashi, N.: Model-checking higher-order functions. In: Proceedings of PPDP 2009 (to appear 2009)
6. Kobayashi, N., Tabuchi, N., Unno, H.: Higher-order multi-parameter tree transducers and recursion schemes for program verification. Preprint (2009)
7. Kobayashi, N., Ong, C.H.L.: Complexity of model checking recursion schemes for fragments of the modal mu-calculus. In: Proceedings of ICALP 2009. LNCS. Springer, Heidelberg (2009)
8. Sabelfeld, A., Myers, A.C.: Language-based information-flow security. IEEE J. Selected Areas in Communications 21(1), 5–19 (2003)
9. Loader, R.: Finitary pcf is not decidable. Theoretical Computer Science 266(1-2), 341–364 (2001)
10. Lindholm, T., Yellin, F.: The Java Virtual Machine Specification, 2nd edn. Addison Wesley, Reading (1999)
11. Pottier, F., Skalka, C., Smith, S.F.: A systematic approach to static access control. ACM Transactions on Programming Languages and Systems 27(2), 344–382 (2005)
12. Fournet, C., Gordon, A.D.: Stack inspection: Theory and variants. ACM Transactions on Programming Languages and Systems 25(3), 360–399 (2003)
13. Abadi, M., Fournet, C.: Access control based on execution history. In: Proceedings of the Network and Distributed System Security Symposium (NDSS 2003). The Internet Society, San Diego (2003)
14. Wang, J., Takata, Y., Seki, H.: HBAC: A model for history-based access control and its model checking. In: Gollmann, D., Meier, J., Sabelfeld, A. (eds.) ESORICS 2006. LNCS, vol. 4189, pp. 263–278. Springer, Heidelberg (2006)
15. Necula, G.C.: Proof-carrying code. In: Proceedings of ACM SIGPLAN/SIGACT Symposium on Principles of Programming Languages, pp. 106–119 (1997)

Deducibility Constraints[*]

Sergiu Bursuc[1], Hubert Comon-Lundh[1,2], and Stéphanie Delaune[1]

[1] LSV, CNRS & ENS Cachan & INRIA project SECSI
[2] AIST, Tokyo

Abstract. In their work on tractable deduction systems, D. McAllester and later D. Basin and H. Ganzinger have identified a property of inference systems (the locality property) that ensures the tractability of the Entscheidungsproblem.

On the other hand, deducibility constraints are sequences of deduction problems in which some parts (formulas) are unknown. The problem is to decide their satisfiability and to represent the set of all possible solutions. Such constraints have also been used for deciding some security properties of cryptographic protocols.

In this paper we show that local inference systems (actually a slight modification of such systems) yield not only a tractable deduction problem, but also decidable deducibility constraints. Our algorithm not only allows to decide the existence of a solution, but also gives a representation of all solutions.

1 Introduction

Deciding whether a given statement can be derived from hypotheses, using a set of formal inference rules, is one of the famous issues in proof theory, known as the *Entscheidungsproblem*. This is undecidable for first-order logic and untractable for propositional logic. There are however several formal proof systems for which the problem is tractable, for instance Horn propositional logic, but also the so-called Dolev-Yao intruder deduction rules. D. McAllester [13] observed that *any* inference system which is *local* yields a tractable Entscheidungsproblem. D. Basin and H. Ganzinger [1] proved that locality is equivalent to a saturation property of the set of inference rules.

The Dolev-Yao inference system is local (and saturated with respect to the subterm ordering). This is why deciding whether a message can be computed by an attacker from a finite set of messages can be performed in polynomial (actually linear) time in this formal proof system. Now, if we consider an active attacker, we need not only to solve the Entscheidungsproblem, but a more general problem in which some statements and proofs are unknown: this corresponds to the attacker's choices. This was formalized in [14], using *deducibility constraints*. There are many historical examples of deducibility constraints in mathematics: Fermat gave a proof of his famous theorem, in which parts were missing; filling the holes amounts to solve a deducibility constraint (in formal arithmetic).

[*] This work has been partially supported by the ANR-07-SESU-002 AVOTÉ.

A. Datta (Ed.): ASIAN 2009, LNCS 5913, pp. 24–38, 2009.
© Springer-Verlag Berlin Heidelberg 2009

The starting point of the present work is the problem of lifting the results of D. McAllester, D. Basin and H. Ganzinger from deducibility to deducibility constraints. For the security protocols, this corresponds to moving from a passive adversary to an active adversary.

We consider formal inference systems without AC-symbols (as in [1]). We also assume that there is a single unary predicate symbol (this corresponds to the attacker knowledge in security protocols). Then we prove that, for any inference system that is saturated in some suitable way (we call it *good*), the deducibility constraints are decidable. Actually, we prove more: we provide with a constraint simplification algorithm that yields *solved forms*. This allows not only to decide the existence of a solution, but also to represent all solutions. Such a feature is used in [7] for deciding trace properties such as authentication and key cycles in security protocols, and also in [11] for deciding game-theoretic security properties such as abuse-freeness. Our results generalize [7] to any good inference system. Finally, we claim that our transformation rules are simple: we simply guess the last inference step and reflect this on the constraint solving. The difficult part is then the design of a complete and terminating strategy.

As in [1], an advantage of our approach is the ability to complete the original inference system; if the inference system is not good (hence we cannot apply directly our results), we may run a saturation procedure, that will yield a good inference system. Of course, such a procedure may not terminate, in which case we can still use our results on the limit (infinite) inference system, but getting an effective algorithm for solving deducibility constraints requires more work, which is out of the scope of this paper.

Related work. The present work is a strict extension of [7]: we consider a class of inference systems instead of a particular one. The intruder theories that are described by a subterm convergent rewriting system can also be casted as good inference systems (but the converse is false). Hence, as far as trace properties are concerned, we also generalize [2,4]. Note however that [2] also considers equivalence properties, that are not covered (yet) by our work. There are also several examples of formal (intruder) proof systems that yield decidable deducibility constraints [16,8,6,5,10]. All these works consider AC-symbols and are incomparable with our results.

Structure of the paper. In Section 2, we introduce good inference systems and their properties. Then, in Section 3, we introduce deducibility constraints. In Section 4, we provide with a set of constraint transformation rules, that is parametrized by any good inference system and that we prove both sound and complete: the solutions of the constraint are the same as the solutions of the solved forms that are obtained by applying the transformation rules. In Section 5, we give a complete and terminating strategy. Due to a lack of space, the proofs are given in [3].

2   Preliminaries

In what follows, we assume that $\mathcal{F}$ is a (ranked) alphabet of *function symbols*. *Terms* are built on this set of function symbols and a set of variables $\mathcal{X}$. *Ground terms* are terms without variables. For any term t (and, by extension, set of terms or any formal expression), $var(t)$ is the set of variable symbols occurring in t and $st(t)$ denotes the set of *subterms* of t defined as usual.

2.1 Inference Systems

We use a natural deduction style for inference systems. An *inference rule* consists in a finite set of terms $\{u_1, \ldots, u_n\}$, the *premises*, and a term u, the *conclusion* such that $var(u) \subseteq var(\{u_1, \ldots, u_n\})$. It is displayed

$$\frac{u_1 \quad \cdots \quad u_n}{u}$$

It may also be convenient to use a deducibility predicate symbol I, in which case the inference rules are simply Horn clauses $I(u_1), \ldots, I(u_n) \to I(u)$.

Example 1. Consider the signature $\mathcal{F} = \{\text{enc}/3, \text{pub}/1, \text{priv}/1, \langle, \rangle/2\}$. The symbols enc and $\langle, \rangle$ represent respectively probabilistic encryption and pairing, pub (resp. priv) represents the public key (resp. private key) construction. A possible set of "Dolev-Yao" inference rules for public-key encryption is:

$$\text{(E)} \quad \frac{x \quad y \quad z}{\text{enc}(x, y, z)} \qquad \text{(D)} \quad \frac{\text{enc}(\text{pub}(y), x, z) \quad \text{priv}(y)}{x} \qquad \text{(K)} \quad \frac{x}{\text{pub}(x)}$$

$$\text{(P)} \quad \frac{x \quad y}{\langle x, y \rangle} \qquad \text{(Proj}_1) \quad \frac{\langle x, y \rangle}{x} \qquad \text{(Proj}_2) \quad \frac{\langle x, y \rangle}{y}$$

Other relevant examples of inference systems are obtained by adding signature schemes, hash functions, symmetric encryption ...

A *proof*, with hypotheses H and conclusion t is a tree, whose nodes are labeled with terms and such that, if a node is labeled s and its sons are labeled $s_1, \ldots, s_n$, then either $n = 0$ (this is a leaf node), and $s \in H$, or else there is an inference rule whose premises are $u_1, \ldots, u_n$ and conclusion is u and a substitution θ such that $u\theta = s$ and, for every i, $u_i\theta = s_i$. We write $H \vdash t$ when there exists a proof with hypotheses H and conclusion t.

We let $\text{step}(\pi)$ be the set of terms labeling the proof π and $\text{leaves}(\pi)$ be the multiset of the terms that labels the leaves of π. If π is a proof, we let $\text{last}(\pi)$ be the last inference step in π, $\text{premises}(\pi)$ be the proofs of the premises of $\text{last}(\pi)$ and $\text{conc}(\pi)$ be its conclusion. More formally,

$$\text{if} \quad \pi = \frac{\pi_1 \quad \cdots \quad \pi_n}{u} \quad \text{then} \quad \begin{cases} \text{last}(\pi) = \dfrac{\text{conc}(\pi_1) \quad \cdots \quad \text{conc}(\pi_n)}{u} \\[2mm] \text{premises}(\pi) = \{\pi_1, \ldots, \pi_n\} \\[2mm] \text{conc}(\pi) = u \end{cases}$$

Example 2. Consider the following proof tree π. Actually, π is a proof in the Dolev-Yao inference system presented in Example 1.

$$\cfrac{\texttt{enc(pub}(k),a,r) \quad \cfrac{\langle \texttt{priv}(k),a\rangle}{\texttt{priv}(k)}\,(\mathsf{Proj}_1)}{a}\,(\mathsf{D})$$

We have that $\texttt{premises}(\pi) = \{\texttt{enc(pub}(k),a,r), \cfrac{\langle\texttt{priv}(k),a\rangle}{\texttt{priv}(k)}\}$, $\texttt{conc}(\pi) = a$,

$\texttt{last}(\pi){=}\cfrac{\texttt{enc(pub}(k),a,r)\ \texttt{priv}(k)}{a}$, $\texttt{leaves}(\pi){=}\{\texttt{enc(pub}(k),a,r),\langle\texttt{priv}(k),a\rangle\}$.

2.2   Good Inference Systems

In the following definitions, we introduce our notion of saturation. Informally, if there is a proof such that some intermediate step is too large (we call this a bad proof and the large step is called a bad pattern), then there must be a simpler proof of the same statement.

If $\mathsf{R} = \cfrac{s_1 \ \cdots \ s_n}{s_0}$ is an inference rule, we let $\mathsf{Max}(\mathsf{R})$ be the multiset of the maximal terms s_i, w.r.t. the subterm ordering $\lhd$.

Definition 1 (bad proof / pattern). *A bad proof is a proof π of the form:*

$$\cfrac{u_1 \ \cdots \ u_n \quad \cfrac{v_1 \ \cdots \ v_m}{u_{n+1}}\,\mathsf{R}_1 \quad u_{n+2} \ \cdots \ u_{n+k}}{v}\,\mathsf{R}_2$$

such that $\mathsf{R}_1 = \cfrac{s_1 \ \cdots \ s_m}{s}$, $\mathsf{R}_2 = \cfrac{t_1 \ \cdots \ t_{n+k}}{t}$, $s \in \mathit{Max}(\mathsf{R}_1)$ *and* $t_{n+1} \in \mathit{Max}(\mathsf{R}_2)$.
A bad pattern *in a proof π is a subproof of π of the form:*

$$\cfrac{\pi_2^1 \ \cdots \ \pi_2^{i-1} \quad \cfrac{\pi_1^1 \ \cdots \ \pi_1^m}{\mathit{conc}(\pi_2^i)}\,\mathsf{R}_1 \quad \pi_2^{i+1} \ \cdots \ \pi_2^n}{v}\,\mathsf{R}_2$$

such that the following proof is a bad proof.

$$\cfrac{\mathit{conc}(\pi_2^1) \ \cdots \ \mathit{conc}(\pi_2^{i-1}) \quad \cfrac{\mathit{conc}(\pi_1^1) \ \cdots \ \mathit{conc}(\pi_1^m)}{\mathit{conc}(\pi_2^i)} \quad \mathit{conc}(\pi_2^{i+1}) \ \cdots \ \mathit{conc}(\pi_2^n)}{v}$$

If $\pi = \mathsf{R}\theta$ is an instance of an inference rule R and $\mathsf{Max}(\mathsf{R}) = \{s_1,\dots,s_k\}$, then $\mu(\pi)$ is the multiset $\{s_1\theta,\dots,s_k\theta\}$. If π is a proof, $\mu(\pi)$ is defined as the multiset of $\mu(\pi')$ for all inference steps π' of π. Formally, if $\texttt{premises}(\pi) = \{\pi_1,\dots,\pi_n\}$, we have that:

$$\mu(\pi) = \mu(\pi_1) \uplus \cdots \uplus \mu(\pi_n) \uplus \mu(\texttt{last}(\pi)).$$

Multisets are ordered using the multiset extensions of their elements: if $\succeq$ is an ordering, we let $\succeq_m$ be its multiset extension.

Definition 2 (good inference system). *An inference system is* good *if there is a total well-founded extension $\prec$ of the subterm ordering $\lhd$ such that, for any bad proof π, there is a proof π' of $\texttt{leaves}(\pi) \vdash \texttt{conc}(\pi)$ with $\texttt{leaves}(\pi') \subseteq \texttt{leaves}(\pi)$ (multiset inclusion), $\mu(\pi') \, (\prec_m)_m \, \mu(\pi)$, and $\mu(\pi') \neq \mu(\pi)$.*

Example 3. The Dolev-Yao inference system described in Example 1 is good. Indeed, all bad proofs are of one of the following forms

$$\frac{\texttt{pub}(u_1) \quad u_2 \quad u_3}{\dfrac{\texttt{enc}(\texttt{pub}(u_1), u_2, u_3) \quad \texttt{priv}(u_1)}{u_2}} \qquad \frac{u_1 \quad u_2}{\dfrac{\langle u_1, u_2 \rangle \quad i = 1, 2}{u_i}}$$

Obviously, for all such π there is a smaller, trivial, proof π' of $\texttt{leaves}(\pi) \vdash \texttt{conc}(\pi)$ such that $\texttt{leaves}(\pi') \subseteq \texttt{leaves}(\pi)$ and $\mu(\pi') \, (\prec_m)_m \, \mu(\pi)$ for any total well-founded extension $\prec$ of the subterm ordering.

Now, we give another example in which the inference system is no longer finite. We consider blind signatures, as described in [9], that are used in some e-voting protocols. The inference system is not good. However, we may complete it and get an infinite, yet recursive, good inference system.

Example 4. We add the following rules to the system of Example 1:

$$(\mathsf{S}) \quad \frac{x \quad y}{\texttt{sign}(x, y)} \qquad (\mathsf{C}) \quad \frac{\texttt{sign}(x, y)}{x}$$

$$(\mathsf{B}) \quad \frac{x \quad y}{\texttt{blind}(x, y)} \qquad (\mathsf{UB}_1) \quad \frac{\texttt{blind}(x, y) \quad y}{x} \qquad (\mathsf{UB}_2) \quad \frac{\texttt{sign}(\texttt{blind}(x, y), z) \quad y}{\texttt{sign}(x, z)}$$

Because of the rule (UB_2), the system not good. The following proof π is bad:

$$\frac{\dfrac{\texttt{sign}(\texttt{blind}(\texttt{blind}(x, x_1), x_2), y) \quad x_2}{\texttt{sign}(\texttt{blind}(x, x_1), y)} \quad x_1}{\texttt{sign}(x, y)}$$

There is no other proof π' of $\texttt{leaves}(\pi) \vdash \texttt{sign}(x, y)$ such that $\texttt{leaves}(\pi') \subseteq \texttt{leaves}(\pi)$. Thus, for any total well-founded extension $\prec$ of $\lhd$, there is no proof π' of $\texttt{leaves}(\pi) \vdash \texttt{sign}(x, y)$ such that $\texttt{leaves}(\pi') \subseteq \texttt{leaves}(\pi)$ and $\mu(\pi') \, (\prec_m)_m \, \mu(\pi)$. However, we may add all shortcuts that correspond to bad proofs. Let $b_n(x, x_1, \ldots, x_n)$ be defined by $b_1(x, x_1) = \texttt{blind}(x, x_1)$ and $b_{n+1}(x, x_1, \ldots, x_{n+1}) = \texttt{blind}(b_n(x, x_1, \ldots, x_n), x_{n+1})$. We add the following rules (for every $n \geq 1$) and the resulting system is a good inference system.

$$\frac{\texttt{sign}(b_n(x, x_1, \ldots, x_n), y) \quad x_1 \quad \cdots \quad x_n}{\texttt{sign}(x, y)}$$

2.3 Some Properties of Good Inference Systems

Definition 3 (simple proof). *Let* $H_1 \subseteq H_2 \subseteq \cdots \subseteq H_n$. *A proof* π *of* $H_i \vdash u$ *is* left-minimal *if for any* $j < i$ *such that* $H_j \vdash u$, π *is a proof of* $H_j \vdash u$. *A proof is* simple *if it does not contain any bad pattern and all its subproofs are left-minimal.*

Example 5. Consider the Dolev-Yao inference system given in Example 1. Let $H_1 = \{\texttt{enc}(\texttt{pub}(k), a, r), \texttt{priv}(k), a\}$, $H_2 = H_1 \cup \{\langle a, b \rangle\}$. We have that $H_2 \vdash a$. Indeed, the proofs π_1, π_2 and π_3 described below are witnesses of this fact:

$$\frac{\langle a, b \rangle}{a} \qquad \frac{\texttt{enc}(\texttt{pub}(k), a, r) \quad \texttt{priv}(k)}{a} \qquad \frac{\dfrac{a \quad a}{\langle a, a \rangle}}{a}$$

The proofs π_2 is simple whereas π_1 and π_3 are not. Note that proof of $H_2 \vdash a$ reduced to a leaf is also a simple proof.

Lemma 1. *Consider a good inference system. Let* $H_1 \subseteq H_2 \subseteq \cdots \subseteq H_n$ *be an increasing sequence of sets of terms and* $i \in \{1, \ldots, n\}$. *If* π *is a proof of* $H_i \vdash u$ *then there is a simple proof of* $H_i \vdash u$.

From now on, we only consider good inference systems. The rules of such systems can be divided in three sets.

- The *composition rules* whose conclusion is the only maximal term. Any rule $I(x_1), \ldots, I(x_n) \to I(\mathsf{f}(x_1, \ldots, x_n))$ is a composition, e.g. (P), (E), (S).
- The *decomposition rules* whose all maximal terms are premises, e.g. (D).
- The *versatile rules* whose both the conclusion and some premises are maximal, e.g. (UB$_2$).

In what follows, we also assume that:

1. any composition rule has a conclusion $\mathsf{f}(x_1, \ldots, x_n)$ where $x_1, \ldots, x_n$ are variables. This is the case in our application area: each function symbol is either public (and there is such a rule) or private.
2. any versatile rule satisfies the following properties:
   (a) each strict subterm of the conclusion is a subterm of some premise.
   (b) each premise that is not maximal in the rule is a strict subterm of another premise of that rule.

These conditions are satisfied in Examples 1 and 4. Besides these examples, any intruder theory that can be presented by a finite subterm-convergent rewrite system satisfies our hypotheses. These hypotheses might not be necessary for our result, but we use them in our proof.

We now classify the proofs, according to the type of the last proof step. This generalizes the classical composition/decomposition classification:

Lemma 2 (locality). *Let* π *be a proof of* $H \vdash u$ *without bad pattern, one of the following occurs:*

- $last(\pi)$ is a composition and $step(\pi) \subseteq st(H \cup \{u\})$;
- π is reduced to a leaf or $last(\pi)$ is a decomposition and $step(\pi) \subseteq st(H)$;
- $last(\pi)$ is (an instance of) a versatile rule and $step(\pi') \subseteq st(H)$ for any strict subproof π' of π.

This is proved by observing that any proof in which a maximal conclusion is also a maximal premise of the next rule can be simplified, according to the definition of good inference systems.

3   Deducibility Constraints

The following definition of (deducibility) constraints has been proved to be relevant in the context of security protocols verification (see, e.g. [15,16,7]).

Definition 4. A constraint system D is a formula of the form $\exists \tilde{z}.[C \mid \mathsf{E}]$ where:

- $\tilde{z}$ is a sequence of variables;
- $\mathsf{E}(D) = \mathsf{E}$ is a set of equations in solved form, identified to a substitution θ_E;
- C is a conjunction of deducibility constraints $H_1 \Vdash u_1 \wedge \ldots \wedge H_n \Vdash u_n$ where $var(C) \cap dom(\theta_\mathsf{E}) = \emptyset$, $H_1, \ldots, H_n$ are finite sets of terms, $u_1, \ldots, u_n$ are terms, and such that monotony and origination are satisfied:
  - Monotony: $\emptyset \neq H_1 \subseteq H_2 \subseteq \ldots \subseteq H_n$;
  - Origination: $var(H_i) \subseteq var(\{u_j \mid H_j \subsetneq H_i\})$ for $1 \leq i \leq n$.

We let $fvar(D) = var(D) \setminus \tilde{z}$ and $\mathsf{LH}(D) = \{H_1, \ldots, H_n\}$.

Definition 5 (solution). Given an inference system, a solution of a constraint system $D = \exists \tilde{z}.[C \mid \mathsf{E}]$ is a ground substitution σ with $dom(\sigma) = fvar(D)$ such that there is a ground substitution τ with $dom(\tau) = \tilde{z}$ such that:

- $H(\sigma \cup \tau) \vdash u(\sigma \cup \tau)$ for every $H \Vdash u \in C$, and
- $u(\sigma \cup \tau) = v(\sigma \cup \tau)$ for every $u = v \in \mathsf{E}$.

We let $Sol(D)$ be the set of solutions of D.

In the context of security protocols, any solution will correspond to a choice of messages that are constructed by the attacker and that are accepted by the honest parties.

Example 6. We consider the Dolev-Yao inference system given in Example 1.

$$D := \begin{cases} H_1 = a \Vdash x_0 \ \wedge \ a \Vdash x_1 \\ H_2 = \mathtt{enc}(x_0, \langle b, x_1 \rangle, r), \ \mathtt{priv}(a), \ a \Vdash b \end{cases}$$

$H_1 \subseteq H_2$ and the variables x_0, x_1 occur first on the right. Thus, D is a constraint system. $\sigma = \{x_0 \mapsto \mathtt{pub}(a), x_1 \mapsto \langle a, a \rangle\}$ is a solution of D. Here, there are no bounded variables nor equations. This is the case for constraint systems that represent the security protocol executions. Bounded variables and equations may however be introduced by our constraint solving rules.

Putting together Definitions 4 and 5, we get the following problem, whose decision is the subject of this paper:

> Given an inference system and a constraint system D, does there exist a substitution σ such that $\sigma \in Sol(D)$? We also want to find an effective representation of all solutions.

Notation. Let $D = \exists \tilde{z}.[C \mid \mathsf{E}]$ be a constraint system. For every variable $x \in var(D)$, we let H_x be the smallest set $H \in \mathsf{LH}(D)$ such that there is a constraint $H \Vdash u \in D$ with $x \in var(u) \smallsetminus var(H)$. In other words, H_x is the left hand side of the deducibility constraint that introduced the variable x for the first time. By origination and monotony, this is defined for all $x \in var(C)$. By convention, $H_x = \emptyset$ when x does not occur in C.

4   Transformation of Deducibility Constraints

We show here that we can solve deducibility constraints in such a way that *we do not miss any solution* (as in [7]). The basic idea of the transformation rules is very straightforward, and that is what makes it appealing: we simply guess the last step of the proof, performing a backwards proof search together with narrowing the variables of the constraint. If $\mathsf{R} = I(u_1), \ldots, I(u_n) \to I(u)$ is guessed as the last rule in the proof of $H\sigma \vdash v\sigma$, we simply perform:

$$\exists \tilde{z}.[C \wedge H \Vdash v \mid \mathsf{E}] \rightsquigarrow \exists \tilde{z}'.[C\theta \wedge H\theta \Vdash u_1\theta \wedge \ldots \wedge H\theta \Vdash u_n\theta \mid \mathsf{E}']$$

where $\tilde{z}' = \tilde{z} \cup var(\mathsf{R})$, $\theta = \mathsf{mgu}(u, v)$ and $\mathsf{E}' = \mathsf{E} \cup \theta$.

This hardly terminates, even for very simple proof systems and ground goals. Consider the rule (Proj_1) only. We get:

$$H \Vdash v \rightsquigarrow \exists x_1, x_2.[H \Vdash \langle v, x_2 \rangle \mid x_1 = v]$$
$$\rightsquigarrow \exists x_1, x_2, y_1, y_2.[H \Vdash \langle\langle v, x_2 \rangle, y_2 \rangle \mid x_1 = v \wedge y_1 = \langle v, x_2 \rangle] \rightsquigarrow \ldots$$

And similarly for (P) (below, we assume that H is a ground set of terms):

$$H \Vdash x \rightsquigarrow \exists x_1, x_2.[H \Vdash x_1 \wedge H \Vdash x_2 \mid x = \langle x_1, x_2 \rangle] \rightsquigarrow \ldots$$

First, we do not aim at explictly enumerating all possible solutions, but only compute *solved forms*, that are a convenient representation of all these solutions. Typically, $H \Vdash v$ will be solved when v is a variable. This rules out the second above non-terminating example.

For decomposition or versatile rules, we may still get the first non-terminating behavior. That is where we use locality: we control the application of such rules, roughly requesting that maximal premises are subterms of H. This is however not complete, as Lemma 2 shows only that, in case of a versatile or decomposition rule, the premises are subterms of the hypotheses *at the ground level*. In other words, if we guessed that the last rule, in the proof of an instance σ of $H \Vdash v$, is a decomposition, we only know that the premises of the last proof step are in $st(H\sigma)$. We use then the property of subterms: $st(H\sigma) = st(H)\sigma \cup st(\sigma)$. If the premises are in $st(H)\sigma$, everything is fine: we can guess subterms of H that are the premises. Otherwise, it is not so straightforward, as σ is unknown. That is where we need some additional strategies.

Another difficulty comes from the introduction of variables. If we keep on introducing variables and equations, the left hand sides of deducibility constraints may grow, hence their subterms too. Then guessing a subterm of H as a premise does not necessarily yield a bounded number of terms.

4.1   Transformation Rules

The rules of Figure 1 are applied non-deterministically. When new variables are introduced (in the Dec rule) they are assumed to be fresh, by renaming.

(Axiom) $\exists \tilde{z}.[C \wedge H \Vdash u \mid \sigma] \rightsquigarrow \exists \tilde{z}.[C\theta \mid \sigma \cup \theta]$
$$\text{where } \theta = \mathsf{mgu}(u, v),\ v \in H \text{ and } u \notin \mathcal{X}$$

(Triv) $\exists \tilde{z}.[C \wedge H \Vdash x \wedge H' \Vdash x \mid \sigma] \rightsquigarrow \exists \tilde{z}.[C \wedge H \Vdash x \mid \sigma]$
$$\text{when } H \subseteq H'$$

(Comp) $\exists \tilde{z}.[C \wedge H \Vdash \mathsf{f}(u_1, \ldots, u_n) \mid \sigma] \rightsquigarrow \exists \tilde{z}.[C \wedge H \Vdash u_1 \wedge \ldots \wedge H \Vdash u_n \mid \sigma]$
$$\text{if } \mathsf{f} \text{ is a public symbol}$$

(Dec) $\exists \tilde{z}.[C \wedge H \Vdash v \mid \sigma] \rightsquigarrow \exists \tilde{z} \cup \tilde{x}.[C\theta \wedge H\theta \Vdash w_1\theta \wedge \ldots H\theta \Vdash w_n\theta \mid \sigma \cup \theta]$
$$\wedge H'\theta \Vdash v_1\theta \wedge \ldots \wedge H'\theta \Vdash v_m\theta$$

where:

- $\mathsf{R} = \dfrac{v_1 \ \cdots \ v_m \ w_1 \ \cdots \ w_n}{w}$ is a decomposition or a versatile rule such that $\mathsf{Max}(\mathsf{R}) \subseteq \{w_1, \ldots, w_n\}$ and $\tilde{x} = var(\mathsf{R})$;
- $\theta = \mathsf{mgu}(\langle w, w_1, \ldots, w_n \rangle, \langle v, u_1, \ldots, u_n \rangle)$, $u_1, \ldots, u_n \in st(H) \smallsetminus \mathcal{X}$, and $v \notin \mathcal{X}$;
- H' is a left member of a deducibility constraint such that $H' \subsetneq H$.

Fig. 1. Transformation of deducibility constraints

The Dec rule deserves some explanation. We guessed here a versatile or decomposition rule. The premises $w_1, \ldots, w_n$ will be those whose instances correspond to a term in $st(H)\sigma$: we can guess the corresponding terms in $st(H)$, namely $u_1, \ldots, u_n$. The other premises (that are then subterms in the substitution part) are constrained to be proved with strictly less hypotheses. We will show that this can always be assumed, hence that we get completeness.

Example 7. Consider the constraint system D given in Example 6. First, considering the rule (Proj_1) and applying Dec to the third constraint yields:

$$\exists x', y'.[a \Vdash x_0, a \Vdash x_1, \mathsf{enc}(x_0, \langle b, x_1 \rangle, r), \mathsf{priv}(a), a \Vdash \langle b, x_1 \rangle \mid \{x' \mapsto b, y' \mapsto x_1\}].$$

Now, considering (D) and applying again Dec to the third constraint yields:

$$D' = \begin{cases} \exists x, y, z, x', y'.[\, a \Vdash x_0\theta, \quad a \Vdash x_1\theta \\ \qquad H_2\theta \Vdash \text{enc}(x_0\theta, \langle b, x_1\theta \rangle, r) \\ \qquad H_2\theta \Vdash \text{priv}(a) \ \mid \ \theta \cup \{x' \mapsto b, y' \mapsto x_1\}] \end{cases}$$

where $\theta = \text{mgu}(\langle x, \text{enc}(\text{pub}(y), x, z), \text{priv}(y) \rangle, \langle \langle b, x_1 \rangle, \text{enc}(x_0, \langle b, x_1 \rangle, r), \text{priv}(a) \rangle)$
$\quad = \{x \mapsto \langle b, x_1 \rangle, y \mapsto a, z \mapsto r, x_0 \mapsto \text{pub}(a)\}.$

Lemma 3 (soundness). *Let D be a constraint system such that $D \rightsquigarrow D'$, then D' is a constraint system and $Sol(D') \subseteq Sol(D)$.*

The transformation rules of Figure 1 also preserve the following invariant.

Definition 6 (uniquely determined). *Let $D = \exists \tilde{z}.[C \mid E]$ be a constraint system. D is* uniquely determined *if for any ground substitution σ such that $dom(\sigma) = fvar(D)$, there are ground terms $u_1, \ldots, u_\ell$ such that either $\text{mgu}(E\sigma) = \bot$ or $\text{mgu}(E\sigma) = \{z_1 = u_1, \ldots, z_\ell = u_\ell\}$ where $\tilde{z} = \{z_1, \ldots, z_\ell\}$. In that case we let $\bar{\sigma}$ be $\sigma \cup \text{mgu}(E\sigma)$. ($\bar{\sigma}$ is a solution of the constraint system $[C \mid E]$.)*

Example 8. Let D' be the constraint system given in Example 7. We have that $fvar(D) = \{x_0, x_1\}$. Once values are assigned to x_0, x_1, there is a unique substitution τ that satisfies the equations in $E(D')$.

Lemma 4. *Let D be a constraint system that is uniquely determined and D' be such that $D \rightsquigarrow D'$. Then D' is uniquely determined.*

Using our transformation rules, solving deducibility constraint systems can be reduced to solving simpler constraint systems that we call solved.

Definition 7. *A constraint system $D = \exists \tilde{z}.[H_1 \Vdash x_1 \wedge \ldots \wedge H_n \Vdash x_n \mid E]$ is in* solved form *when $x_1, \ldots, x_n$ are distinct variables.*

Solved deducibility constraint systems are particulary simple since they always have a solution.

Lemma 5. *A solved form has always at least one solution.*

4.2   Completeness

Let $H_1 \subseteq H_2 \subseteq \ldots \subset H_n$ be a sequence of sets of terms. Let π be a proof of $H_i \vdash u$ for some i $(1 \leq i \leq n)$. We associate to π, the minimal set $\text{Hyp}(\pi) \in \{H_1, \ldots, H_n\}$ containing the leaves of π. Note that $\text{Hyp}(\pi) \subseteq H_i$. Given a constraint system $D = \exists \tilde{z}.[C \mid E]$ that is uniquely determined and a solution σ, a simple proof w.r.t. D is a simple proof w.r.t. the sequence of sets of terms $\text{LH}(D)\bar{\sigma}$.

We first show that either the subterms occurring in proofs are subterms of the hypotheses, or else their simple proofs end with a composition or a versatile rule.

Lemma 6. *Let D be a constraint system of the form $[C \mid \mathsf{E}]$. Let $H \in \mathsf{LH}(D)$ be such that for every $y \in var(H)$ there is a constraint $H_y \Vdash y \in D$. Let σ be a solution of D and v be a term such that $H\sigma \vdash v$. Let $u \in st(v)$. Then:*

1. *either $u \in (st(H) \setminus \mathcal{X})\sigma$;*
2. *or $H\sigma \vdash u$ and any simple proof π of $H\sigma \vdash u$ ends with a composition or a versatile rule.*

To prove this lemma, we consider the set Π of simple proofs of $H\sigma \vdash v$ and we prove the lemma by induction on the pair (H, d) where d is the size of a minimal proof in Π.

Now, we define the complexity of the proofs witnessing that σ is a solution of D and show that there is always a rule yielding a strictly smaller complexity, until we reach a solved form. Let $D = \exists \tilde{z}.[C \mid \mathsf{E}]$ be a uniquely determined constraint system and σ be a solution of D.

- If $H \Vdash u \in C$ then $\mathsf{PS}(H \Vdash u, \sigma)$ is the size (i.e. number of nodes) of a simple proof of $H\bar{\sigma} \vdash u\bar{\sigma}$ that has a minimal size.
- If $\mathsf{LH}(D) = \{H_1, \ldots, H_n\}$ with $H_1 \subsetneq \ldots \subsetneq H_n$, then the *level* $\mathsf{lev}(H \Vdash u, D)$ of a deducibility constraint $H \Vdash u \in C$ is the index i such that $H = H_i$.

The measure PS is extended to constraint systems by letting, for any solution σ of D, $\mathsf{PS}(D, \sigma)$ be the multiset of pairs $(\mathsf{lev}(H \Vdash u, D), \mathsf{PS}(H \Vdash u, \sigma))$ for all deducibility constraints $H \Vdash u \in D$. The multisets $\mathsf{PS}(D, \sigma)$ are compared using the multiset extension of the lexicographic composition of the orderings.

Note that the number of different levels in a constraint system might decrease, but it may never increase.

Lemma 7. *If D is a constraint system that is uniquely determined and $\sigma \in Sol(D)$, then either D is in solved form or else there is a D' such that $D \rightsquigarrow D'$, $\sigma \in Sol(D')$, and $\mathsf{PS}(D, \sigma) > \mathsf{PS}(D', \sigma)$.*

Proof. (sketch) If D is not in solved form, there must be a constraint $H \Vdash u \in D$ such that u is not a variable. We consider such a constraint, with a minimal left hand side. Then, depending on the last rule of a minimal size simple proof of $H\sigma \vdash u\sigma$, we may apply some transformation, that yields a smaller PS:

- *If the proof is reduced to a leaf,* then we use the Axiom rule.
- *If the last rule is a composition,* then we apply Comp to D, yielding a smaller PS.
- *If the last rule is versatile or a decomposition,* we have to show that the conditions of Dec are met in order to conclude. To prove this, we rely on Lemma 2 and Lemma 6.   □

Then, we prove the following lemma by induction on $\mathsf{PS}(D, \sigma)$, applying Lemma 7 for the induction step. Lemma 4 allows us to ensure that the resulting constraint system is uniquely determined and to apply our induction hypothesis.

Lemma 8 (completeness). *If D is a constraint system that is uniquely determined and $\sigma \in Sol(D)$, then there is a solved deducibility constraint D' such that $D \rightsquigarrow^* D'$ and $\sigma \in Sol(D')$.*

(Active) $\exists \tilde{z}.[A \mid F \mid E] \mapsto_A \exists \tilde{z} \cup \tilde{x}.[A' \mid F \mid E \cup \theta]$

> if $A \rightsquigarrow \exists \tilde{x}.[A' \mid \theta]$ using Axiom, Triv, Comp; or Dec on $H \Vdash v$ and there exists $x \in var(v)$ such that $\mathsf{lev}(x, A) = \mathsf{lev}(H, A)$.We assume that $\mathsf{mgu}(E \cup \theta) \neq \perp$.

(Freeze) $\exists \tilde{z}.[A \wedge H \Vdash v \mid F \mid E] \mapsto \exists \tilde{z} \cup \tilde{x}.[A \wedge H \Vdash u_1 \wedge \ldots H \Vdash u_n \mid$
$$F \wedge H' \Vdash v_1 \wedge \ldots \wedge H' \Vdash v_m \mid E \cup \theta]$$

where:

- $R = \dfrac{v_1 \quad \cdots \quad v_m \quad w_1 \quad \cdots \quad w_n}{w}$ is a decomposition or a versatile rule such that $\mathsf{Max}(R) \subseteq \{w_1, \ldots, w_n\}$ and $\tilde{x} = var(R)$;
- $\theta = \mathsf{mgu}(\langle w, w_1, \ldots, w_n \rangle, \langle v, u_1, \ldots, u_n \rangle)$, $u_1, \ldots, u_n \in st(H) \smallsetminus \mathcal{X}$, and $v \notin \mathcal{X}$;
- H' is a left member of a deducibility constraint in A such that $H' \subsetneq H$;
- $\mathsf{mgu}(E \cup \theta) \neq \perp$ and $\mathsf{lev}(x, A \wedge H \Vdash v) < \mathsf{lev}(H, A \wedge H \Vdash v)$ for any $x \in var(v)$.

(Open) $\exists \tilde{z}.[A \mid F \mid E] \mapsto_O \exists \tilde{z}.[(A \cup F)\theta \mid \emptyset \mid \theta]$
$$\text{when } A \text{ in solved form and } \theta = \mathsf{mgu}(E)$$

Fig. 2. Transformation of extended constraint systems

5 Termination

In order to get termination, we add some control on the transformation rules.

5.1 Our Strategy

For every variable x and constraint system D, the *level* $\mathsf{lev}(x, D)$ of x is the level of H_x in D, if $x \in var(D)$, and is 0 otherwise. The deducibility constraints of D are split into an *active part* $\mathsf{Act}(D)$ and a *frozen part* $\mathsf{Fr}(D)$.

Definition 8 (extended constraint system). *An* extended constraint system D *is a formula* $\exists \tilde{z}.[A \mid F \mid E]$ *where:*

- *$\tilde{z}$ is a sequence of variables;*
- *$E(D) \stackrel{\text{def}}{=} E$ is a set of equations (not necessarily in solved form) with $\mathsf{mgu}(E) \neq \perp$;*
- *$\mathsf{Act}(D) \stackrel{\text{def}}{=} A$, the active part of D, and $\mathsf{Fr}(D) \stackrel{\text{def}}{=} F$, the frozen part of D, are sets of deducibility constraints; A and $(A \cup F)\mathsf{mgu}(E)$ are constraint systems.*

Let $\theta = \mathsf{mgu}(E)$. A solution of $\exists \tilde{z}.[A \mid F \mid E]$ is a solution of $\exists \tilde{z}.[(A \cup F)\theta \mid \theta]$. The system D is in solved form when $\mathsf{Fr}(D) = \emptyset$ and $\mathsf{Act}(D)\theta$ is in solved form.

The rules are described in Figure 2. The transformation relation defined by these rules is denoted $\mapsto$. Sometimes, we use $\mapsto_{A/F}$ instead of $\mapsto_A \cup \mapsto_F$.

In the initial constraint system, nothing is frozen. All rules only apply to the active part and all rules (except Dec) only modify the active part.

- When the rule Dec is applied to a constraint $H \Vdash v$ such that, for some variable $x \in var(v)$, we have that $\mathsf{lev}(x, \mathsf{Act}(D)) = \mathsf{lev}(H, \mathsf{Act}(D))$, it also contributes only to the active part.

– Otherwise, when for all $x \in var(v)$, $\mathsf{lev}(x, \mathsf{Act}(D)) < \mathsf{lev}(H, \mathsf{Act}(D))$, then only the constraints $H \Vdash u_1 \wedge \ldots \wedge H \Vdash u_n$ are kept in the active part, and the remainder falls in the frozen part.

When $\mathsf{Act}(D)$ is in solved form (and only then), we open the fridge and pour the frozen part into the active one, performing all necessary replacements.

First, we have to establish the soundness of the transformation rules. The main point is to show that the active part remains a constraint system.

Lemma 9 (soundness). *Let D be an extended constraint system such that $D \mapsto D'$ then D' is an extended constraint system and $Sol(D') \subseteq Sol(D)$.*

If there is a loop on the active part by using only **Active** and **Freeze**, i.e. $D \mapsto^*$ $D_1 \mapsto^*_{\mathsf{A/F}} D_2$ and $\mathsf{Act}(D_1) = \mathsf{Act}(D_2)$, we remove all the branches that begin with this prefix. We will show that this strategy is both:

– *complete*: for any D, for any $\sigma \in Sol(D)$, there is a sequence $D \mapsto^* D'$ authorized by the strategy such that $\sigma \in Sol(D')$ and D' is in solved form.
– *terminating*: there are no infinite transformation sequences.

5.2   Termination of Our Strategy

Now, we clarify the role of the fridge, by showing that the level of a variable in the active part is never increasing. Moreover, if new variables are introduced in the active part, their level is strictly smaller than the level of an older variable, whose respective level strictly decreased.

Lemma 10. *If $D \mapsto_{\mathsf{A/F}} D'$, then:*

1. $\mathsf{lev}(x, \mathsf{Act}(D')) \leq \mathsf{lev}(x, \mathsf{Act}(D))$ *for every $x \in var(\mathsf{Act}(D))$.*
2. *Let $M = var(\mathsf{Act}(D')) \setminus var(\mathsf{Act}(D))$. If $M \neq \emptyset$ then there exists $x \in var(\mathsf{Act}(D))$ such that $\mathsf{lev}(z, \mathsf{Act}(D')) < \mathsf{lev}(x, \mathsf{Act}(D))$ for any $z \in M \cup \{x\}$.*

Now, we get a first termination lemma:

Lemma 11. *There is no infinite transformation sequence without opening the fridge.*

The reason for this is that either we do not introduce variables in which case there must be a loop (this is forbidden by the strategy) or else, thanks to Lemma 10, there is a level ℓ such that the level of some variable at level ℓ strictly decreases, while all new variables have a strictly smaller level than ℓ.

Finally, we cannot open very often the fridge:

Lemma 12. *Let D be an extended constraint system such that $\mathsf{E}(D) = \mathsf{Fr}(D) = \emptyset$. In any transformation sequence starting with D, we can open at most $2|\mathsf{LH}(D)| + |\mathsf{MLH}(D)|$ times the fridge – $\mathsf{MLH}(D)$ is the maximal set of hypotheses in $\mathsf{LH}(D)$.*

The idea is that the maximal level variables x occur in a constraint $H \Vdash x$ when we are about to open the fridge. Furthermore, in the fridge, all variables have a strictly smaller level. It follows that $H \Vdash x$ will not participate any more in any transformation: further transformations only take place at lower levels. More precisely, we show that between two openings, the number of levels or the number of distinct terms in the maximal left hand side decreases; otherwise in the resulting system further transformations only take place at lower levels.

From the previous lemmas, we derive the following corollary.

Corollary 1 (termination). *Our strategy is strongly terminating: there is no infinite transformation sequence of (extended) deducibility constraints.*

5.3   Completeness of Our Strategy

For an extended constraint system $D = \exists \tilde{z}.[\mathsf{A} \mid \mathsf{F} \mid \mathsf{E}]$, we let:

$$\mathsf{Open}(D) = \exists \tilde{z}.[(\mathsf{A} \cup \mathsf{F})\mathsf{mgu}(\mathsf{E}) \mid \mathsf{mgu}(\mathsf{E})]$$

and we say that D is uniquely determined if $\mathsf{Open}(D)$ is uniquely determined. Note that by definition of Open, we have that $Sol(D) = Sol(\mathsf{Open}(D))$ and "uniquely determined" is preserved by $\mapsto$.

The following corollary ensures that PS is decreasing on the active part.

Corollary 2 (of Lemma 7). *Let D be a uniquely determined extended constraint system such that $\mathsf{Act}(D)$ is not in solved form and $\sigma \in Sol(D)$. Then there is a D' such that $D \mapsto_{\mathsf{A}/\mathsf{F}} D'$ and $\sigma \in Sol(D')$.*

Moreover, $\mathsf{PS}(\mathsf{A}, \overline{\sigma}|_{var(\mathsf{A})}) > \mathsf{PS}(\mathsf{A}', \overline{\sigma}|_{var(\mathsf{A}')})$ where $\mathsf{A} = \mathsf{Act}(D)$, $\mathsf{A}' = \mathsf{Act}(D')$ and $\overline{\sigma}$ is the extension of σ w.r.t. D'.

Thanks to this, if there is a loop on the active part, we can close the branch, still having a complete strategy:

Lemma 13. *Our strategy is complete.*

6   Conclusion

We gave a simple set of transformation rules that allows to derive a complete and effective representation of all solutions of a deducibility constraint. This works for any good inference system that satisfies some additional syntactic conditions. We believe that this is the starting point of several further works:

1. It would be nice to remove the additional syntactic restrictions (or to prove that they are necessary)
2. Getting a full generalization of [1], requires to introduce predicate symbols.
3. We need to enrich the syntax of constraints, in order to get effective algorithms for infinite (recursive) good inference systems.

4. Our transformation rules are not only preserving all solutions, but also all simple proofs, i.e. some witnesses that they are indeed solutions. This suggests that the same transformation rules can be used for the decision of the symbolic equivalence of constraint systems.
5. Covering all current decision results requires an extension that includes AC-symbols.

References

1. Basin, D., Ganzinger, H.: Automated complexity analysis based on ordered resolution. Journal of the ACM 48(1), 70–109 (2001)
2. Baudet, M.: Deciding security of protocols against off-line guessing attacks. In: Proc.12th ACM Conference on Computer and Communications Security (CCS 2005), Alexandria, Virginia, USA, pp. 16–25. ACM Press, New York (2005)
3. Bursuc, S., Comon-Lundh, H., Delaune, S.: Deducibility constraints. Research Report LSV-09-17, LSV, ENS Cachan, France, 36 pages (2009)
4. Chevalier, Y., Kourjieh, M.: Key substitution in the symbolic analysis of cryptographic protocols. In: Arvind, V., Prasad, S. (eds.) FSTTCS 2007. LNCS, vol. 4855, pp. 121–132. Springer, Heidelberg (2007)
5. Chevalier, Y., Küsters, R., Rusinowitch, M., Turuani, M.: Deciding the security of protocols with Diffie-Hellman exponentiation and products in exponents. In: Pandya, P.K., Radhakrishnan, J. (eds.) FSTTCS 2003. LNCS, vol. 2914, pp. 124–135. Springer, Heidelberg (2003)
6. Chevalier, Y., Küsters, R., Rusinowitch, M., Turuani, M.: An NP decision procedure for protocol insecurity with xor. In: Kolaitis [13]
7. Comon-Lundh, H., Cortier, V., Zalinescu, E.: Deciding security properties of cryptographic protocols. application to key cycles. Transaction on Computational Logic (to appear 2009)
8. Comon-Lundh, H., Shmatikov, V.: Intruder deductions, constraint solving and insecurity decision in preence of exclusive or. In: Kolaitis [12]
9. Delaune, S., Kremer, S., Ryan, M.D.: Verifying privacy-type properties of electronic voting protocols. Journal of Computer Security 17(4), 435–487 (2009)
10. Delaune, S., Lafourcade, P., Lugiez, D., Treinen, R.: Symbolic protocol analysis for monoidal equational theories. Information and Computation 206(2-4) (2008)
11. Kähler, D., Küsters, R.: Constraint Solving for Contract-Signing Protocols. In: Abadi, M., de Alfaro, L. (eds.) CONCUR 2005. LNCS, vol. 3653, pp. 233–247. Springer, Heidelberg (2005)
12. Kolaitis, P. (ed.): 18th Annual IEEE Symposium on Logic in Computer Science. IEEE Comp. Soc, Los Alamitos (2003)
13. McAllester, D.: Automatic recognition of tractability in inference relations. Journal of the ACM 40(2) (1993)
14. Millen, J., Shmatikov, V.: Constraint solving for bounded-process cryptographic protocol analysis. In: Proc. 8th ACM Conference on Computer and Communications Security, CCS 2001 (2001)
15. Millen, J., Shmatikov, V.: Symbolic protocol analysis with products and Diffie-Hellman exponentiation. In: Proc. 16th Computer Security Foundation Workshop (CSFW 2003), pp. 47–62. IEEE Comp. Soc. Press, Los Alamitos (2003)
16. Rusinowitch, M., Turuani, M.: Protocol insecurity with a finite number of sessions, composed keys is NP-complete. Theoretical Computer Science, 1-3 (2003)

Automated Security Proof for Symmetric Encryption Modes[*]

Martin Gagné[2], Pascal Lafourcade[1], Yassine Lakhnech[1],
and Reihaneh Safavi-Naini[2]

[1] Université Grenoble 1, CNRS,VERIMAG, France
[2] Department of Computer Science, University of Calgary, Canada

Abstract. We presents a compositional Hoare logic for proving semantic security of modes of operation for symmetric key block ciphers. We propose a simple programming language to specify encryption modes and an assertion language that allows to state invariants and axioms and rules to establish such invariants. The assertion language consists of few atomic predicates. We were able to use our method to verify semantic security of several encryption modes including Cipher Block Chaining (CBC), Cipher Feedback mode (CFB), Output Feedback (OFB), and Counter mode (CTR).

1 Introduction

A block cipher algorithm (e.g. AES, Blowfish, DES, Serpent and Twofish) is a symmetric key algorithm that takes a fixed size input message block and produces a fixed size output block. A mode of operation is a method of using a block cipher on an arbitrary length message. Important modes of operation are Electronic Code Book (ECB), Cipher Block Chaining (CBC), Cipher FeedBack mode (CFB), Output FeedBack (OFB), and Counter mode (CTR). Modes of operations have different applications and provide different levels of security and efficiency. An important question when a mode of operation is used for encryption is the level of security that the mode provides, assuming the underlying block cipher is secure. The answer to this question is not straightforward. For example if one uses the naive ECB mode with a "secure" block cipher, then the encryption scheme obtained is not even IND-CPA secure. Others, like CBC or CTR, will provide confidentiality only if the initial vector (IV) is chosen adequately.

Recent years have seen an explosion of new modes of operation for block cipher (IACBC, IAPM [19], XCB [23], TMAC [18,20], HCTR [5], HCH [7], EMU [15], EMU* [12], PEP [6], OMAC [16,17], TET [13], CMC [14], GCM [24], EAX [4], XEX [25], TAE, TCH, TBC [22,28] to name only a few). These new modes of operation often offer improved security guarantees, or additional security features. They also tend to be more complex than the traditional modes of operations,

[*] This work was supported by ANR SeSur SCALP, SFINCS, AVOTE and iCORE.

A. Datta (Ed.): ASIAN 2009, LNCS 5913, pp. 39–53, 2009.
© Springer-Verlag Berlin Heidelberg 2009

and arguments for proving their security can similarly become much more complicated – sometimes so complicated that flaws in the security proofs could go unnoticed for years.

Proofs generated by automated verification tools can provide us with an independent argument for the security of modes of operation, thereby increasing our confidence in the security of cryptographic protocols. While the rules used by the prover must also be proven by humans, and are therefore also susceptible to error, they tend to be much simpler than the protocols they will be used to check, which ensures that mistakes are far less likely to go unnoticed. In this paper, we take a first step towards building an automated prover for modes of operation, and show how to automatically generate proofs for many traditional block cipher modes of operation.

CONTRIBUTIONS: We propose a compositional Hoare logic for proving semantic security of modes of operation for symmetric key block ciphers. We notice that many modes use a small set of operations such as xor, concatenation, and selection of random values. We introduce a simple programming language to specify encryption modes and an assertion language that allows to state invariants and axioms and rules to establish such invariants. The assertion language requires only four predicates: one that allows us to express that the value of a variable is indistinguishable from a random value when given the values of a set of variables, one that states that an expression has not been yet submitted to the block cipher, and two bookkeeping predicates that allow us to keep track of 'fresh' random values and counters. Transforming the Hoare logic into an (incomplete) automated verification procedure is quite standard. Indeed, we can interpret the logic as a set of rules that tell us how to propagate the invariants backwards. Using our method, an automated prover could verify semantic security of several encryption modes including CBC, CFB, CTR and OFB. Of course our system does not prove ECB mode, because ECB is not semantically secure.

RELATED WORK: Security of symmetric encryption modes have been studied for a long time by the cryptographers. In [1] the authors presented different concrete security notions for symmetric encryption in a concrete security framework. For instance, they give a security analysis of CBC mode. In [2] a security analysis of the encryption mode CBC-MAC [21]. In [26] they propose a new encryption mode called OCB for efficient authenticated encryption and provide a security analysis of this new mode. Many other works present proofs of encryption modes.

Other works try to encode security of symmetric encryption modes as a non-interference property for programs with deterministic encryption. For example, [9] presents a computationally sound type system with exact security bounds for such programs. This type system has been applied to verify some symmetric encryption modes. The logic presented in this paper can be used to give a more structured soundness proof for the proposed type system. Moreover, we believe that our logic is more expressive and can be more easily adapted to more encryption modes.

A first important feature of our method is that it is not based on a global reasoning and global program transformation as it is the case for the game-based approach [3,27].

In [8], the authors proposed an automatic method for proving semantic security for asymmetric generic encryption schemes. Our work continues that line of work. We extend the input language and axioms of the Hoare logic of [8] in order to capture symmetric encryption modes.

OUTLINE: In Section 2 we introduce the material for describing the encryption modes. In Section 3, we present our Hoare Logic for analyzing the semantic security of encryption modes described with the grammar given in the previous section. Finally before concluding in the last section, we apply our method to some examples in Section 4.

2   Definitions

2.1   Notation and Conventions

For simplicity, over this paper, we assume that all variables range over large domains, whose cardinality is exponential in the security parameter η. We also assume that all programs have length polynomial in η.

A block cipher is a function $\mathcal{E} : \{0,1\}^k \times \{0,1\}^\eta \to \{0,1\}^\eta$ such that for each $K \in \{0,1\}^k$, $\mathcal{E}(K,\cdot)$ is a permutation. It takes as input a k-bit key and an η-bit message block, and returns an η-bit string. We often denote by $\mathcal{E}(x)$ the application of the block cipher to the message block x. We omit the key used every time to simplify the notation, but it is understood that a key was selected at random at the beginning of the experiment and remains the same throughout.

For a mode of operation M, we denote by $\mathcal{E}_M$ the encryption function described by M using block cipher $\mathcal{E}$.

For a probability distribution $\mathcal{D}$, we denote by $x \xleftarrow{\$} \mathcal{D}$ the operation of sampling a value x according to distribution $\mathcal{D}$. If S is a finite set, we denote by $x \xleftarrow{\$} S$ the operation of sampling x uniformly at random among the values in S.

Given two distribution ensembles $X = \{X_\eta\}_{\eta \in \mathbb{N}}$ and $X' = \{X'_\eta\}_{\eta \in \mathbb{N}}$, an algorithm $\mathcal{A}$ and $\eta \in \mathbb{N}$, we define the *advantage* of $\mathcal{A}$ in distinguishing X_η and X'_η as the following quantity:

$$\mathsf{Adv}(\mathcal{A}, \eta, X, X') = \Pr[x \xleftarrow{\$} X_\eta : \mathcal{A}(x) = 1] - \Pr[x \xleftarrow{\$} X'_\eta : \mathcal{A}(x) = 1].$$

Two distribution ensembles X and X' are called *indistinguishable*, denoted by $X \sim X'$, if $\mathsf{Adv}(\mathcal{A}, \eta, X, X')$ is negligible as a function of η for every probabilistic polynomial-time algorithm $\mathcal{A}$.

2.2   Grammar

We introduce our language for defining a generic encryption mode. The commands are given by the grammar of Figure 1, where:

$$c ::= x \xleftarrow{\$} \mathcal{U} \mid x := \mathcal{E}(y) \mid x := \mathcal{E}^{-1}(y) \mid x := y \oplus z \mid x := y\|z \mid x := y[n,m] \mid$$
$$\mid x := y+1 \mid c_1; c_2$$

Fig. 1. Language grammar

- $x \xleftarrow{\$} \mathcal{U}$ denotes uniform sampling of a value and assigning it to x.
- $x := \mathcal{E}(y)$ denotes application of the block cipher $\mathcal{E}$ to the value of y and assigning the result to x.
- Similarly for $x := \mathcal{E}^{-1}(y)$, where $\mathcal{E}^{-1}$ denotes the inverse function of $\mathcal{E}$.
- $x := y \oplus z$ denotes application of the exclusive-or operator to the values of y and z and assigning the result to x.
- $x := y\|z$ represents the concatenation of the values of y and z.
- $x := y[n,m]$ assigns to x the bits at positions between n and m in the bit-string value of y. I.e., for a bit-string $bs = b_1 \ldots b_k$, where the b_i's are bits, $bs[n,m]$ denotes the bits-string $b_n \ldots b_m$[1]. Then, $x := y[n,m]$ assigns $bs[n,m]$ to x, where bs is the value of y. Here, n and m are polynomials in the security parameter η.
- $x := y+1$ increments by one the value of y and assigns the result to x. The operation is carried modulo 2^η.
- $c_1; c_2$ is the sequential composition of c_1 and c_2.

2.3 Generic Encryption Mode

We can now formally define a mode of encryption.

Definition 1 (Generic Encryption Mode). *A generic encryption mode M is represented by $\mathcal{E}_M(m_1|\ldots|m_i, c_0|\ldots|c_i) : \mathbf{var}\ \boldsymbol{x_i}; c_i$, where $\boldsymbol{x_i}$ is the set of variables used in c_i, all commands of c_i are built using the grammar described in Figure 1, each m_j is a message blocks, and each c_j is a cipher block, both of size n according to the input length of the block cipher $\mathcal{E}$.*

We add the additional block c_0 to the ciphertext because encryption modes are usually generate ciphertexts longer than the message. In all examples in this paper, c_0 will be the initialization vector (IV). The definition can easily be extended for encryption modes that also add one or more blocks at the end.

In Figure 2, we present the famous encryption mode $\mathcal{E}_{CBC}$ for a message of three blocks.

2.4 Semantics

In addition to the variables in Var,[2] we consider a variable $\mathcal{T}_E$ that records the values on which $\mathcal{E}$ was computed and cannot be accessed by the adversary.

---

[1] Notice that $bs[n,m] = \epsilon$, when $m < n$ and $bs[n,m] = bs[n,k]$, when $m > k$.

[2] We denote by Var the complete set of variables in the program, whereas **var** denotes the set of variables in the program that are not input or output variables.

$$\mathcal{E}_{CBC}(m_1|m_2|m_3, IV|c_1|c_2|c_3) :$$

var z_1, z_2, z_3;

$IV \stackrel{\$}{\leftarrow} \mathcal{U}$;

$z_1 := IV \oplus m_1$;

$c_1 := \mathcal{E}(z_1)$;

$z_2 := c_1 \oplus m_2$;

$c_2 := \mathcal{E}(z_2)$;

$z_3 := c_2 \oplus m_3$;

$c_3 := \mathcal{E}(z_3)$;

Fig. 2. Description of $\mathcal{E}_{CBC}$

Thus, we consider states that assign bit-strings to the variables in Var and lists of pairs of bit-strings to $\mathcal{T}_E$. Given a state S, $S(\mathcal{T}_E).\mathsf{dom}$ and $S(\mathcal{T}_E).\mathsf{res}$ denote the lists obtained by projecting each pair in $S(\mathcal{T}_E)$ to its first and second element respectively.

The state also contains two sets of variables, F and C, which are used for bookkeeping purposes. The set F contains the variables with values that were sampled at random or obtained as a result of the computation of the block cipher, and have not yet been operated on. Those values are called *fresh* random values. The set C contains the variables whose value are the most recent increment of a counter that started at a fresh random value.

A program takes as input a *configuration* $(S, \mathcal{E})$ and yields a distribution on configurations. A configuration is composed of a state S, a block cipher $\mathcal{E}$. Let $\Gamma_\mathcal{E}$ denote the set of configurations and $\mathrm{DIST}(\Gamma_\mathcal{E})$ the set of distributions on configurations. The semantics is given in Table 1. In the table, $\delta(x)$ denotes the Dirac measure, i.e. $\Pr[x] = 1$ and $\mathcal{T}_E \mapsto S(\mathcal{T}_E) \cdot (x, y)$ denotes the addition of element (x, y) to $\mathcal{T}_E$. Notice that the semantic function of commands can be lifted in the usual way to a function from $\mathrm{DIST}(\Gamma_\mathcal{E})$ to $\mathrm{DIST}(\Gamma_\mathcal{E})$. That is, let $\phi : \Gamma_\mathcal{E} \rightarrow \mathrm{DIST}(\Gamma_\mathcal{E})$ be a function. Then, ϕ defines a unique function $\phi^* : \mathrm{DIST}(\Gamma_\mathcal{E}) \rightarrow \mathrm{DIST}(\Gamma_\mathcal{E})$ obtained by point-wise application of ϕ. By abuse of notation we also denote the lifted semantics by $[\![c]\!]$.

A notational convention. It is easy to see that commands never alter $\mathcal{E}$. Therefore, we can, without ambiguity, write $S' \stackrel{\$}{\leftarrow} [\![c]\!](S, \mathcal{E})$ instead of $(S', \mathcal{E}) \stackrel{\$}{\leftarrow} [\![c]\!](S, \mathcal{E})$.

Here, we are only interested in distributions that can be constructed in polynomial time. We denote their set by $\mathrm{DIST}(\Gamma, \mathcal{F})$, where $\mathcal{F}$ is a family of block ciphers, and is defined as the set of distributions of the form:

$$[\mathcal{E} \stackrel{\$}{\leftarrow} \mathcal{F}(1^\eta); S \stackrel{\$}{\leftarrow} [\![p]\!](I, \mathcal{E}) : (S, \mathcal{E})]$$

where p is a program with a polynomial number of commands, and I is the "initial" state, in which all variables are undefined and all lists and sets are empty.

Table 1. The semantics of the programming language

$$\llbracket x \stackrel{\$}{\leftarrow} \mathcal{U} \rrbracket (S, \mathcal{E}) = [u \stackrel{\$}{\leftarrow} \mathcal{U} : (S\{x \mapsto u, \mathsf{F} \mapsto \mathsf{F} \cup \{x\}, \mathsf{C} \mapsto \mathsf{C} \setminus \{x\}\}, \mathcal{E})]$$

$$\llbracket x := \mathcal{E}(y) \rrbracket (S, \mathcal{E}) =$$
$$\begin{cases} \delta(S\{x \mapsto v, F \mapsto F \cup \{x\} \setminus \{y\}, \mathsf{C} \mapsto \mathsf{C} \setminus \{x\}\}, \mathcal{E}) \text{ if } (S(y), v) \in S(\mathcal{T}_E) \\ \delta(S\{x \mapsto v, F \mapsto F \cup \{x\} \setminus \{y\}, \mathsf{C} \mapsto \mathsf{C} \setminus \{x\}, \mathcal{T}_E \mapsto S(\mathcal{T}_E) \cdot (S(y), v)\}, \mathcal{E}) \\ \qquad \text{if } (S(y), v) \notin S(\mathcal{T}_E) \text{ and } v = \mathcal{E}(S(y)) \end{cases}$$

$$\llbracket x := \mathcal{E}^{-1}(y) \rrbracket (S, \mathcal{E}) = \delta(S\{x \mapsto \mathcal{E}^{-1}(S(y)), F \mapsto F \setminus \{x, y\}, \mathsf{C} \mapsto \mathsf{C} \setminus \{x\}\}, \mathcal{E})$$

$$\llbracket x := y \oplus z \rrbracket (S, \mathcal{E}) = \delta(S\{x \mapsto S(y) \oplus S(z), F \mapsto F \setminus \{x, y, z\}, \mathsf{C} \mapsto \mathsf{C} \setminus \{x\}\}, \mathcal{E})$$

$$\llbracket x := y || z \rrbracket (S, \mathcal{E}) = \delta(S\{x \mapsto S(y) || S(z), F \mapsto F \setminus \{x, y, z\}, \mathsf{C} \mapsto \mathsf{C} \setminus \{x\}\}, \mathcal{E})$$

$$\llbracket x := y[n, m] \rrbracket (S, \mathcal{E}) = \delta(S\{x \mapsto S(y)[n, m], F \mapsto F \setminus \{x, y\}, \mathsf{C} \mapsto \mathsf{C} \setminus \{x\}\}, \mathcal{E})$$

$$\llbracket x := y + 1 \rrbracket (S, \mathcal{E}) =$$
$$\begin{cases} \delta(S\{x \mapsto S(y) + 1, C \mapsto C \cup \{x\} \setminus \{y\}, F \mapsto F \setminus \{x, y\}\}, \mathcal{E}) \text{ if } y \in S(F) \text{ or } y \in S(C) \\ \delta(S\{x \mapsto S(y) + 1, F \mapsto F \setminus \{x, y\}, \mathsf{C} \mapsto \mathsf{C} \setminus \{x\}\}, \mathcal{E}) \text{ otherwise} \end{cases}$$

$$\llbracket c_1 ; c_2 \rrbracket = \llbracket c_2 \rrbracket \circ \llbracket c_1 \rrbracket$$

2.5   Security Model

Ideal Cipher Model
We prove the modes of encryption secure in the ideal cipher model. That is, we assume that the block cipher is a pseudo-random function.[3] This is a standard assumption for proving the security of any block-cipher-based scheme.

The advantage of an algorithm $\mathcal{A}$ against a family of pseudo-random function is defined as follows.

Definition 2. *Let $P : \{0, 1\}^k \times \{0, 1\}^n \to \{0, 1\}^n$ be a family of functions and let $\mathcal{A}$ be an algorithm that takes an oracle and returns a bit. The prf-advantage of $\mathcal{A}$ is defined as follows.*

$$Adv_{\mathcal{A}, P}^{prf} = Pr[K \stackrel{\$}{\leftarrow} \{0, 1\}^k; \mathcal{A}^{P(K, \cdot)} = 1] - Pr[R \stackrel{\$}{\leftarrow} \Phi_n; \mathcal{A}^{R(\cdot)} = 1]$$

where Φ_n is the set of all functions from $\{0, 1\}^n$ to $\{0, 1\}^n$.

The security of a symmetric mode of operation is usually proven by first showing that the mode of operation would be secure if $\mathcal{E}$ was a random function in Φ_n. As a result, an adversary $\mathcal{A}$ against the encryption scheme can be transformed into an adversary $\mathcal{B}$ against the block cipher (as a pseudo-random function) with a similar running time, such that $\mathcal{B}$'s prf-advantage is similar to $\mathcal{A}$'s advantage in breaking the encryption scheme.

Encryption Security
Semantic security for a mode of encryption is defined as follows.

Definition 3. *Let $\mathcal{E}_M(m_1| \ldots |m_i, c_0| \ldots |c_i) : \mathbf{var}\ \boldsymbol{x}_i; c_i$ be a generic encryption mode. $A = (A_1, A_2)$ be an adversary and $X \in \mathrm{DIST}(\Gamma, \mathcal{E})$. For $\eta \in \mathbb{N}$, let*

---

[3] While block ciphers are really families of permutations, it is well known that pseudo-random permutations are indistinguishable from pseudo-random functions if the block size is large enough.

$$Adv_{A,M}^{ind-CPA}(\eta, X)$$
$$= 2 * Pr[(S, \mathcal{E}) \xleftarrow{\$} X;$$
$$(x_0, x_1, p, s) \xleftarrow{\$} A_1^{\mathcal{O}_1}(\eta); b \xleftarrow{\$} \{0, 1\};$$
$$S' \xleftarrow{\$} [\![c_p]\!](S\{m_1| \dots |m_p \mapsto x_b\}, \mathcal{E}):$$
$$A_2^{\mathcal{O}_2}(x_0, x_1, s, S'(c_0| \dots |c_p)) = b] - 1$$

where $\mathcal{O}_1 = \mathcal{O}_2$ are oracles that take a pair (m, j) as input, where m is a string and j is the block length of m, and answers using the jth algorithm in $\mathcal{E}_M$. A_1 outputs x_0, x_1 such that $|x_0| = |x_1|$ and are composed of p blocks. The mode of operation M is semantically (IND-CPA) secure if $Adv_{A,M}^{ind-CPA}(\eta, X)$ is negligible for any constructible distribution ensemble X and polynomial-time adversary A.

It is important to note that in this definition, an adversary against the scheme is only given oracle access to the encryption mode $\mathcal{E}_M$, and *not* to the block cipher $\mathcal{E}$ itself.

Our method verifies the security of an encryption scheme by proving that the ciphertext is indistinguishable from random bits. It is a classical result that this implies semantic security.

3 Proving Semantic Security

In this section, we present our Hoare logic for proving semantic (IND-CPA) security for generic encryption mode defined with our language. We prove that our logic is sound although not complete. Our logic can be used to annotate each command of our programming language with a set of invariants that hold at each point of the program for any execution.

3.1 Assertion Language

We consider new predicates in order to consider properties of symmetric encryption modes. We use a Hoare Logic based on the following invariants:

$$\varphi ::= \mathsf{true} \mid \varphi \wedge \varphi \mid \psi$$
$$\psi ::= \mathsf{Indis}(\nu x; V) \mid F(x) \mid \mathsf{E}(\mathcal{E}, e) \mid Rcounter(e),$$

where $V \subseteq \mathsf{Var}$ and e is an expression constructible out of the variables used in the program and the grammar presented in Section 2. Intuitively:

Indis($\nu x; V$): means that any adversary has negligible probability to distinguish whether he is given results of computations performed using the value of x or a random value, when he is given the values of the variables in V.

E($\mathcal{E}, e$): means that the probability that the value $\mathcal{E}(e)$ has already been computed is negligible.

$F(e)$: means e is a fresh random value.

$RCounter(e)$: means that e is the most recent value of a counter that started at a fresh random value.

More formally, for each invariant ψ, we define that a distribution X satisfies ψ, denoted $X \models \psi$ as follows:

- $X \models \text{true}$.
- $X \models \varphi \wedge \varphi'$ iff $X \models \varphi$ and $X \models \varphi'$.
- $X \models \text{Indis}(\nu x; V)$ iff $[(S, \mathcal{E}) \xleftarrow{\$} X : (S(x, V), \mathcal{E})] \sim [(S, \mathcal{E}) \xleftarrow{\$} X; u \xleftarrow{\$} \mathcal{U}; S' = S\{x \mapsto u\} : (S'(x, V), \mathcal{E})]$
- $X \models \mathsf{E}(\mathcal{E}, e)$ iff $\Pr[(S, \mathcal{E}) \xleftarrow{\$} X : S(e) \in S(\mathcal{T}_E).\text{dom}]$ is negligible.
- $X \models F(e)$ iff $\Pr[(S, E) \xleftarrow{\$} X : e \in S(\mathsf{F})] = 1$.
- $X \models RCounter(e)$ iff $\Pr[(S, E) \xleftarrow{\$} X : e \in S(\mathsf{C})] = 1$.

3.2 Hoare Logic Rules

We present a set of rules of the form $\{\varphi\}\mathsf{c}\{\varphi'\}$, meaning that execution of command c in any distribution that satisfies φ leads to a distribution that satisfies φ'. Using Hoare logic terminology, this means that the triple $\{\varphi\}\mathsf{c}\{\varphi'\}$ is valid. We group rules together according to their corresponding commands. We do not provide rules for the commands $x := \mathcal{E}^{-1}(y)$ or $x := y[n, m]$ since those commands are only used during decryption.

Notation: For a set V, we write V, x as a shorthand for $V \cup \{x\}$, $V - x$ as a shorthand for $V \setminus \{x\}$, and $\text{Indis}(\nu x)$ as a shorthand for $\text{Indis}(\nu x; \text{Var})$.

Random Assignment:

- (R1) $\{true\}\ x \xleftarrow{\$} \mathcal{U}\ \{F(x) \wedge \text{Indis}(\nu x) \wedge \mathsf{E}(\mathcal{E}, x)\}$
- (R2) $\{\text{Indis}(\nu y; V)\}\ x \xleftarrow{\$} \mathcal{U}\ \{\text{Indis}(\nu y; V, x)\}$

Increment:

- (I1) $\{F(y)\}\ x := y + 1\ \{RCounter(x) \wedge \mathsf{E}(\mathcal{E}, x)\}$
- (I2) $\{RCounter(y)\}\ x := y + 1\ \{RCounter(x) \wedge \mathsf{E}(E, x)\}$
- (I3) $\{\text{Indis}(\nu z; V)\}\ x := y + 1\ \{\text{Indis}(\nu z; V - x)\}$ if $z \neq x, y$ and $y \notin V$

Xor operator:

- (X1) $\{\text{Indis}(\nu y; V, y, z)\}x := y \oplus z\{\text{Indis}(\nu x; V, x, z)\}$ where $x, y, z \notin V$,
- (X2) $\{\text{Indis}(\nu y; V, x)\}x := y \oplus z\{\text{Indis}(\nu y; V)\}$ where $x \notin V$,
- (X3) $\{\text{Indis}(\nu t; V, y, z)\}\ x := y \oplus z\ \{\text{Indis}(\nu t; V, x, y, z)\}$ if $t \neq x, y, z$ and $x, y, z \notin V$
- (X4) $\{F(y)\}\ x := y \oplus z\ \{\mathsf{E}(\mathcal{E}, x)\}$ if $y \neq z$

Concatenation:

- (C1) $\{\text{Indis}(\nu y; V, y, z)\} \wedge \{\text{Indis}(\nu z; V, y, z)\}\ x := y\|z\ \{\text{Indis}(\nu x; V, x)\}$ if $y, z \notin V$
- (C2) $\{\text{Indis}(\nu t; V, y, z)\}\ x := y\|z\ \{\text{Indis}(\nu t; V, x, y, z)\}$ if $t \neq x, y, z$

Block cipher:

- (B1) $\{\mathsf{E}(\mathcal{E}, y)\}\ x := \mathcal{E}(y)\ \{F(x) \wedge \text{Indis}(\nu x) \wedge \mathsf{E}(\mathcal{E}, x)\}$
- (B2) $\{\mathsf{E}(\mathcal{E}, y) \wedge \text{Indis}(\nu z; V)\}\ x := \mathcal{E}(y)\ \{\text{Indis}(\nu z; V)\}$ provided $z \neq x$

- (B3) $\{\mathsf{E}(\mathcal{E}, y) \wedge Rcounter(z)\}\ x := \mathcal{E}(z)\ \{Rcounter(z)\}$ provided $z \neq x$
- (B4) $\{\mathsf{E}(\mathcal{E}, y) \wedge \mathsf{E}(\mathcal{E}, z)\}\ x := \mathcal{E}(y)\ \{\mathsf{E}(\mathcal{E}, z)\}$ provided $z \neq x, y$
- (B5) $\{\mathsf{E}(\mathcal{E}, y) \wedge F(z)\}\ x := \mathcal{E}(y)\ \{F(z)\}$ provided $z \neq x, y$

Finally, we add a few rules whose purpose is to preserve invariants that are unaffected by the command.

Generic preservation rules:

Assume that $z \neq x, w, v$ and c is either $x \xleftarrow{\$} \mathcal{U}$, $x := w\|v$, $x := w \oplus v$, or $x := w + 1$:

- (G1) $\{\mathsf{Indis}(\nu z; V)\}\ \mathsf{c}\ \{\mathsf{Indis}(\nu z; V)\}$ provided $w, v \in V$
- (G2) $\{\mathsf{E}(\mathcal{E}, z)\}\ \mathsf{c}\ \{\mathsf{E}(\mathcal{E}, z)\}$
- (G3) $\{RCounter(z)\}\ \mathsf{c}\ \{RCounter(z)\}$
- (G4) $\{F(z)\}\ \mathsf{c}\ \{F(z)\}$

3.3 Proof Sketches

Due to space restrictions, we cannot present formal proofs of all our rules here. We present quick sketches instead to give the reader some intuition as to why each rule holds. The complete proofs are available in our full manuscript [11].

Rules for random assignment

In rule (R1), $F(x)$ simply follows from the definition of $F(\cdot)$, and $\mathsf{Indis}(\nu x)$ should be obvious since x has just been sampled at random, independently of all other values. Also, since the block cipher has been computed only on a polynomial number of values, out of an exponential domain, the probability that x has been queried to the block cipher is clearly negligible. Rule (R2) is easily proven using the fact that, at this point, x is independent from all other values in the program.

Rules for increment

For rules (I1) and (I2) the behavior of $RCounter(\cdot)$ easily follows from its definition. Note that since we have either $F(y)$ or $RCounter(y)$, y (and x) were obtained by repeatedly applying $+1$ to a random value r, i.e. $x = r + k$ for some number k. Since $\mathcal{E}$ was computed only on a polynomial number of values, the probability of being less than k away from one of those values is negligible, therefore the probability that x has been queried to the block cipher is negligible. In (I3), if $\mathsf{Indis}(\nu z; V)$ holds, then clearly $\mathsf{Indis}(\nu z; V - x)$ holds as well, and the values in $V - x$ are unchanged by the command.

Rules for Xor

Rules (X1) and (X2) are proven by considering y as a one-time pad applied to z. As a result, one of x or y will be indistinguishable from random provided that the other is not known. For (X3), one simply notes that x is easy to construct from y and z, so if t is indistinguishable from random given y and z, then it is also indistinguishable from random given x, y and z. For rule (X4), since y is fresh, it is still independent from all other values, from z in particular. It then follows that x has the same distribution as y and is independent from all values except y and therefore, the probability that it has been queried to $\mathcal{E}$ is negligible for the same reason that y is.

Rules for concatenation

Rules (C1) and (C2) follow simply from the observation that the concatenation of two independent random strings is a random string.

Rules for block cipher

To prove (B1), in the Ideal Cipher Model, $\mathcal{E}$ is sampled at random among all possible functions $\{0,1\}^\eta \rightarrow \{0,1\}^\eta$. Since y has never been queried to the block cipher, $x := \mathcal{E}(y)$ is indistinguishable from an independent random value, and so possess the same invariants as if $x \xleftarrow{\$} \mathcal{U}$ had been executed. Rules (B2) to (B5) simply preserve invariants that are unaffected by the computation of the block cipher on a value that has never been queried before.

Generic preservation rules

The conditions for applying those rules, particularly $z \neq x, w, v$ were designed specifically so that the command would have no effect on the invariant. The invariant is therefore preserved.

As a result of all this, we have the following:

Proposition 1. *In the Ideal Cipher Model, the Hoare triples given in the previous rules are valid.*

As a result, our method can be used to prove the semantic security of an encryption mode by proving that, from the adversary's point of view, the ciphertexts are indistinguishable from random bits.

Proposition 2. *Let $\mathcal{E}_M(m_1|\ldots|m_i, c_0|\ldots|c_i) : \mathbf{var}\ \boldsymbol{x_i}; c_i$ be a generic encryption mode describe with our language, and let $IO = \{m_1, \ldots, m_i, c_0, \ldots, c_i\}$. If $\{true\}c_i \bigwedge_{k=0}^{i}\{Indis(\nu c_k; IO)\}$ is valid for every i, then $\mathcal{E}_M$ is IND-CPA secure in the Ideal Cipher Model.*

We conclude with the following, which states that our method of proving security of encryption modes is sound in the standard model.

Proposition 3. *Let $\mathcal{E}_M$ be an encryption mode proven secure in the Ideal Cipher Model using the method of Proposition 2. If there exists a standard model algorithm A such that $Adv_{A,M}^{ind-CPA}(\eta, X)$ is non-negligible, then there exists an algorithm B such that $Adv_{B,\mathcal{E}}^{prf}$ is non-negligible.*

4   Examples

In this section we apply our method to the traditional encryption modes (CBC), (CFB), (OFB) and (CTR) in respectively Figure 3, 4, 5 and 6. For simplicity, we consider messages consisting of only 3 blocks. The reader can easily be convinced that the same invariant propagation holds for any finite number of

$\mathcal{E}_{CBC}(m_1|m_2|m_3, IV|c_1|c_2|c_3)$
var IV, z_1, z_2, z_3;

$IV \xleftarrow{\$} \mathcal{U};$	$\{\mathsf{Indis}(\nu IV; \mathsf{Var}) \wedge F(IV) \wedge \mathsf{E}(\mathcal{E}, IV)\}$	(R1)
$z_1 := IV \oplus m_1;$	$\{\mathsf{Indis}(\nu IV; \mathsf{Var} - z_1) \wedge \mathsf{E}(\mathcal{E}, z_1)\}$	(X2)(X4)
$c_1 := \mathcal{E}(z_1);$	$\{\mathsf{Indis}(\nu IV; \mathsf{Var} - z_1)$	(B2)
	$\wedge\ \mathsf{Indis}(\nu c_1; \mathsf{Var}) \wedge F(c_1)\}$	(B1)
$z_2 := c_1 \oplus m_2;$	$\{\mathsf{Indis}(\nu IV; \mathsf{Var} - z_1)$	(G1)
	$\wedge\ \mathsf{Indis}(\nu c_1; \mathsf{Var} - z_2) \wedge \mathsf{E}(\mathcal{E}, z_2)\}$	(X2)(X4)
$c_2 := \mathcal{E}(z_2);$	$\{\mathsf{Indis}(\nu IV; \mathsf{Var} - z_1) \wedge \mathsf{Indis}(\nu c_1; \mathsf{Var} - z_2)$	(B2)
	$\wedge\ \mathsf{Indis}(\nu c_2; \mathsf{Var}) \wedge F(c_2)\}$	(B1)
$z_3 := c_2 \oplus m_3;$	$\{\mathsf{Indis}(\nu IV; \mathsf{Var} - z_1) \wedge \mathsf{Indis}(\nu c_1; \mathsf{Var} - z_2)$	(G1)
	$\wedge\ \mathsf{Indis}(\nu c_2; \mathsf{Var} - z_3) \wedge \mathsf{E}(\mathcal{E}, z_3)\}$	(X2)(X4)
$c_3 := \mathcal{E}(z_3);$	$\{\mathsf{Indis}(\nu IV; \mathsf{Var} - z_1) \wedge \mathsf{Indis}(\nu c_1; \mathsf{Var} - z_2)$	(B2)
	$\wedge\ \mathsf{Indis}(\nu c_2; \mathsf{Var} - z_3) \wedge Indis(\nu c_3; \mathsf{Var})\}$	(B1)

Fig. 3. Analysis of CBC encryption mode

$\mathcal{E}_{CFB}(m_1|m_2|m_3, IV|c_1|c_2|c_3)$
var IV, z_1, z_2, z_3;

$IV \xleftarrow{\$} \mathcal{U};$	$\{\mathsf{Indis}(\nu IV) \wedge F(IV) \wedge \mathsf{E}(\mathcal{E}, IV)\}$	(R1)
$z_1 := \mathcal{E}(IV);$	$\{\mathsf{Indis}(\nu IV) \wedge \mathsf{Indis}(\nu z_1) \wedge F(z_1)\}$	(B1)(B2)
$c_1 := z_1 \oplus m_1;$	$\{\mathsf{Indis}(\nu IV) \wedge \mathsf{Indis}(\nu c_1; \mathsf{Var} - z_1) \wedge \mathsf{E}(\mathcal{E}, c_1)\}$	(G1)(X1)(X4)
$z_2 := \mathcal{E}(c_1);$	$\{\mathsf{Indis}(\nu IV) \wedge \mathsf{Indis}(\nu c_1; \mathsf{Var} - z_1) \wedge F(z_2)\}$	(B1)(B2)
$c_2 := z_2 \oplus m_2;$	$\{\mathsf{Indis}(\nu IV) \wedge \mathsf{Indis}(\nu c_1; \mathsf{Var} - z_1)$	(G1)
	$\wedge\ \mathsf{Indis}(\nu c_2; \mathsf{Var} - z_2) \wedge \mathsf{E}(\mathcal{E}, c_2)\}$	(X1) (X4)
$z_3 := \mathcal{E}(c_2);$	$\{\mathsf{Indis}(\nu IV) \wedge \mathsf{Indis}(\nu c_1; \mathsf{Var} - z_1)$	(B2)
	$\wedge\ \mathsf{Indis}(\nu c_2; \mathsf{Var} - z_2) \wedge F(z_3)\}$	(B1)
$c_3 := z_3 \oplus m_3;$	$\{\mathsf{Indis}(\nu IV) \wedge \mathsf{Indis}(\nu c_1; \mathsf{Var} - z_1)$	(G1)
	$\wedge\ \mathsf{Indis}(\nu c_2; \mathsf{Var} - z_2)$	(X1)
	$\wedge\ \mathsf{Indis}(\nu c_3; \mathsf{Var} - z_3)\}$	

Fig. 4. Analysis of CFB encryption mode

blocks. In order to prove IND-CPA security of these encryption schemes we have to prove that $c_0 = IV, c_1, c_2, c_3$ are indistinguishable from random bitstrings when given $m_1, m_2, m_3, c_0, c_1, c_2$ and c_3. Of course our method fails in analyzing ECB encryption mode and the "counter" version of CBC, which are two insecure operation modes.

CBC & CFB : In Figure 3 and 4, we describe the application of our set of rules on CBC and CFB examples. The analysis of these two encryption modes are similar.

OFB : The order of the commands in our description of OFB may seem strange, but it is not without reason. The variable z_{i+1} must be computed before c_i because no rule can preserve the invariant $\mathsf{E}(\mathcal{E}, z_i)$ through the computation of c_i.

$\mathcal{E}_{OFB}(m_1|m_2|m_3, IV|c_1|c_2|c_3)$
var IV, z_1, z_2, z_3;

$IV \xleftarrow{\$} \mathcal{U}$;	$\{\text{Indis}(\nu IV; \text{Var}) \wedge F(IV) \wedge \text{E}(\mathcal{E}, IV)\}$	(R1)
$z_1 := \mathcal{E}(IV)$;	$\{\text{Indis}(\nu IV; \text{Var}) \wedge \{F(z_1) \wedge \text{E}(\mathcal{E}, z_1) \wedge \text{Indis}(\nu z_1; \text{Var})\}$	(B1)(B2)
$z_2 := \mathcal{E}(z_1)$;	$\{\text{Indis}(\nu IV; \text{Var}) \wedge \text{Indis}(\nu z_1; \text{Var}) \wedge \text{E}(\mathcal{E}, z_2)$	(B1)(B2)
	$\wedge F(z_2) \wedge \text{Indis}(\nu z_2; \text{Var})\}$	
$c_1 := m_1 \oplus z_1$;	$\{\text{Indis}(\nu IV; \text{Var}) \wedge \text{Indis}(\nu c_1; \text{Var} - z_1) \wedge \text{E}(\mathcal{E}, z_2)$	(G1)(G2)(X1)
	$\wedge F(z_2) \wedge \text{Indis}(\nu z_2; \text{Var})\}\}$	(G4)
$z_3 := \mathcal{E}(z_2)$;	$\{\text{Indis}(\nu IV; \text{Var}) \wedge \text{Indis}(\nu c_1; \text{Var} - z_1) \wedge \text{E}(\mathcal{E}, z_3)$	(B1)(B2)
	$\wedge \text{Indis}(\nu z_2; \text{Var}) \wedge F(z_3) \wedge \text{Indis}(\nu z_3; \text{Var})\}$	(B2)
$c_2 := m_2 \oplus z_2$;	$\{\text{Indis}(\nu IV; \text{Var}) \wedge \text{Indis}(\nu c_1; \text{Var} - z_1)\}$	(G1)
	$\wedge \text{Indis}(\nu c_2; \text{Var} - z_2) \wedge \text{Indis}(\nu z_3; \text{Var})$	(X1)
$c_3 := m_3 \oplus z_3$;	$\{\text{Indis}(\nu IV; \text{Var}) \wedge \text{Indis}(\nu c_1; \text{Var} - z_1)\}$	(G1)
	$\wedge \text{Indis}(\nu c_2; \text{Var} - z_2) \wedge \text{Indis}(\nu c_3; \text{Var} - z_3)$	(X1)

Fig. 5. Analysis of OFB encryption mode

$\mathcal{E}_{CTR}(m_1|m_2|m_3, IV|c_1|c_2|c_3)$
var IV, z_1, z_2, z_3;

$IV \xleftarrow{\$} \mathcal{U}$;	$\{\text{Indis}(\nu IV; \text{Var}) \wedge F(IV) \wedge \text{E}(\mathcal{E}, IV)\}$	(R1)
$ctr1 := IV + 1$;	$\{\text{Indis}(\nu IV; \text{Var} - ctr1)$	(I3)
	$\wedge Rcounter(ctr1) \wedge \text{E}(\mathcal{E}, ctr1)\}$	(I1)
$z_1 := \mathcal{E}(ctr1)$;	$\{\text{Indis}(\nu IV; \text{Var} - ctr1) \wedge Rcounter(ctr1)$	(B2)(B3)
	$\wedge F(z_1) \wedge \text{E}(\mathcal{E}, z_1) \wedge \text{Indis}(\nu z_1; \text{Var})\}$	(B1)
$c_1 := m_1 \oplus z_1$;	$\{\text{Indis}(\nu IV; \text{Var} - ctr1) \wedge Rcounter(ctr1)$	(G1)(G3)
	$\wedge \text{Indis}(\nu c_1; \text{Var} - z_1)\}$	(X1)
$ctr2 := ctr1 + 1$;	$\{\text{Indis}(\nu IV; \text{Var} - ctr1 - ctr2)$	(I3)
	$\wedge \text{Indis}(\nu c_1; \text{Var} - z_1)$	(G1)
	$\wedge Rcounter(ctr2) \wedge \text{E}(\mathcal{E}, ctr2)\}$	(I2)
$z_2 := \mathcal{E}(ctr2)$;	$\{\text{Indis}(\nu IV; \text{Var} - ctr1 - ctr2)$	(B2)
	$\wedge \text{Indis}(\nu c_1; \text{Var} - z_1) \wedge Rcounter(ctr2)$	(B1)
	$\wedge F(z_2) \wedge \text{E}(\mathcal{E}, z_2) \wedge \text{Indis}(\nu z_2; \text{Var})\}$	(B3)
$c_2 := m_2 \oplus z_2$;	$\{\text{Indis}(\nu IV; \text{Var} - ctr1 - ctr2)$	(G1)
	$\wedge \text{Indis}(\nu c_1; \text{Var} - z_1) \wedge Rcounter(ctr2)$	(G3)
	$\wedge \text{Indis}(\nu c_2; \text{Var} - z_2)\}$	(X1)
$ctr3 := ctr2 + 1$;	$\{\text{Indis}(\nu IV; \text{Var} - ctr1 - ctr2 - ctr3)$	(I3)
	$\wedge \text{Indis}(\nu c_1; \text{Var} - z_1) \wedge \text{E}(\mathcal{E}, ctr3)$	(I2)
	$\wedge \text{Indis}(\nu c_2; \text{Var} - z_2) \wedge Rcounter(ctr3)\}$	(G1)
$z_3 := \mathcal{E}(ctr3)$;	$\{\text{Indis}(\nu IV; \text{Var} - ctr1 - ctr2 - ctr3)$	(B2)
	$\wedge \text{Indis}(\nu c_1; \text{Var} - z_1)$	(B1)
	$\wedge \text{Indis}(\nu c_2; \text{Var} - z_2) \wedge Rcounter(ctr3)$	(B3)
	$\wedge F(z_3) \wedge \text{E}(\mathcal{E}, z_3) \wedge \text{Indis}(\nu z_3; \text{Var})\}$	
$c_3 := m_3 \oplus z_3$;	$\{\text{Indis}(\nu IV; \text{Var} - ctr1 - ctr2 - ctr3)$	(G1)
	$\wedge \text{Indis}(\nu c_1; \text{Var} - z_1)$	(X1)
	$\wedge \text{Indis}(\nu c_2; \text{Var} - z_2)$	
	$\wedge \text{Indis}(\nu c_3; \text{Var} - z_3)\}$	

Fig. 6. Analysis of CTR encryption mode

CTR : This scheme is the only one of the four encryption modes we have studied that uses the increment command. The analysis is presented in Figure 6. We can see how the *RCounter* invariant is used for proving the IND-CPA security of this mode.

5   Conclusion

We proposed an automatic method for proving the semantic security of symmetric encryption modes. We introduced a small programming language in order to describe these modes. We construct a Hoare logic to make assertions about variables and propagate the assertions with the execution of the commands in the language. If the program which represents an encryption mode satisfies some invariants at the end of our automatic analysis then we conclude that the encryption mode is IND-CPA secure.

Future work: An obvious extension to our work would be to add a loop construct to our grammar. This would remove the necessity of having a different program for each message length within a mode of operation. We are also considering an extension of our work to prove CCA security of encryption modes using approaches such as the one proposed in [10] or the method proposed in [8]. Another more complex and challenging direction is to propose an extended version of our Hoare Logic in order to be able to analyze "modern" encryption modes which use more complex mathematical operation or primitives, or to try to use our method to prove security properties of other block-cipher based construction, such as unforgeability for block-cipher based MACs, or collision-resistance for block-cipher based hash functions.

References

1. Bellare, M., Desai, A., Jokipii, E., Rogaway, P.: A concrete security treatment of symmetric encryption. In: Annual IEEE Symposium on Foundations of Computer Science, p. 394 (1997)
2. Bellare, M., Kilian, J., Rogaway, P.: The security of the cipher block chaining message authentication code. J. Comput. Syst. Sci. 61(3), 362–399 (2000)
3. Bellare, M., Rogaway, P.: Code-based game-playing proofs and the security of triple encryption. Cryptology ePrint Archive, Report 2004/331 (2004), http://eprint.iacr.org/
4. Bellare, M., Rogaway, P., Wagner, D.: The EAX mode of operation. In: Roy, B., Meier, W. (eds.) FSE 2004. LNCS, vol. 3017, pp. 389–407. Springer, Heidelberg (2004)
5. Chakraborty, D., Nandi, M.: An improved security bound for HCTR, pp. 289–302 (2008)
6. Chakraborty, D., Sarkar, P.: A new mode of encryption providing a tweakable strong pseudo-random permutation. In: Robshaw, M.J.B. (ed.) FSE 2006. LNCS, vol. 4047, pp. 293–309. Springer, Heidelberg (2006)
7. Chakraborty, D., Sarkar, P.: HCH: A new tweakable enciphering scheme using the hash-counter-hash approach. IEEE Transactions on Information Theory 54(4), 1683–1699 (2008)

8. Courant, J., Daubignard, M., Ene, C., Lafourcade, P., Lahknech, Y.: Towards automated proofs for asymmetric encryption schemes in the random oracle model. In: Proceedings of the 15th ACM Conference on Computer and Communications Security (CCS 2008), Alexandria, USA (October 2008)

9. Courant, J., Ene, C., Lakhnech, Y.: Computationally sound typing for noninterference: The case of deterministic encryption. In: Arvind, V., Prasad, S. (eds.) FSTTCS 2007. LNCS, vol. 4855, pp. 364–375. Springer, Heidelberg (2007)

10. Desai, A.: New paradigms for constructing symmetric encryption schemes secure against chosen-ciphertext attack. In: Bellare, M. (ed.) CRYPTO 2000. LNCS, vol. 1880, pp. 394–412. Springer, Heidelberg (2000)

11. Gagné, M., Lafourcade, P., Lakhnech, Y., Safavi-Naini, R.: Automated security proof for symmetric encryption modes (manuscript 2009), http://pages.cpsc.ucalgary.ca/~mgagne/TR_Asian.pdf

12. Halevi, S.: EME*: Extending EME to handle arbitrary-length messages with associated data. In: Canteaut, A., Viswanathan, K. (eds.) INDOCRYPT 2004. LNCS, vol. 3348, pp. 315–327. Springer, Heidelberg (2004)

13. Halevi, S.: Invertible universal hashing and the tet encryption mode. In: Menezes, A. (ed.) CRYPTO 2007. LNCS, vol. 4622, pp. 412–429. Springer, Heidelberg (2007)

14. Halevi, S., Rogaway, P.: A tweakable enciphering mode. In: Boneh, D. (ed.) CRYPTO 2003. LNCS, vol. 2729, pp. 482–499. Springer, Heidelberg (2003)

15. Halevi, S., Rogaway, P.: A parallelizable enciphering mode. In: Okamoto, T. (ed.) CT-RSA 2004. LNCS, vol. 2964, pp. 292–304. Springer, Heidelberg (2004)

16. Iwata, T., Kurosawa, K.: OMAC: One-key CBC MAC. In: Johansson, T. (ed.) FSE 2003. LNCS, vol. 2887, pp. 129–153. Springer, Heidelberg (2003)

17. Iwata, T., Kurosawa, K.: On the security of a new variant of OMAC. In: Lim, J.-I., Lee, D.-H. (eds.) ICISC 2003. LNCS, vol. 2971, pp. 67–78. Springer, Heidelberg (2004)

18. Iwata, T., Kurosawa, K.: Stronger security bounds for OMAC, TMAC, and XCBC. In: Johansson, T., Maitra, S. (eds.) INDOCRYPT 2003. LNCS, vol. 2904, pp. 402–415. Springer, Heidelberg (2003)

19. Jutla, C.S.: Encryption modes with almost free message integrity. In: Pfitzmann, B. (ed.) EUROCRYPT 2001. LNCS, vol. 2045, pp. 529–544. Springer, Heidelberg (2001)

20. Kurosawa, K., Iwata, T.: TMAC: Two-key CBC MAC. In: Joye, M. (ed.) CT-RSA 2003. LNCS, vol. 2612, pp. 33–49. Springer, Heidelberg (2003)

21. Jaulmes, É., Joux, A., Valette, F.: On the security of randomized CBC-MAC beyond the birthday paradox limit: A new construction. In: Daemen, J., Rijmen, V. (eds.) FSE 2002. LNCS, vol. 2365, p. 237. Springer, Heidelberg (2002)

22. Liskov, M., Rivest, R.L., Wagner, D.: Tweakable block ciphers. In: Yung, M. (ed.) CRYPTO 2002. LNCS, vol. 2442, pp. 31–46. Springer, Heidelberg (2002)

23. McGrew, D.A., Fluhrer, S.R.: The security of the extended codebook (XCB) mode of operation (2007)

24. McGrew, D.A., Viega, J.: The security and performance of the galois/counter mode (GCM) of operation. In: Canteaut, A., Viswanathan, K. (eds.) INDOCRYPT 2004. LNCS, vol. 3348, pp. 343–355. Springer, Heidelberg (2004)

25. Rogaway, P.: Efficient instantiations of tweakable blockciphers and refinements to modes OCB and PMAC. In: Lee, P.J. (ed.) ASIACRYPT 2004. LNCS, vol. 3329, pp. 16–31. Springer, Heidelberg (2004)

26. Rogaway, P., Bellare, M., Black, J., Krovetz, T.: OCBa block-cipher mode of operation for efficient authenticated encryption. In: CCS 2001: Proceedings of the 8th ACM conference on Computer and Communications Security, pp. 196–205. ACM, New York (2001)
27. Victor Shoup. Sequences of games: a tool for taming complexity in security proofs (2004), http://eprint.iacr.org/2004/332
28. Wang, P., Feng, D., Wu, W.: On the security of tweakable modes of operation: TBC and TAE. In: Zhou, J., López, J., Deng, R.H., Bao, F. (eds.) ISC 2005. LNCS, vol. 3650, pp. 274–287. Springer, Heidelberg (2005)

Noninterference with Dynamic Security Domains and Policies

Robert Grabowski and Lennart Beringer

Ludwig-Maximilians-Universität
D-80538 München, Germany
{robert.grabowski,lennart.beringer}@ifi.lmu.de

Abstract. Language-based information flow analysis is used to statically examine a program for information flows between objects of different security domains, and to verify these flows follow a given policy.

When the program is distributed as mobile code, it may access resources whose domains depend on the client environment, or may face different security policies. In proof-carrying code scenarios, it is desirable to give a single proof that the program executes securely in any of these situations.

This paper presents an object-oriented, Java-like language with runtime security types that can be inspected to ensure that flows between accessed objects are actually allowed before operations inducing these flows are performed. A type system is used to statically prove that the flow tests included in the program are sufficient, such that a noninterference property for the program is ensured regardless of the domains of objects and the effective security policy. Also, the paper outlines how the concepts of the type system are transferred to a bytecode language.

1 Introduction

The goal of information flow security is to control the flow of information between data objects of a computing system, like variables, files, or sockets. More precisely, each object is assigned a *security domain*. An *information flow policy* defines the allowed flows between objects of these domains. Programs that transfer data between objects in a manner that respects a transitive end-to-end flow policy are called *noninterferent* [1]. A way to verify this property is to perform a static analysis prior to the execution [2].

While the language-based approach has evolved into a larger research field [3], most works assume the objects a program uses and their domains can be statically inferred. In mobile code scenarios, however, the program is executed in different client environments, where the set of available data objects and their domains as well as the security policy typically vary.

For example, consider a program that opens a specific file and appends some data to it. The security of the program clearly depends on the domain of the contents of the accessed file and of the appended data as well as on the information flow policy. This makes it impossible to certify programs with current proof-carrying code (PCC) techniques [4], as the code producer has no or little

A. Datta (Ed.): ASIAN 2009, LNCS 5913, pp. 54–68, 2009.
© Springer-Verlag Berlin Heidelberg 2009

information about the environments the program is executed in, and therefore cannot prove security statically.

Another application scenario is an address book with entries whose fields have varying, user-defined confidentiality levels. A backup application should preserve these levels and the security guarantee in the backup copy, while a program that synchronizes the data with some less trusted cloud storage service should only transmit those contact profile fields that have been declared public. In general, a program should be able to adapt to the security environment.

A solution is to introduce language support for querying or reflecting the domains of objects and the security policy, such that potentially insecure operations can be guarded with an appropriate flow test.

Previous work. The JIF language [5] contains constructs for dynamic label tests which have been formalized in the functional language λ_{DSec} [6]. Security domains can be used as values, enabling a constrained form of dependent pair and function types. In the imperative language RTI [7], data is associated with roles (sets of principals) which may be updated and queried programmatically to ensure that data flows securely. In the functional language λ^{deps^+} [8], all values are explicitly paired with their security domains, such that an external monitor program may throw invalid flow exceptions as required.

While all three approaches tackle aspects of dynamic information flow security in expressive and sophisticated ways, they are in our opinion not directly applicable to the mobile code scenario, as their analyses depend on a known security policy. Also, the analyses are defined only on the source code, and there is no translation given for an analysis on a lower level, e.g. bytecode.

The DSD language. In this paper, we present a Java-like object-oriented language called DSD (for "Dynamic Security Domains"). It features a light-weight extension in form of abstract domains and flow operators that can be used to query dynamic domains and the security policy at runtime. The analysis does not make any assumptions about the available set of security domains or the flow policy by reasoning over the domains abstractly. With a single proof, programs can be shown secure for *any* object domains and security policies.

Moreover, the choice of a mild extension of Java makes it possible to transfer the analysis to the bytecode level by building on existing work on certified compilation that preserves security types [9,10,11]. The mechanism gives an end-to-end noninterference guarantee for compiled code suitable for PCC contexts.

In the language, we allow a very restricted form of dependent types for objects: each object has a special field f_δ that can be used as the symbolic domain of other fields. Likewise, we assume each method has a special variable x_δ that can be used as a type for the other variables.

For the file append example above, a file with a dynamic domain could be modelled as an object of a class `File` whose pseudo-specification is shown in figure 1. The *value* of the field f_δ is used as the runtime security domain of the field *contents*. Existing files and their security domains as given by the environment can then be modelled as objects initially present on the heap.

```
class File {
   fδ: Domain⊥ ;
   contents: Stringfδ ;

   append(xδ: Domain⊥ , s: Stringxδ) {
      if xδ ⊑ this.fδ then this.contents := this.contents + s;
                      else skip; // or some error-handling code
   }
}
```

Fig. 1. File class

The method *append* takes a string s whose security type is explicitly passed in an additional domain argument x_δ. Since appending s to the file contents induces a flow of information, the contents update is guarded by a test whether the domain of the string (x_δ) is lower or equal to the domain of the file contents $(this.f_\delta)$ with respect to the effective security policy. The method is secure, since the critical assignment to *this.contents* is only executed if the induced flow is permitted in the client environment. The well-typedness of the methods proves that the file operations act securely in any particular client environment.

Outline of the analysis. We present a type system in the style of Volpano, Smith, and Irvine [12] and Banerjee and Naumann [13]. Since the domains are not statically available, the analysis is performed by collecting symbolic information about the domain fields and variables. For instance, the expression $x_\delta \sqsubseteq this.f_\delta$ evaluates to true in the **then** branch of the *append* method. The system aims to derive as much as possible from such information by employing a technique similar to Hoare logic, and verifies the flow tests in the program are sufficient.

This work extends a previous paper [14], featuring a more standard object-oriented language with dynamic methods including domain variables and constraint annotations, and improves the analysis with flexible constraint sets, updatable domain variables and fields, and a more clarified abstract reasoning.

Main contributions. This paper makes the following contributions:

- an object-oriented language with dynamic domains modelled explicitly as field and variables (section 2),
- security types that refer symbolically to these fields and variables, and a generalized termination-insensitive noninterference property (section 3), and
- a sound type system with abstract reasoning on the domain variable order (sections 4-5).

Furthermore, we briefly explain how the described dynamic security domains and concepts of the type system can be translated to the bytecode level (section 6). The presented type system for DSD has also been implemented as a prototypic type inference algorithm for a subset of Java with dynamic domain annotations [15]. For space reasons, this implementation is not discussed here.

2 The DSD Language

2.1 Syntax

The syntax of DSD is shown below. We use several disjoint sets of identifiers for variables ($x \in \mathcal{X}$), fields ($f \in \mathcal{F}$), classes ($C \in \mathcal{C}$), and methods ($m \in \mathcal{M}$). The notation $\bar{e}$ denotes a sequence of argument expressions.

$$e \in \mathcal{E} ::= n \mid x \mid e.f \mid e \; \mathbf{op} \; e \mid \top \mid \bot \mid e \sqcup e \mid e \sqsubseteq e$$
$$P \in \mathcal{P} ::= P \; ; P \mid \mathbf{if} \; e \; \mathbf{then} \; P \; \mathbf{else} \; P \mid \mathbf{while} \; e \; \mathbf{do} \; P \mid$$
$$\mathbf{skip} \mid x := e \mid e.f := e \mid x := \mathbf{new} \; C \mid x := e.m(\bar{e})$$

The syntax is split into expressions and programs (statements). It forms an imperative object-oriented language, with some additional expressions ($\top$, $\bot$, and operators $\sqcup$ and $\sqsubseteq$) to refer abstractly to security domains, as well as arbitrary side-effect free operators (denoted by $e \; \mathbf{op} \; e$). The syntax does not depend on the concrete security domains and the policy, which are understood to be given by the environment in which the program is executed.

2.2 Domain Lattice and Semantics

The flow policy on the client is specified by a *domain lattice* $(\mathcal{D}, \leq, \vee, H, L)$. Given two security domains $k_1, k_2 \in \mathcal{D}$, the order $k_1 \leq k_2$ expresses that information may flow from k_1 to k_2. To simplify presentation, we call the top-most domain in the lattice H (highest security) and the bottom-most domain L (lowest security), and assume a fixed domain lattice $\mathcal{D}$ for now.

We use a standard object-oriented state model. It consists of a store, i.e. a variable valuation, and a heap where objects are allocated:

states:	$\sigma \in \Sigma = \mathcal{S} \times \mathcal{H}$	values: $v \in \mathcal{V} ::= n \mid k \mid a \mid null$
stores:	$s \in \mathcal{S} = \mathcal{X} \rightharpoonup \mathcal{V}$	addresses: $a \in \mathcal{A}$
heaps:	$h \in \mathcal{H} = \mathcal{A} \rightharpoonup \mathcal{O}$	domains: $k \in \mathcal{D}$
objects:	$(C, F) \in \mathcal{O} = \mathcal{C} \times (\mathcal{F} \rightharpoonup \mathcal{V})$	numbers: $n \in \mathbb{N}$

There is a notable extension to the standard model: It is assumed there is a special variable identifier $x_\delta \in \mathcal{X}$, and a special field identifier $f_\delta \in \mathcal{F}$. We additionally require that a well-formed store s must contain x_δ, and all objects on a well-formed heap h must include the field f_δ. These assumptions are merely to simplify the presentation of type environments, which may refer to these special variables or fields. The analysis could later be extended to objects with none or many of these fields with arbitrary names.

Given a domain lattice $\mathcal{D}$, the interpretation of expressions in a program state σ is defined by a denotational semantics $\llbracket e \rrbracket_\sigma$. In particular, abstract domain expressions are interpreted in the concrete domain lattice:

$$\llbracket \top \rrbracket_\sigma = H \qquad \llbracket e_1 \sqcup e_2 \rrbracket_\sigma = \llbracket e_1 \rrbracket_\sigma \vee \llbracket e_2 \rrbracket_\sigma$$
$$\llbracket \bot \rrbracket_\sigma = L \qquad \llbracket e_1 \sqsubseteq e_2 \rrbracket_\sigma = \llbracket e_1 \rrbracket_\sigma \leq \llbracket e_2 \rrbracket_\sigma$$

For programs, we use a big-step operational semantics $\sigma_1 \xrightarrow{P} \sigma_2$ which states that if P is executed in state σ_1, it terminates in state σ_2. The definition is completely standard, with the exception that $x := \mathbf{new}\ C$ initializes the value of the f_δ field of the newly created object with the domain L. For reasons of limited space, the full semantics is not given here.

For the dynamic method dispatch, we use the functions margs and mtable that describe for each method the names of the formal arguments as well as the (dynamic-class dependent) implementations:

$$\text{margs} : \mathcal{M} \to \overline{\mathcal{X}} \qquad \text{mtable} : \mathcal{C} \times \mathcal{M} \rightharpoonup \mathcal{P}$$

Again to simplify the presentation, we require that each method includes x_δ at the first argument position. Methods are called dynamically depending on the dynamic type of the called object. A method is executed with a new store consisting of the formal parameters $\text{margs}(m)$ initially bound to the actual argument values, a special variable *this* containing the caller object, as well as a special return variable *ret* whose contents is assigned to the variable x after the method has terminated. With *ret*, no special return syntax is needed.

3   Noninterference

Our type system employs variable and field type environments. The types focus on information flow security, hence we consider only programs that are well-typed with respect to data types.

3.1   Type Environments

Type environments assign symbolic security domains to variables and fields:

$$\Gamma : \mathcal{X} \rightharpoonup \{\top, \bot, x_\delta\}$$
$$\text{ft} : \mathcal{F} \to \{\top, \bot, f_\delta\}$$

A variable typing Γ associates a symbolic security domain with the variables of the active method body. The types $\top$ or $\bot$ refer abstractly to the top-most and bottom-most domain of $\mathcal{D}$, respectively. A variable typed with the special symbol x_δ has the domain that is stored in the variable x_δ at runtime. A variable typing Γ is well-formed if $x_\delta \in \text{dom}(\Gamma)$ and $\Gamma(x_\delta) = \bot$.

A field typing ft associates a type with each field of an object. A field typed with f_δ has the domain that is stored in the field f_δ of the same object. A field typing ft is well-formed if $\text{ft}(f_\delta) = \bot$. Issues of subtyping, inheritance, and well-formedness are handled uniformly by giving a type for each field *identifier*. In the following, we assume a fixed well-formed field typing ft and leave it implicit. (Other types for $\Gamma(x_\delta)$ and $\text{ft}(f_\delta)$ will be discussed later.)

3.2   Type Interpretation

Types of variables and fields are interpreted as security domains in $\mathcal{D}$, given stores s and field valuations F, respectively:

$$[\![\top]\!]_s = H \qquad\qquad [\![\top]\!]_F = H$$
$$[\![\bot]\!]_s = L \qquad\qquad [\![\bot]\!]_F = L$$
$$[\![x_\delta]\!]_s = s(x_\delta) \qquad\quad [\![f_\delta]\!]_F = F(f_\delta)$$

The interpretation is well-defined, as every store includes x_δ and every object has a field f_δ. If $[\![\varGamma(x)]\!]_s \leq k$, we say x is *visible at k in s*; similar for fields.

3.3   Equivalence of States

In preparation for the definition of noninterference, we define when two states are equivalent with respect to a security domain $k \in \mathcal{D}$. To capture related allocations of different fresh addresses in two parallel runs, we parametrize equivalence by a partial bijection β, as presented in [13]. Two addresses a, a' are *indistinguishable* if $\beta(a) = a'$. Two domains, numbers, or null values are indistinguishable if they are equal. We write $v \sim_\beta v'$ for indistinguishable values.

For $k \in \mathcal{D}$, two stores are *k-equivalent* with respect to a variable typing $\varGamma$ if all variables visible at k have indistinguishable values:

$$s \sim_\beta^{\varGamma,k} s' \iff \forall x \in \mathrm{dom}(\varGamma).\ [\![\varGamma(x)]\!]_s \leq k \Rightarrow s(x) \sim_\beta s'(x)$$

Note that the relation is symmetric because $[\![\varGamma(x)]\!]_s = [\![\varGamma(x)]\!]_{s'}$: the well-formedness condition $\varGamma(x_\delta) = \bot$ ensures that x_δ itself contains the same domain in both states, therefore $\varGamma(x)$ is always interpreted as the same domain.

Two heaps are k-equivalent if all β-related objects are k-equivalent. Two objects are k-equivalent if they have the same fields and if all fields visible at k have indistinguishable values. In particular, this means that $F(f_\delta) = F'(f_\delta)$.

$$h \sim_\beta^k h' \iff \mathrm{dom}(\beta) \subseteq \mathrm{dom}(h) \wedge \mathrm{rng}(\beta) \subseteq \mathrm{dom}(h') \wedge$$
$$\forall a \in \mathrm{dom}(\beta).\ h(a) \sim_\beta^k h(\beta(a))$$
$$(C,F) \sim_\beta^k (D,F') \iff C = D \wedge \forall f \in \mathrm{dom}(F).\ [\![\mathrm{ft}(f)]\!]_F \leq k \Rightarrow F(f) \sim_\beta F'(f)$$

Finally, we extend k-equivalence point-wise to program states:

$$(s,h) \sim_\beta^{\varGamma,k} (s',h') \iff s \sim_\beta^{\varGamma,k} s' \wedge h \sim_\beta^k h'$$

3.4   Noninterference

Using the definition of state equivalence, we now define information flow security for a program P as a standard termination-insensitive noninterference property.

Definition 1. *P is secure with respect to variable typing $\varGamma$ if for all domains $k \in \mathcal{D}$, for all states $\sigma_1, \sigma_2, \sigma_1', \sigma_2'$ and for all partial bijections β,*

$$\sigma_1 \sim_\beta^{\varGamma,k} \sigma_1' \wedge \sigma_1 \xrightarrow{P} \sigma_2 \wedge \sigma_1' \xrightarrow{P} \sigma_2' \Rightarrow \sigma_2 \sim_\gamma^{\varGamma,k} \sigma_2'$$

for some partial bijection $\gamma \supseteq \beta$.

The property implies that all objects that are β-related before the execution stay related after the execution. The extended bijection γ captures the fact that new addresses may have been allocated and related in both executions.

As noninterference with dynamic security domains may rely on the values of domain fields and variables, we parametrize the above definition by certain state predicates Q and Q' that hold before and after the execution. We write $\sigma \models Q$ if σ satisfies Q, and will instantiate these predicates in the next section.

Definition 2. *Let Q and Q' be state predicates, and P a program. P is (Q, Q')-valid if for all states σ_1 and σ_2 such that $\sigma_1 \xrightarrow{P} \sigma_2$, $\sigma_1 \models Q$ implies $\sigma_2 \models Q'$. P is (Q, Q')-secure with respect to Γ if it is secure w.r.t. Γ and (Q, Q')-valid.*

4   Reasoning with Abstract Security Domains

4.1   Labels

As x_δ and f_δ may occur symbolically in variable and field types, the type system infers abstract domains as types for expressions. These abstract domains are called *labels*, and are a subset of expressions:

$$
\begin{aligned}
\text{access paths:} & \qquad \pi ::= x \mid \pi.f \\
\text{labels:} & \qquad \mathcal{L} \ni \ell ::= \top \mid \bot \mid x_\delta \mid \pi.f_\delta \mid \ell \sqcup \ell
\end{aligned}
$$

An f_δ field can appear in a label if the object to which it belongs is referenced in a normalized form, i.e. by an access path π of the form $x.f_1.f_2.\ldots.f_n$. This restriction is needed since objects are used syntactically in labels.

The type system assigns a label to each expression. For example, if $\Gamma(y) = x_\delta$ and $\Gamma(z) = \top$, the expression $y + z$ is assigned the label $x_\delta \sqcup \top$. Every label is an expression that evaluates to a security domain. If an expression e is typed with a label ℓ, then e depends in state σ on data of domains at most $[\![\ell]\!]_\sigma$. Since labels are special expressions, DSD features a very constrained form of dependent types.

4.2   Ordering Labels

Information flow type systems with static domains contain a number of side conditions $k_1 \leq k_2$ which require that information may flow from security domains k_1 to k_2 according to the security policy. Our type system has no static information about the values of labels at runtime. It is nevertheless possible to define an abstract order on labels by exploiting the fact that elements in $\mathcal{D}$ (to which labels evaluate) are ordered as a lattice. For example, it can be inferred that data may always flow from an expression labeled with $\bot$ to an expression labeled with $x_\delta \sqcup y.f_\delta$, as the evaluation of $\bot$ is always the lowest element in $\mathcal{D}$.

The following rules define the order over labels. (Assume $Q = \emptyset$ for now.) We additionally define a label equality $\equiv$ mirroring idempotence, commutativity, and associativity of the join operator, as well as antisymmetry of the order.

$$\dfrac{}{\bot \sqsubseteq_Q \ell} \qquad \dfrac{}{\ell \sqsubseteq_Q \top} \qquad \dfrac{}{\ell \sqsubseteq_Q \ell \sqcup \ell'} \qquad \dfrac{\ell_1 \sqsubseteq_Q \ell_2 \quad \ell_2 \sqsubseteq_Q \ell_3}{\ell_1 \sqsubseteq_Q \ell_3} \qquad \dfrac{\ell_1 \sqsubseteq_Q \ell_3 \quad \ell_2 \sqsubseteq_Q \ell_3}{\ell_1 \sqcup \ell_2 \sqsubseteq_Q \ell_3} \qquad \dfrac{(\ell_1, \ell_2) \in Q}{\ell_1 \sqsubseteq_Q \ell_2}$$

The label order rules that are justified by properties of the domain lattice are usually not sufficient to typecheck a program, as the validity of flows may depend on the actual values of domain fields and variables. This is the reason why the language features label flow tests, i.e. conditional statements of the form **if** $\ell_1 \sqsubseteq \ell_2$ **then** P_1 **else** P_2. For the subprogram P_1, we can assume that an information flow from $[\![\ell_1]\!]_\sigma$ to $[\![\ell_2]\!]_\sigma$ is permitted; otherwise, the branch will not be taken during the execution. The typing judgements for programs are therefore parametrized over a set $Q \subseteq \mathcal{L} \times \mathcal{L}$ containing label pairs. A pair $(\ell_1, \ell_2) \in Q$ expresses the assumption that a flow from ℓ_1 to ℓ_2 is allowed.

The set Q thus stores abstract information about f_δ fields and x_δ variables at a point of execution. Since Q gives requirements for suitable program states, we also call it the *constraint set*. (Constraint sets are the state predicates that were used in the definition of noninterference.)

Definition 3. *A program state σ satisfies a constraint set Q, written $\sigma \models Q$, if for all pairs $(\ell_1, \ell_2) \in Q$ it holds that $[\![\ell_1]\!]_\sigma \leq [\![\ell_2]\!]_\sigma$.*

The following theorem states that the rules for label order and equality are sound with respect to their interpretation in satisfying program states.

Theorem 1 (Soundness of label order and equality rules). *Given a set of constraints Q, two labels ℓ and ℓ' and a state σ satisfying Q, then*

1. *$\ell_1 \sqsubseteq_Q \ell_2$ implies $[\![\ell_1]\!]_\sigma \leq [\![\ell_2]\!]_\sigma$, and*
2. *$\ell_1 \equiv \ell_2$ implies $[\![\ell_1]\!]_\sigma = [\![\ell_2]\!]_\sigma$.*

Proof. By induction over the derivation of the label order and equality.

In fact, $(\mathcal{L}, \sqsubseteq_Q, \sqcup, \top, \bot)$ forms a semi-lattice over the (infinite) set of labels, where labels related by $\equiv$ refer to the same lattice point. It can be shown that if σ satisfies Q, the evaluation function $[\![\cdot]\!]_\sigma$ is a homomorphism that embeds the label lattice into the domain lattice.

The evaluation function not only depends on the program state σ, but also on $\mathcal{D}$ and its lattice operators. If we fix the state σ, then Q can as well be interpreted as the set of those domain lattices $(\mathcal{D}, \leq)$ whose structure includes the pairwise domain positionings which are abstractly described by label pairs in Q. A label test thus collects information about the program state and the structure of the domain policy at once.

5   Type System

The type system is mostly syntax-directed, and follows the separation of expressions and programs. We mainly discuss the extensions and differences to the type systems by Volpano, Smith, and Irvine [12] and Banerjee and Naumann [13].

5.1 Typing Expressions

The typing rules for expressions are shown in figure 2. A typing judgement $\Gamma \vdash e : \ell$ means that the expression e has a label ℓ, i.e. it depends in a specific program state σ on information of security domain $[\![\ell]\!]_\sigma$ at most. In particular, the type of a variable x, which is looked up in the environment Γ, is from the set $\{\top, \bot, x_\delta\}$ and thus a label. For field access, we define the *qualified field type*

$$\mathsf{ft}_\pi(f) := \begin{cases} \pi.f_\delta & \text{if } \mathsf{ft}(f) = f_\delta \\ \mathsf{ft}(f) & \text{else} \end{cases}$$

to transform the field type f_δ into a label by prepending an access path π that is supposed to reference the object whose field f is accessed.

$$\frac{}{\Gamma \vdash n : \bot} \qquad \frac{c \in \{\top, \bot\}}{\Gamma \vdash c : \bot} \qquad \frac{}{\Gamma \vdash x : \Gamma(x)} \qquad \frac{\Gamma \vdash \pi : \ell}{\Gamma \vdash \pi.f : \mathsf{ft}_\pi(f) \sqcup \ell}$$

$$\frac{\circ \in \{\mathbf{op}, \sqcup, \sqsubseteq\} \qquad \Gamma \vdash e_1 : \ell_1 \qquad \Gamma \vdash e_2 : \ell_2}{\Gamma \vdash e_1 \circ e_2 : \ell_1 \sqcup \ell_2}$$

Fig. 2. Expression type system

5.2 Typing Programs

For programs, we derive a typing judgement $\Gamma, pc \vdash Q \{P\} Q'$, which means a program P is secure if executed in states satisfying Q, and finishes in states satisfying Q'. The rules for the derivation system are shown in figure 3. Basically, the rules combine a Hoare logic-style reasoning on program predicates (constraint sets) with an information flow type system that uses labels instead of domains.

As in [13], the *program counter label* pc is actually a pair of labels (pc_s, pc_h), which is used to capture the lower bound of side effects on the store and the heap, respectively, in order to prevent indirect information flows. Using a pair of labels improves precision when method calls are involved.

The interesting rules are the ones for label tests and assignments. The rule for label tests works like the ordinary rule for conditionals, but also adds the label comparison to the pre-set of the **then** branch, since the condition holds when the execution takes that branch. No negative label order information is added for the **else** branch, since it does not improve the precision of the type system, and also might introduce self-contradicting constraint sets.

A variable assignment is typable if the induced flows can be abstractly shown secure, i.e. if the flows between labels are justified by the pre-condition set Q. It is also possible to update the x_δ variable, but only if it can be inferred that the new domain, given by the expression e, is at least as high as the old one. Therefore, one can change the runtime type of data e.g. from L to H.

$$\frac{\Gamma, pc \vdash Q_0 \{P\} Q_0' \quad Q \Rightarrow Q_0 \quad Q_0' \Rightarrow Q'}{\Gamma, pc \vdash Q \{P\} Q'}$$

$$\Gamma, pc \vdash Q \{\mathbf{skip}\} Q \qquad \frac{\Gamma, pc \vdash Q \{P_1\} Q' \quad \Gamma, pc \vdash Q' \{P_2\} Q''}{\Gamma, pc \vdash Q \{P_1 \,;\, P_2\} Q''} \qquad \frac{\Gamma \vdash e : \ell \quad \Gamma, pc \sqcup \ell \vdash Q \{P\} Q}{\Gamma, pc \vdash Q \{\mathbf{while}\ e\ \mathbf{do}\ P\} Q}$$

$$\frac{\Gamma \vdash e : \ell \quad \Gamma, pc \sqcup \ell \vdash Q \{P_1\} Q' \quad \Gamma, pc \sqcup \ell \vdash Q \{P_2\} Q'}{\Gamma, pc \vdash Q \{\mathbf{if}\ e\ \mathbf{then}\ P_1\ \mathbf{else}\ P_2\} Q'} \qquad \frac{\Gamma \vdash \ell_1 \sqsubseteq \ell_2 : \ell \quad \Gamma, pc \sqcup \ell \vdash Q, \ell_1 \sqsubseteq \ell_2 \{P_1\} Q' \quad \Gamma, pc \sqcup \ell \vdash Q \{P_2\} Q'}{\Gamma, pc \vdash Q \{\mathbf{if}\ \ell_1 \sqsubseteq \ell_2\ \mathbf{then}\ P_1\ \mathbf{else}\ P_2\} Q'}$$

$$\frac{\begin{array}{c}\Gamma \vdash e : \ell \\ \ell \sqcup pc_s \sqsubseteq_Q \Gamma(x) \\ x = x_\delta \Rightarrow x \sqsubseteq_Q e \\ x \notin pc\end{array}}{\Gamma, pc \vdash Q'[e/x] \cup Q \{x := e\} Q'} \qquad \frac{\begin{array}{c}\Gamma \vdash \pi : \ell_1 \quad \Gamma \vdash e : \ell_2 \\ \ell_1 \sqcup \ell_2 \sqcup pc_h \sqsubseteq_Q \mathsf{ft}_\pi(f) \\ f = f_\delta \Rightarrow \pi.f \sqsubseteq_Q e \\ f \notin pc \quad f \notin Q'[e/\pi.f]\end{array}}{\Gamma, pc \vdash Q'[e/\pi.f] \cup Q \{\pi.f := e\} Q'}$$

$$\frac{pc_s \sqsubseteq_Q \Gamma(x) \quad x \notin pc \quad x \neq x_\delta \quad x \notin Q'}{\Gamma, pc \vdash Q' \cup Q \{x := \mathbf{new}\ C\} Q', x.f_\delta \leq \bot}$$

$$\frac{\begin{array}{c}\Gamma \vdash \pi : \ell_{this} \quad \Gamma \vdash \bar{e} : \bar{\ell} \quad \mathsf{mtype}(m)[\bar{e}_{\#1}/x_\delta] = \ell'_{this}, \bar{\ell}' \xrightarrow{pc_h'} \ell_{ret} \\ \ell_{this} \sqsubseteq_Q \ell'_{this} \quad \bar{\ell} \sqsubseteq_Q \bar{\ell}' \quad pc_h \sqcup \ell_{this} \sqsubseteq_Q pc_h' \quad \ell_{ret} \sqcup \ell_{this} \sqcup pc_s \sqsubseteq_\emptyset \Gamma(x) \\ \mathsf{mreq}(m)[\bar{e}/\mathsf{margs}(m)][\pi/this] = Q \quad \mathsf{mens}(m)[x/ret] = Q' \\ x \notin pc \quad x \neq x_\delta\end{array}}{\Gamma, pc \vdash Q \{x := \pi.m(\bar{e})\} Q'}$$

where

- $id \notin \ell$ if and only if the identifier id does not syntactically occur in ℓ
- $Q \Rightarrow Q'$ if and only if $\forall (\ell_1, \ell_2) \in Q'.\ \ell_1 \sqsubseteq_Q \ell_2$
- $pc \sqcup \ell = (pc_s \sqcup \ell, pc_h \sqcup \ell)$

Fig. 3. Program type system

The set Q' is used for backward reasoning, in order to be able to make assertions about the post-value of x. The reason why Q is added is that one might need the pre-state of x in the premises of the rule. Note that $Q'[e/x]$ and Q do not need to be disjoint; in fact, they may even be identical. The constraint set assertions can be derived in Hoare logic by combining the rules for assignment and consequence of the logic. The rule for assigning to fields works similarly. Side conditions of the form $x \notin pc$ ensure that the evaluation of pc remains invariant.

The rule for method calls relies on given method annotations. More precisely, the *(security) type of a method* is a tuple $(t_{this}, \bar{t}, t_h, t_{ret})$ that assigns variable types to formal arguments of a method, where t is a meta-variable ranging over the possible variable types $\{\top, \bot, x_\delta\}$. We denote this by writing

$$\mathsf{mtype}(m) = t_{this}, \bar{t} \xrightarrow{t_h} t_{ret},$$

to be read as: in method m, *this* has type t_{this}, the arguments $\mathsf{margs}(m)$ have types $\bar{t}$, *ret* has type t_{ret}, and no fields below t_h are updated.

In the rule for method calls, these variable types are turned into labels by substituting x_δ with the first argument expression in the sequence, which is supposed to contain the domain value for x_δ. It is then checked whether the passed arguments and *this* have labels lower than their formal labels, and whether the return value has a label lower than the assigned variable. Also, the lower bound of the caller's heap side effect must be lower than the method's lower bound.

We also use functions

$$\mathsf{mreq}, \mathsf{mens} : \mathcal{M}(m) \to \mathcal{L} \times \mathcal{L}$$

to annotate method declarations with required (pre-)constraint sets and ensured (post-)constraint sets. Required sets may refer to the local variables, and ensured sets may refer to *ret*. The appropriate variable substitutions are performed before they can be compared with the caller's constraint sets. We can now formulate that a method is well-typed if its declared type can actually be derived.

Definition 4. *Let m be a method with* $\mathsf{mtype}(m) = t_{this}, \bar{t} \xrightarrow{t_h} t_{ret}$ *and constraint sets* $\mathsf{mreq}(m) = Q$ *and* $\mathsf{mens}(m) = Q'$. *Then, m is well-typed if for all implementations P of m, the judgment* $\Gamma, (\bot, t_h) \vdash Q \{P\} Q'$ *can be derived, where*

$$\Gamma = [\mathsf{margs}(m) \mapsto \bar{t}][this \mapsto t_{this}][ret \mapsto t_{ret}].$$

5.3   Soundness

The following is the main soundness theorem.

Theorem 2. *If $\Gamma, (\bot, \bot) \vdash Q \{P\} Q'$ and all methods are well-typed, then P is (Q, Q')-secure with respect to Γ.*

The proof of the theorem is by induction over the operational semantics. The full proof can be found on the first author's homepage [16].

We observe that the theorem actually states security for any given domain lattice: The semantics, state equivalence and security notion are parametric in the lattice $\mathcal{D}$. However, the syntax, the type environments and the typing rules only refer to labels and do not depend on the concrete security policy. Therefore, if a program is typable, it is secure with respect to any given security policy $(\mathcal{D}, \leq)$. As motivated in the introduction, this enables a single verification of a program that is executed in different environments with varying security policies.

5.4   Meta-label Monotonicity

The soundness proof relies on an intrinsic property of the type system: a security label ℓ derived as a type always interprets to a domain that is at least as confidential as the interpretation of the (meta-)label of ℓ.

Lemma 1. *If $\Gamma \vdash e : \ell$ and $\Gamma \vdash \ell : \ell'$, then $\llbracket \ell' \rrbracket_\sigma \leq \llbracket \ell \rrbracket_\sigma$ for any state σ.*

To put it in informal terms: the fact that something is public can never be itself a secret. The property seems to be common in languages where security types are accessible programmatically; RTI [7] for example has a similar requirement on security roles.

For precisely that reason, we chose $\bot$ as the type for domain variables and fields. If we admitted for instance $\Gamma(x_\delta) = \top$, a consistent type system would need to ensure that every x_δ-typed variable actually gets a label that is at least $\top$, which is not very useful.

6   Dynamic Security Domains at the Bytecode Level

This section outlines how the described dynamic security domains can be expressed on the bytecode level, i.e. for an unstructured language that operates on a stack. Since the described concepts are directly re-used, the type system is mainly suitable for results of the compilation from DSD.

A bytecode program P is a mapping of program points i to instructions I with the following syntax:

$$lit ::= \top \mid \bot \mid n$$
$$op ::= \sqcup \mid \sqsubseteq \mid \ldots$$
$$I ::= \mathsf{push}\ lit \mid \mathsf{pop} \mid \mathsf{prim}\ op \mid \mathsf{load}\ x \mid \mathsf{store}\ x \mid \mathsf{ifeq}\ i \mid \mathsf{goto}\ i \mid$$
$$\mathsf{new}\ C \mid \mathsf{putfield}\ f \mid \mathsf{getfield}\ f \mid \mathsf{call}\ m \mid \mathsf{return}$$

Instructions are interpreted with respect to program states (i, s, h, ρ) where i is the program point, s and h are stores and heaps as before, and ρ is an operand stack, i.e. a list of values. The small-step operational semantics for each instruction is omitted here, but can be found e.g. in [10].

The type system is based on the system by Barthe et al. [11], but requires the derivation of some additional information. Figure 4 is meant to illustrate the following explanations; it shows the bytecode program that corresponds to the introductory example **if** $x_\delta \sqsubseteq this.f_\delta$ **then** P_1 **else** P_2, and gives a possible derivation of the required auxiliary mappings, assuming $\Gamma(this) = \top$.

In contrast to the original type system, we use labels instead of domains again. Since labels remain a subset of expressions of the high-level DSD language, it is necessary to "disassemble" instructions that are used to construct labels. This is accomplished by deriving judgements of the form

$$i \vdash E \Rightarrow E'$$

i	$\mathbf{E}(i)$	$\mathbf{Q}(i)$	$\mathbf{S}(i)$	$\mathbf{pc}(i)$	$P(i)$
1	ϵ	$\emptyset$	ϵ	$\bot$	load x_δ
2	$"x_\delta"$	$\emptyset$	$\bot$	$\bot$	load $this$
3	$"this" :: "x_\delta"$	$\emptyset$	$\top :: \bot$	$\bot$	getfield f_δ
4	$"this.f_\delta" :: "x_\delta"$	$\emptyset$	$\top :: \bot$	$\bot$	prim $\sqsubseteq$
5	$"x_\delta \sqsubseteq this.f_\delta"$	$\emptyset$	$\top$	$\bot$	ifeq 17
6	ϵ	$\emptyset$	ϵ	$\top$	(instructions of P_2...)
$\vdots$					
17	ϵ	$\{x_\delta \sqsubseteq this.f_\delta\}$	ϵ	$\top$	(instructions of P_1...)

Fig. 4. Type derivation of the compilation of **if** $x_\delta \sqsubseteq this.f_\delta$ **then** P_1 **else** P_2

where E and E' are sequences of (high-level language) expressions and thus abstractions of the stack values. The judgement means that the execution of the instruction at i in a state with a stack described by E leads to a new state where the stack is described by E'. The system induces a mapping $\mathbf{E}$ that associates each program point with a list of expressions that describe the stack whenever that point is reached. (Instead of an expression, one may also describe a stack entry with a special symbol that indicates "don't know", hence $\mathbf{E}$ always exists.)

Using the stack expressions, we can compute local pre- and post-constraint sets for each instruction by deriving judgements

$$\mathbf{E} \vdash i : Q \;\Rightarrow\; i' : Q'$$

which say that if a state satisfies Q and program point i' is reachable via the instruction $P(i)$, then the new state satisfies Q'. Together with a consequence rule, this gives a mapping $\mathbf{Q}$ from each program point to a constraint set.

Finally, the main typing judgment has the form

$$\Gamma, \mathbf{Q}, \mathbf{E}, \mathbf{pc}, i \vdash S \Rightarrow S'$$

which models the small-step semantics abstractly by giving stack typings S and S', which are sequences of labels describing the security of the stack values at position i and the following position. The component $\mathbf{pc}$ is a mapping of instruction points to triples of labels (pc_s, pc_h, pc_ρ) that give the lower bound on side effects on the store, the heap, and the stack at each position. As is standard, whenever a "high" branching is performed, the program counter label is lifted for every instruction within the *control dependence region* [17] of the branching instruction.

If the rules induce a mapping $\mathbf{S}$ of program points to stack typings, then the program is well-typed, and (according to the soundness property) also secure. The soundness proof shows that the rules define a weak bisimulation of two executions where instructions with a "high" program counter label are shown to have no visible effect.

7   Discussion

We presented an object-oriented language with runtime tests of security domains, which makes programs possible that safely access dynamically typed data. This section highlights further benefits of DSD and outlines open work.

Modular security design. The encapsulation of data and security domains supports a modular software design. In the introductory example, the caller of *append* does not need to deal with security-related aspects of the file's contents if an error recovery mechanism for the **else** case is implemented. Alternatively, it is possible with the presented framework to pass the proof obligation $x_\delta \sqsubseteq this.f_\delta$ to the method caller by annotating the method accordingly.

Erasure and declassification in DSD. As the domain fields and variables can be inspected and compared during execution, it is possible to perform various security-related operations. For example, a file can be classified as confidential simply by setting its f_δ field to H, or information can be *erased* by overwriting the *contents* field with a harmless value and then setting f_δ to L. The last scenario is secure but currently not typable.

When the contents is not overwritten, the above operation amounts to *declassification*. Though it is hard to find an appropriate weakening of the noninterference property, the explicit change of security types (f_δ) in DSD represents a novel syntactic way of declassification.

Type preserving compilation. For PCC scenarios, it is desirable to compile DSD programs to bytecode such that the bytecode translation is typable with the bytecode type system if the original program was typable with the high-level system. The compilation may take the structure of the high-level program into account to compute the control dependence regions. Both the compilation and the type preservation proof are currently work in progress.

Implementation. As mentioned in the introduction, we have encoded the DSD language into a subset of the Java language by using Java annotations for field types and method signatures. Furthermore, we have developed a prototypic implementation of a type inference as a plugin for the integrated development environment Eclipse [15].

Expressivity and complexity. We plan to give a larger example program to better demonstrate the expressivity of the type system. Also, although the focus of PCC lies on efficient verifiability, it would be interesting to investigate the complexity of the analysis, or to give empirical benchmark results of the implementation.

Acknowledgements

This work was supported by the Information Society Technologies programme of the European Commision, Future and Emerging Technologies under the IST-2005-015905 MOBIUS project, and by the DFG-funded project InfoZert, grant number Be 3712/2-1. We would like to thank Gilles Barthe and Daniel Hedin (IMDEA Software Madrid) as well as Alexander Knapp, Florian Lasinger, and Martin Hofmann (LMU Munich) for their helpful input and comments.

References

1. Goguen, J.A., Meseguer, J.: Security policies and security models. In: Proceedings of the 1982 Symposium on Security and Privacy, pp. 11–20. IEEE Computer Society Press, Los Alamitos (1982)
2. Denning, D.E., Denning, P.J.: Certification of programs for secure information flow. Commun. ACM 20(7), 504–513 (1977)
3. Sabelfeld, A., Myers, A.C.: Language-based information-flow security. IEEE Journal on Selected Areas in Communications – special issue on Formal Methods for Security 21(1), 5–19 (2003)
4. Necula, G.C.: Proof-carrying code. In: Proceedings of the 24th ACM Symposium on Principles of Programming Languages, pp. 106–119. ACM Press, New York (1997)
5. Myers, A.C.: JFlow: Practical Mostly-Static Information Flow Control. In: Proceedings of the 26th ACM Symposium on Principles of Programming Languages (POPL), pp. 228–241. ACM Press, New York (1999)
6. Zheng, L., Myers, A.C.: Dynamic security labels and static information flow control. Int. J. Inf. Secur. 6(2), 67–84 (2007)
7. Bandhakavi, S., Winsborough, W., Winslett, M.: A trust management approach for flexible policy management in security-typed languages. In: Proceedings of 21st IEEE Computer Security Foundations Symposium, pp. 33–47. IEEE Computer Society, Los Alamitos (2008)
8. Shroff, P., Smith, S., Thober, M.: Dynamic dependency monitoring to secure information flow. In: Proceedings of the 20th IEEE Computer Security Foundations Symposium, Washington, DC, USA, pp. 203–217. IEEE Computer Society, Los Alamitos (2007)
9. Barthe, G., Pichardie, D., Rezk, T.: A certified lightweight non-interference java bytecode verifier. In: De Nicola, R. (ed.) ESOP 2007. LNCS, vol. 4421, pp. 125–140. Springer, Heidelberg (2007)
10. Barthe, G., Rezk, T.: Non-interference for a JVM-like language. In: TLDI 2005: Proceedings of the 2005 ACM SIGPLAN international workshop on Types in languages design and implementation, pp. 103–112 (2005)
11. Barthe, G., Rezk, T., Naumann, D.A.: Deriving an Information Flow Checker and Certifying Compiler for Java. In: S&P, pp. 230–242. IEEE Computer Society, Los Alamitos (2006)
12. Volpano, D., Smith, G., Irvine, C.: A sound type system for secure flow analysis. J. Computer Security 4(3), 167–187 (1996)
13. Banerjee, A., Naumann, D.A.: Stack-based access control and secure information flow. J. Funct. Program. 15(2), 131–177 (2005)
14. Grabowski, R.: Noninterference for Mobile Code with Dynamic Security Domains. In: International Workshop on Proof-Carrying Code, Pittsburgh, USA (Post-proceedings to appear, 2008)
15. Lasinger, F., Grabowski, R.: DSecCheck: Implementation of the DSD type system as an Eclipse plug-in (2009), http://www.tcs.ifi.lmu.de/~grabow/dsd
16. Grabowski, R.: Proofs for the soundness of the DSD type system (2009), http://www.tcs.ifi.lmu.de/~grabow/dsd
17. Ball, T.: What's in a region? or computing control dependence regions in near-linear time for reducible control flow. LOPLAS 2(1-4), 1–16 (1993)

A Critique of Some Chaotic-Map and Cellular Automata-Based Stream Ciphers

Matt Henricksen

Institute for Infocomm Research,
A*STAR, Singapore
mhenricksen@i2r.a-star.edu.sg

Abstract. Designing symmetric ciphers based on chaotic maps or cellular automata has a long but rarely successful history. In this paper, we examine some symmetric ciphers based on chaotic maps and cellular automata, and indicate how to reconcile design techniques for these primitives with current methodologies.

Keywords: Chaotic maps, cellular automata, symmetric cryptology.

1 Introduction

Cryptology, which pertains to information secrecy, lies at the core of information security. For reasons of efficiency, encryption is predominantly conducted using symmetric cryptology, realized through primitives (block ciphers, stream ciphers) for which the sender and receiver of the hidden information share a key.

Because of the recent ECRYPT eSTREAM competition [1], there has been a great deal of research into stream ciphers in the past few years. eSTREAM sought to identify stream ciphers that are secure and fast in hardware and/or software. Many of the submissions to the eSTREAM competition relied on upgrades to traditional shift-register based designs, on table swapping permutations, on to very novel designs. Only two of the thirty-four candidates were based on the principle of iterating a chaotic map, or Cellular Automaton (CA).

This belies the observation that there is a steady but almost orthogonal interest in designing symmetric ciphers based upon these principles, despite their being quickly and regularly broken. It is rare to see a design of a chaotic-map or CA based cipher a skilled cryptanalyst, and it is also clear that the lessons of mainstream cipher design are not always heard by the designers of chaotic-map-based schemes. Mainsteam cryptographers tend to view ciphers based on chaotic maps and cellular automata suspiciously [4]. Stream cipher technology is not yet mature [1], and this is sufficient reason not to abandon further study in chaotic-map based designs. Another reason is diversity. Many stream ciphers rely on the non-linearity given by s-boxes or on the guarantees of periodicity of word-based Linear Feedback Shift Registers (LFSRs), but a recent style of side-channel attack [24] utilizes the non-constant access time of both s-boxes and LFSRs on machines that utilize cache. The response by the cryptographic community has been a trend to design stream ciphers using a trinity of instructions

A. Datta (Ed.): ASIAN 2009, LNCS 5913, pp. 69–78, 2009.

- addition, rotation and exclusive-or, all of which are constant-time fast operations on modern computer architectures. But addition is only slightly non-linear with respect to rotation and exclusive-or, and such limited diversity in stream cipher design may not be robust given development of attack technologies such as algebraic attacks. As chaotic-map based designs tend to eschew s-boxes and LFSRs, it is an interesting source of 'genetic diversity'.

This paper attempts to bridge some of the gaps between conventional stream cipher design, and design of stream ciphers based upon chaotic maps and CAs. Many of these ciphers (or their specifications) share the same deficiencies. In Section 2, we give a handful of case studies of three types of cipher, including real-valued chaotic maps, fixed-value integer chaotic-maps and integer-based cellular automata. In Section 3, we give guidelines on how to design chaotic-map based and CA-based stream ciphers that can compete successfully with mainstream stream ciphers. In Section 4, we provide concluding notes.

2   Case Studies

Chaotic-map ciphers have a long history, dating back to Shannon's observation [19] that chaotic maps, such as the Baker's map, can be used to perform good mixing transformations.

2.1   Ciphers Based on Real-Valued Chaotic Maps

Real-valued chaotic maps appear at first sight to be a good match to encryption systems. Chaotic systems are very sensitive to initial conditions and system parameters. Depending upon the initial states, they may exhibit exponential sensitivity to minor changes. Iterating these maps gives the appearance of random behaviour, in which two similar values quickly diverge [1]. Information about the initial state is therefore lost. The parameters of the system can be determined using keys, and the trajectory of the system used for encryption.

Baptista's scheme. One of the most famous chaotic-map ciphers is the Baptista scheme [5], in which the logistic map $X_{n+1} = bX_n(1 - X_n)$ is used with values $b \in [0, 4]$ and $X_0 \in [0, 1]$. The range of the logistic map is partitioned into 256 sites, each assigned to an ASCII character. Ergodicity dictates that the trajectory of the map eventually visits all sites. A single character is encrypted by iterating the logistic map from its initial conditions until the target site for that character is reached. The encryption of the character is the number of iterations required to reach the target. Initial states are chained; the initial state of the second character is the final state of the first.

Irrespective of the security merits (the scheme was successfully attacked by Alvarez et al. [3]), it is obvious that such a scheme cannot compete efficiently with modern symmetric cryptosystems. The latter do not divide the plaintext or

---

[1] This property is not unique to chaotic maps. It is an integral part of symmetric ciphers, as measured by the Strict Avalanche Criterion.

ciphertext alphabet into ASCII characters, but rather into the native word size of the processor (ie. alphabets with 2^{32}, 2^{64} or 2^{128} characters) so can process the equivalent of multiple ASCII characters in the time it takes the Baptista scheme to process one, assuming that the update functions are equivalent. It is possible to further subdivide the target sites, but real-number valued schemes such as Baptista's already suffer from precision problems. *Ciphers that output bytes at a time are likely to be very slow and outmoded [2], and do not take full advantage of the efficiency of word-based instructions.*

It is also obviously the case that the round function of Baptista's scheme is not efficient relative to those of mainstream stream ciphers. Modern symmetric cryptosystems use simple operations such as exclusive-or, or addition, or table lookups which can be implemented to execute in less than a single cycle on a super-scalar architecture. The logistic map of Baptista's scheme uses real numbers, for which multiplication may be implemented with a latency of four cycles on recent architectures [11], but much slower on older machines. Given that the encryption of a single character takes several tens of thousands of iterations, the scheme is not competitive with stream ciphers that generate throughput in the order of gigabytes/second. It is very difficult for the cryptographer to take this kind of inefficient scheme seriously[3]. When proposing new schemes based on real-valued chaotic maps, the designers should optimize their cipher implementations and report speeds in terms of number of computer cycles required to generate one byte. If the speed can not be reported in terms of single-digit cycles, then the cipher is unlikely to be viewed positively.

Other schemes iterate chaotic maps a certain number of times and release part of the final state as the output. There are exotic variations involving multidimensional chaotic maps. For example, in a typical scheme, the state of the stream cipher is contained in two variables X and Y. The least significant bits of Y selects one of the following two-dimensional maps:

1. Baker's map

$$S(x, y) = \begin{cases} (2x, \frac{y}{2}) & \text{for } (0 \le x < \frac{1}{2}) \\ (2 - 2x, 1 - \frac{y}{2}) & \text{for } (\frac{1}{2} < x < 1) \end{cases}$$

2. Kaplan-Yorke map

$$x_{n+1} = 2x_n \bmod 1$$
$$y_{n+1} = ay_n + cos(4\pi x_n)$$

---

[2] RC4 is a notable and rare exception.

[3] While security was considered the paramount property of ciphers around a decade ago, efficiency has emerged as a primary consideration. There are now many ciphers that are both fast and secure. Cryptographers are not interested in slow ciphers - eSTREAM chose the fastest of the secure for their portfolio. Hence it does not matter what novel security features a new cipher possesses if it is not fast.

The value of X modulo some map-dependant constant selects how many times the map is iterated during one clock for the stream cipher. The modulus exists because for the Kaplan-Yorke map, the period is extremely low and it should not be permitted to iterate more than six times, while the Baker's map may be allowed to iterate more than twenty-times. This instantly raises a number of problems.

Firstly, if different maps contain significantly different operations or different constraints on how many times they can be iterated, then the attacker may mount a timing attack very simply by measuring the amount of time (with microsecond precision) between each output of keystream. For example, in this case if each iteration of a map takes 1 millisecond, then a delay of 20 millisecond indicates the Baker's map was iterated, and the least significant bit of Y has been leaked. The Kaplan-Yorke map is guaranteed to be slow because it implements a cosine operation, which takes around 100 cycles on most Intel processors [11]. In the time it takes to implement a single cosine, a conventional stream cipher can generate 128 bits of keystream.

The second problem is of periodicity. Many of the chaotic maps require their parameters to be within very specific ranges in order to guarantee chaotic behavior. Even then, the period of the maps is extremely small, compared to those of LFSRs (a 128-bit LFSR with a primitive polynomial has a guaranteed period of $2^{128} - 1$). Software and hardware efficiency dictates that it is not feasible to check whether the starting parameters for a chaotic map or LFSR will be successful in inducing pseudo-random behaviour, so many chaotic maps can not provide the necessary guarantees for periodicity in the way that conventional stream cipher design demands.

2.2   Ciphers Based on Fixed-Value Integer Chaotic-Maps

Basing a chaotic-map on fixed-point integer values allows the algorithm can be implemented in the general purpose registers, offering better throughput on simple instructions. The precision issue disappears because (for a given word size) there is no disagreement between processors on how to implement integer arithmetic.

Rabbit. [7] harnesses the pseudo-random properties of real-valued chaotic maps, but discretizes them to 32-bit words. Rabbit is probably the most successful stream cipher based upon chaotic maps, as one of the four finalists in the eS-TREAM software portfolio, with an excellent performance of 3.7 cycles/byte on the Pentium III. The designers of Rabbit submitted an extensive cryptanalysis alongside the specification. Third-party cryptanalysis includes a moderately serious distinguisher with complexity 2^{158} [14].

The Rabbit state consists of eight 32-bit state variables and eight 32-bit state counters. The update function is defined as

$$x_{j,i+1} = g_{j,i} + g_{j-1,i} \lll r_{i,1} + g_{j-2,i} \lll r_{i,2}, r_i \in \{8, 16\}$$

where

$$g_{j,i} = ((x_{j,i} + c_{j,1})^2 \oplus ((x_{j,1} + c_{j,1})^2 \gg 32)) \bmod 2^{32}$$

The g function can be implemented using four 32-bit multiplications. On recent Intel processors with SSE2 (eg. the Core Duo), two 32-bit multiplications can be conducted simultaneously with a latency of a single cycle. But on older machines, multiplication is a problematic operation: on the Intel Pentium 4, the SSE2 latency is six cycles, and the general register latency is as much as 17 cycles. On that machine, the throughput of Rabbit falls to 9.5 cycles [10]. This emphasizes the need to choose operations carefully, although in Rabbit's case a good compromise between blazing efficiency on common machines, and sturdy performance on legacy machines seems to have made.

Rabbit's update function exhibits very good diffusion due to the fact that each state variable is updated using a non-linear combination of three state variables and three counters. This chaining makes it very difficult to perform divide-and-conquer and guess-and-determine attacks. Multiplication as a provider of confusion is less convincing. The use of constant-time operations and non-reliance on s-boxes means that timing and cache-timing attacks do not apply.

2.3   Ciphers Based on Integer-Based Cellular Automata

A popular theme in cipher design, if not a very successful one, is to construct a secretly-keyed CA. The automaton consists of a set of discrete cells in one or more dimensions. Each cell has a set of neighbours defined for a particular distance d. In an automaton with $d = 1$, the neighbours consist of the immediately adjacent cells. The CA state is iterated by determining a new generation of cells, where a set of rules determines the new state for each cell based on its own value and those of its neighbours.

Rule30. The theory of cellular automata was popularized by Steven Wolfram in 1985 [22]. He continued to advance their usage in cryptography in the well-known book *A new kind of science* [23], in which he classified cellular automata into four groups. Only the third, in which nearly all patterns evolve in a pseudo-random or chaotic manner, is suitable for cryptographic usage. In his earlier paper, Wolfram defines an automaton based on rule 30, ie. expressed in $GF(2)$ as $a_i = a_{i-1} \oplus (a_i \text{ OR } a_{i+1})$, alternatively represented below.

Rule 30							
Now	111	110	101	100	011	010	001	000
Next	0	0	0	1	1	1	1	0

Rule 30 was defined in the infancy of cryptography, and Wolfram acknowledges that the construction is highly linear. He justifies its existence by empirically demonstrating that there are no statistical regularities for sequence lengths up to 2^{19}. The usage of statistics to demonstrate the security of a cipher was a common approach in the eighties and the nineties. Nowadays, there is call for ciphers that when keyed with 256-bit keys produce keystream indistinguishable from random, so that distinguishers with extremely low biases (for example, in the order of 2^{-128}) successfully diminish confidence in the ciphers. It is not possible to demonstrate theses biases empirically. In any case, statistical tests go a long way towards proving nothing - for example, Dawson et al. [9] use statistical tests to verify that there is a bias in the second byte of any RC4 keystream, but refute the claim by Mironov [15] that there is also a bias in the first byte, by using statistical analysis of 100,000 randomly initialized keystreams. If they had used more keystreams, they would have discovered a different result: later on, it was indeed demonstrated that there is a bias in the first, and other bytes of RC4 keystream [17] using a significantly large number of keystreams (possible through improved computing power) in conjunction with theoretical analysis. Conversely, even trivially breakable ciphers, such as those comprising several LFSRs with long periods, can pass statistical tests. *Statistics used in isolation can indeed prove anything. They are inadequate as a line of defence.*

Wolfram suggests that the weakness of linearity in the CA can be avoided by non-bijectivity. In this case, the attacker cannot work backwards from the keystream to identify the internal state of the cipher. This idea of non-bijectivity is valid within the output filter, the function that samples the state of the cipher and produces a one-way map of it to provide keystream, but it is a dangerous concept when applied to the update function, which maps the internal state of the cipher at time t to the state at time $t+1$. The state of a stream cipher should always maintain its entropy, otherwise at a later stage an attacker may be able to perform a search with complexity less than that of brute forcing the master key.

MAG. With the passing of 25 years, and in the context of the sophisticated theories of cipher design that mandate highly non-linear components, Wolfram's work on 'Cryptography with CA' is now unconvincing, but it still attracts followers. MAG [21] is a accumulator-based stream cipher based on the Wolfram Rule 30 generalized to 32-bit words. It was entered into the eSTREAM competition as a software candidate, but was quickly archived due to security and efficiency issues.

In the algorithm, cell a_i is compared to neighbour a_{i-1}, and on the basis of their relationship cell a_{i+1} or its complement is exclusive-ored to the accumulator, which is then exclusive-ored to cell a_{i+2}. This cell is used to generate output. As a case study, MAG is an excellent archetype. Firstly, its defence against cryptanalysis attacks is empirical, being based upon statistical testing of fifty samples of output, each sample being ten megabytes long. MAG also uses 'visual cryptanalysis', whereby the keystream is mapped as a picture. The absence of visual artifacts for this one keystream is taken as proof that the keystream is pseudo-random, thereby ignoring the facts that not all keystreams are created equal, and that the human eye is not an effective computer for determining the presence of low-probability biases. While this test is meaningless as a device to detect 2^{-128} probability biases, it is surprisingly common in chaotic-map and CA cipher design papers.

The most interesting thing about MAG is its claim that due to its heritage, it is not subject to the usual cryptanalytic techniques.

> The advantage of [this] approach is: a set of criteria such as linear complexity, nonlinearity, statistics, confusion and diffusion does not have

to be addressed directly as is the case with more complicated system-theoretic approaches. The whole security issue is shifted to the computational irreducibility principle alone. [21, p. 15]

MAG *can* be represented as a conventional cipher design. MAG was cryptanalysed by Simpson et al. [20] in which they demonstrate that MAG can be represented as a traditional cipher structure involving a 127-word register coupled with the accumulator. Their attack on MAG succeeds with a modest thirty-two bytes of keystream. Thus the security by difference defence does not hold.

In MAG, the state update function is close to linear, using only exclusive-or and complementation operations. The output filter, by truncating the 32-bit input to its least significant byte, simultaneously cripples the efficiency of the cipher and leaks large portions of the internal state into keystream. After 127 iterations of the cipher, the entropy of the state is reduced by one-quarter. For an 80-bit key, this reduction allows the remaining key bits to be almost practically brute-forced, and the loss of entropy is fatal. The comparison operation in each cycle adds only one bit of uncertainty to be taken into account by the attacker.

The diffusion in the cipher is extremely poor. During one cycle clock, only one word of the register is altered, and it is only directly influenced by one other word of the register. *This is intrisincally a property of using a cellular automaton with a small neighbourhood.* Comparison with LFSR based ciphers is instructive. Generally large LFSRs will have a large number of taps, meaning that in each cycle, many words will be combined to influence a single word, and the number of words influenced can be increased by having many smaller LFSRs coupled together by some non-linear mechanism. In fact, this non-linear mechanism is likely to be much stronger than the non-linearity in MAG, which is generated through complementation. The linearity of the exclusive-ors means that successive complementations in MAG cancel, and that for any two points in time, the attacker need only to effectively deal with a single complementation operation. No explicit intra-word diffusion elements are present.

Perhaps the most serious mistake of the cipher is that, in its quest for efficiency, MAG inadequately mixes the state before releasing keystream. This is a common problem in many CA-based and chaotic-based ciphers, such as the unnamed CA-based system cryptanalysed by Bao [4]. Bao describes that the "inherent weakness is that it is actually like a one round block cipher" The recent all-in-one symmetric cryptographic primitive Enrupt [16] has strong similiarities to the MAG cipher, although its update function is more complex. As with MAG, the cipher can be represented as a long register coupled to an accumulator, and characterized by a slow-diffusion moderately-linear update function that operates on a small set of neighbouring cells. The advantage Enrupt has over MAG is that it releases keystream from the accumulator rather than from the register, and ensures that the accumulator is updated several times before each keystream is generated. This makes it more difficult for the attacker to retrieve internal state. Nevertheless, Enrupt was convincingly cryptanalysed in its hash function form by Indesteege [13].

3   A Good Design Methodology for Stream Ciphers

The task of designing a good stream cipher involves several iterative stages. In the first, the designer selects a series of simple and efficient operations and combines them in a novel way. In the second, he analyses the design from efficiency and security perspectives. He iterates through these two stages, applying modifications until he has a cipher that provides both good benchmarks, and a series of results that defend the cipher against known attacks, such as time-memory-data tradeoff, guess-and-determine, related key-related IV, algebraic attacks, and so on. Generally the absence of such a defence in the specification paper for a new cipher indicates the second phase has been improperly performed, and therefore the onus of defending the cipher falls inappropriately to third-party cryptographers. The same applies when only basic statistical arguments are present.

Therefore the designer also must be the cryptanalyst. He must ensure that the state size of the cipher is at least double the combined length of the key and IV in order to avoid time-memory-data tradeoff attacks [12]. For software implementations, all operations should be word-based or bitsliced. The algorithm should have no conditional branches, in order to avoid pipeline stalls and timing attacks. The update function should be bijective, and the output filter should be a one-way map. Either or both of these should have some non-linear components. Linear components should have some guarantee of minimum period to ensure that keystream does not quickly become repetitive. Diffusion between different parts of the cipher should be strong and efficient (CA with neighbourhoods of 1 need not apply).

The algorithm should have a key initialization algorithm that mixes in a key and an equal length IV into the state in a non-linear and non-reverisble way. Preferably this should involve reuse of the update function, and occur in two phases - the first, the mixing of the key, and the second the mixing of the IV - to enable agile IV-rekeying.

All of this should occur sufficiently quickly to enable the cipher to be competitive with its contemporaries, but not too efficiently to degrade the security of the cipher. Most importantly, the designer needs to show that he is aware of the latest cryptanalytic techniques, and he has applied them unsuccessfully to his cipher. This is frequently something that is missing from chaotic-map and cellular automata-based specifications.

4   Conclusion

In this paper, we surveyed a number of chaotic-map and cellular automata-based stream ciphers.

Many mainstream ciphers are built upon LFSRs, which have well-understood properties, including guaranteed properties when used with an irreducible primitive polynomial. Contrast this to chaotic maps, which particularly due to their representation as floating-point numbers, with all the associated disadvantages of round-off errors, may have very short or indeterminate periods, or depending upon inappropriate choice of starting parameters, may not be chaotic at all. The limitations of real-valued chaotic-map based ciphers will continue to make them non-competitive in relation to mainstream ciphers. Integer-based chaotic maps schemes are viable, as demonstrated by Rabbit.

Most of the cellular automata-based stream ciphers have very slow diffusion. The exception is Hiji-Bij-Bij [18][4], which is a hybrid cipher that combines two cellular automata with standard stream cipher building blocks. It will be interesting to investigate the suitability of cellular automata with larger neighbourhoods and better diffusion properties.

In this paper, we have attempted to provide guidelines for designers interested in using chaotic maps or cellular automata to build stream ciphers. The most important guidelines are to understand and deploy a wide range of standard cryptanalysis techniques, and to understand the importance of efficiency in this very competitive field.

References

1. eSTREAM PHASE 3 (September 2008),
   http://www.ecrypt.eu.org/stream/index.html
2. State of the Art Stream Ciphers (SASC) 2008 Workshop, Lausanne, Switzerland (February 2008), Special Workshop hosted by the ECRYPT Network of Excellence, http://www.ecrypt.eu.org/stvl/sasc2008/
3. Alvarez, G., Montoya, F., Romera, M., Pastor, G.: Cryptanalysis of an ergodic chaotic cipher. Physics Letters A 311, 172–179 (2003)
4. Bao, F.: Cryptanalysis of a Partially Known Cellular Automata Cryptosystem. IEEE Transactions on Computers 53(11), 1493–1497 (2004)
5. Baptista, M.S.: Cryptography with chaos. Phys. Lett. A 240(50) (1998), http://cmup.fc.up.pt/cmup/murilo.baptista/baptista_PLA1998.pdf
6. Bernstein, D.: The Salsa20 Family of Ciphers. In: Robshaw, M., Billet, O. (eds.) New Stream Cipher Designs: The eSTREAM Finalists. LNCS, vol. 4986, pp. 84–97. Springer, Heidelberg (2008)
7. Boesgaard, M., Vesterager, M., Pedersen, T., Christiansen, J., Scavenius, O.: Rabbit: a new high-performance stream cipher. In: Johansson, T. (ed.) FSE 2003. LNCS, vol. 2887, pp. 325–344. Springer, Heidelberg (2003)
8. Cho, J.Y.: An improved estimate of the correlation of distinguisher for Dragon. In: SASC 2008 [2]. Special Workshop hosted by the ECRYPT Network of Excellence, pp. 11–20 (2008), http://www.ecrypt.eu.org/stvl/sasc2008/
9. Dawson, E., Gustafson, H., Henricksen, M.: Analysis of statistical flaws in the RC4 encryption algorithm. In: 19th British Combinatorics Conference, Bangor, Wales (2003)
10. ECRYPT eSTREAM. The eSTREAM Project - eSTREAM Phase 3 Performance Figures - Intel Pentium 4 (2008), http://www.ecrypt.eu.org/stream/phase3perf/2007a/pentium-4-a/
11. Fog, A.: Instruction tables. Lists of instruction latencies, throughputs and microoperation breakdowns for Intel and AMD CPU's (2009), http://www.agner.org/optimize/instruction_tables.pdf

---

[4] Hiji-Bij-Bij is sureveyed in the long version of this paper.

12. Hong, J., Sarkar, P.: New applications of time memory data tradeoffs. In: Roy, B.K. (ed.) ASIACRYPT 2005. LNCS, vol. 3788, pp. 353–372. Springer, Heidelberg (2005)

13. Indesteege, S.: Practical Collisions for EnRUPT. In: 16th International Workshop on Fast Software Encryption, FSE 2009, Leuven, Belgium (February 2009)

14. Lu, Y., Wang, H., Ling, S.: Cryptanalysis of Rabbit. In: Wu, T.-C., Lei, C.-L., Rijmen, V., Lee, D.-T. (eds.) ISC 2008. LNCS, vol. 5222, pp. 204–214. Springer, Heidelberg (2008)

15. Mironov, I. (Not So) Random Shuffles of RC4. In: Yung, M. (ed.) CRYPTO 2002. LNCS, vol. 2442, pp. 304–319. Springer, Heidelberg (2002)

16. O'Neil, S.: EnRUPT First all-in-one symmetric cryptographic primitive. In: SASC 2008 - The State of the Art of Stream Ciphers. Special Workshop hosted by the ECRYPT Network of Excellence, Lausanne, Switzerland, February 13-14 [2], pp. 259–272., http://www.ecrypt.eu.org/stvl/sasc2008/

17. Paul, G., Rathi, S., Maitra, S.: On non-negligible bias of the first output byte of RC4 towards the first three bytes of the secret key. Des. Codes Cryptography 49(1-3), 123–134 (2008)

18. Sarkar, P.: Hiji-bij-bij: A new stream cipher with a self-synchronizing mode of operation. In: Johansson, T., Maitra, S. (eds.) INDOCRYPT 2003. LNCS, vol. 2904, pp. 36–51. Springer, Heidelberg (2003)

19. Shannon, C.: Communication theory of secrecy systems. Bell System Technical Journal 28, 656–715 (1985)

20. Simpson, L.R., Henricksen, M.: Improved Cryptanalysis of MAG. In: Batten, L.M., Safavi-Naini, R. (eds.) ACISP 2006. LNCS, vol. 4058, pp. 64–75. Springer, Heidelberg (2006)

21. Vuckovac, R.: MAG My Array Generator (a new strategy for random number generation) (2005), http://www.ecrypt.eu.org/stream/ciphers/mag/mag.pdf

22. Wolfram, S.: Cryptography with cellular automata. In: Williams, H.C. (ed.) CRYPTO 1985. LNCS, vol. 218, pp. 429–432. Springer, Heidelberg (1985)

23. Wolfram, S.: A New Kind of Science. Wolfram Media (January 2002)

24. Zenner, E.: A Cache Timing Analysis of HC-256. In: Proceedings of 15th Annual Workshop on Selected Areas in Cryptography. LNCS, Springer, Heidelberg (2008)

A Logic for Formal Verification of Quantum Programs

Yoshihiko Kakutani

Department of Information Science, University of Tokyo
kakutani@is.s.u-tokyo.ac.jp

Abstract. This paper provides a Hoare-style logic for quantum computation. While the usual Hoare logic helps us to verify classical deterministic programs, our logic supports quantum probabilistic programs. Our target programming language is QPL defined by Selinger, and our logic is an extension of the probabilistic Hoare-style logic defined by den Hartog. In this paper, we demonstrate how the quantum Hoare-style logic proves properties of well-known algorithms.

1 Introduction

The Hoare logic is a formal system for verification of programs. The logic was introduced by Hoare in [1], and has been studied technically and practically by many researchers (*e.g.*, [2], [3]). The aim of this work is to provide a kind of Hoare logic which is useful for verification of quantum programs.

Quantum computation is a developing topic in the field of computer science. Traditionally, studies of quantum computation are based on quantum gates and circuits, which are important for realize a quantum computer. Quantum Turing machines are purely abstract setting of quantum computation, and suitable for studies on computational complexity. Since our aim is to verify algorithms and protocols, we focus on neither circuits nor Turing machines but quantum programming languages. Our target language is QPL defined by Selinger in [4]. QPL has clear denotational semantics and its syntax is similar to that of the original Hoare logic. Our formulation of a Hoare-style logic is based on Selinger's denotational semantics.

Probabilistic behavior is one of the features of quantum computation. The usual Hoare logic derives an assertion that a post-condition holds after the termination of a program if a pre-condition holds before the execution. In probabilistic computation, however, it is not deterministic whether a condition is true or false. A probabilistic extension of the Hoare logic defined by den Hartog in [5] can derive a probabilistic assertion of a probabilistic program. We extend this probabilistic Hoare logic to quantum computation: probabilistic states are replaced with quantum mixed states, and formulae are extended with unitary transformations. Our quantum Hoare logic (may be called QHL in this paper) naturally covers den Hartog's logic because QPL has also classical bits. We do not describe a state of a quantum bit directly in our logic, but can describe probability after measurement. Such representation makes the syntax simple.

A. Datta (Ed.): ASIAN 2009, LNCS 5913, pp. 79–93, 2009.

In this paper, we show some practical examples how our quantum Hoare logic verifies properties of algorithms, quantum teleportation [6], Shor's prime factorization [7], a solution of the Deutsch problem [8], and quantum coin tossing [9].

Related Works

There are other extensions of the Hoare logic for quantum computation.

A dynamic logic with quantum computation, LQP, is provided by Baltag and Smets in [10]. LQP is an extension of the propositional dynamic logic, which is an extension of the propositional Hoare logic. LQP is more sophisticated from the viewpoint of program verification than extensions of the quantum logic like [11]. Because LQP is a propositional logic, it cannot describe a probabilistic predicate. It is an advantage that the base of our Hoare logic is a first-order predicate logic.

Another quantum Hoare logic is given by Chadha *et al.* in [12]. Also their logic is based on a probabilistic Hoare logic. While the expressive power of their formulae is strong, the derivation system as a Hoare logic is weak. Our logic supports wider probabilistic Hoare-style derivations, including the `while` loop. Formulation of rules for `while` loop programs is also a contribution of our work. Distinction of pure quantum states from mixed states makes the syntax and semantics of Chadha *et al.*'s logic complicated. Since our semantics based on Selinger's, we can deal with mixed states and classical states uniformly.

D'Hondt and Panangaden studies weakest preconditions on quantum programs in [13]. Their formulation gives another representation of probabilistic conditions. A Hoare-style logic [14] based on [13] is being developed by Ying.

2　Mathematical Preliminaries and Notations

We use some mathematical conventional notations in this paper.

The set of complex numbers is denoted by $\mathbb{C}$, the set of real numbers is denoted by $\mathbb{R}$, the set of integers is denoted by $\mathbb{Z}$, and the set of natural numbers including 0 is denoted by $\mathbb{N}$.

A finite dimensional vector on $\mathbb{C}$ is denoted by a column. The unit vectors $\begin{pmatrix} 1 \\ 0 \end{pmatrix}$ and $\begin{pmatrix} 0 \\ 1 \end{pmatrix}$ in $\mathbb{C}^2$ are denoted by e_0 and e_1, respectively. The unit matrix in $\mathbb{C}^{2^n \times 2^n}$ is denoted by I_n, and the zero matrix is by O_n. The suffix n of I_n or O_n may be omitted. For a matrix A, $A^\dagger$ denotes the adjoint of A. Some special matrices in $\mathbb{C}^{2 \times 2}$ are denoted as follows:

$$E_0 = \begin{pmatrix} 1\,0 \\ 0\,0 \end{pmatrix} \qquad E_1 = \begin{pmatrix} 0\,0 \\ 0\,1 \end{pmatrix} \qquad N = \begin{pmatrix} 0\,1 \\ 1\,0 \end{pmatrix}$$

$$H = \frac{1}{\sqrt{2}} \begin{pmatrix} 1\ \ 1 \\ 1\,{-1} \end{pmatrix} \qquad V = \begin{pmatrix} 1\,0 \\ 0\,i \end{pmatrix}.$$

$H_n \in \mathbb{C}^{2^n \times 2^n}$ is defined as $H_0 = 1$ and $H_{n+1} = H \otimes H_n$. A matrix in $\mathbb{C}^{2n \times 2n}$ may be denoted by $\begin{pmatrix} A\ C \\ B\ D \end{pmatrix}$ with matrices A, B, C, $D \in \mathbb{C}^{n \times n}$.

We show some equations useful in this paper.

$$(E_i \otimes X) \begin{pmatrix} A_0 & C \\ B & A_1 \end{pmatrix} (E_i \otimes Y) = E_i \otimes X A_i Y \qquad H^2 = I$$

$$(e_i^\dagger \otimes X) \begin{pmatrix} A_0 & C \\ B & A_1 \end{pmatrix} (e_i \otimes Y) = X A_i Y \qquad NE_0 N = E_1.$$

We represent a pure state of a quantum bit as a unit vector in $\mathbb{C}^2$. In that case, the first basis vector is identified with the integer 0, and the second basis vector with 1.

In order to distinguish program codes from usual mathematical expressions, we use `typewriter font` for program codes.

3   Quantum Programming Language

In this section, we introduce a quantum programming language, which is a restriction of Selinger's QPL [4]. Though our language does not support recursion, it has still a loop structure.

Definition 1. *The syntax of the quantum programming language is defined as follows.*

$$
\begin{aligned}
P ::= \; &\texttt{skip} \mid P \; ; \; P \\
&\mid \texttt{bit } x \mid \texttt{qbit } x \mid \texttt{discard } x \\
&\mid x \; \texttt{:= 0} \mid x \; \texttt{:= 1} \mid x, \ldots, x \; \texttt{*=} \; U \\
&\mid \texttt{if } x \texttt{ then } P \texttt{ else } P \mid \texttt{while } x \texttt{ do } P \\
&\mid \texttt{measure } x \texttt{ then } P \texttt{ else } P
\end{aligned}
$$

where x ranges over program variables, and U over unitary transformations. A typing context is a sequence which assigns a variable to either `bit` *or* `qbit`*. For typing contexts Γ and Γ', we write $\Gamma \cong \Gamma'$ when Γ' is a permutation of Γ. The typing rules are given in Table 1.*

The syntax `bit` b and `qbit` q mean variable declarations intuitively. The syntax `discard` x closes the scope of the variable x. Each program variable has the type of either classical bits or quantum bits which is declared by `bit` x or `qbit` x respectively.

If a program is well-typed with fixed contexts, the typing derivation is unique up to permutations of contexts. In this paper, we may implicitly identify permutable contexts.

The semantic interpretation of a program is a superoperator on density matrices. It is a usual manner in theoretical physics to represent mixed states as density matrices. For a pure quantum state u, that is, a unit vector, $uu^\dagger$ is a positive hermitian matrix whose trace is 1. A mixed state of u_1 with the probability p_1 and u_2 with the probability p_2 is represented as $p_1 u_1 u_1^\dagger + p_2 u_2 u_2^\dagger$. We remark

Table 1. Typing rules of QPL

$$\frac{}{\langle \Gamma \rangle \ \text{skip} \ \langle \Gamma \rangle} \qquad \frac{\langle \Gamma \rangle \ P \ \langle \Theta \rangle \qquad \langle \Theta \rangle \ Q \ \langle \Delta \rangle}{\langle \Gamma \rangle \ P \ ; \ Q \ \langle \Delta \rangle}$$

$$\frac{}{\langle \Gamma \rangle \ \text{bit} \ b \ \langle b : \text{bit}, \Gamma \rangle} \qquad \frac{}{\langle \Gamma \rangle \ \text{qbit} \ q \ \langle q : \text{qbit}, \Gamma \rangle}$$

$$\frac{}{\langle x : t, \Gamma \rangle \ \text{discard} \ x \ \langle \Gamma \rangle} \qquad \frac{}{\langle b : \text{bit}, \Gamma \rangle \ b := i \ \langle b : \text{bit}, \Gamma \rangle}$$

$$\frac{U \in \mathbb{C}^{2^n \times 2^n}}{\langle q_1 : \text{qbit}, \ldots, q_n : \text{qbit}, \Gamma \rangle \ q_1, \ldots, q_n \ \text{*=} \ U \ \langle q_1 : \text{qbit}, \ldots, q_n : \text{qbit}, \Gamma \rangle}$$

$$\frac{\langle b : \text{bit}, \Gamma \rangle \ P_1 \ \langle \Delta \rangle \qquad \langle b : \text{bit}, \Gamma \rangle \ P_0 \ \langle \Delta \rangle}{\langle b : \text{bit}, \Gamma \rangle \ \text{if} \ b \ \text{then} \ P_1 \ \text{else} \ P_0 \ \langle \Delta \rangle}$$

$$\frac{\langle b : \text{bit}, \Gamma \rangle \ P \ \langle b : \text{bit}, \Gamma \rangle}{\langle b : \text{bit}, \Gamma \rangle \ \text{while} \ b \ \text{do} \ P \ \langle b : \text{bit}, \Gamma \rangle}$$

$$\frac{\langle q : \text{qbit}, \Gamma \rangle \ P_1 \ \langle \Delta \rangle \qquad \langle q : \text{qbit}, \Gamma \rangle \ P_0 \ \langle \Delta \rangle}{\langle q : \text{qbit}, \Gamma \rangle \ \text{measure} \ q \ \text{then} \ P_1 \ \text{else} \ P_0 \ \langle \Delta \rangle}$$

$$\frac{\Gamma \cong \Gamma' \qquad \langle \Gamma' \rangle \ P \ \langle \Delta' \rangle \qquad \Delta' \cong \Delta}{\langle \Gamma \rangle \ P \ \langle \Delta \rangle}$$

that any positive hermitian matrix A is equal to some $\sum_k p_k u_k u_k^\dagger$. A diagonal element of a density matrix indicates the probability that the corresponding basis vector is observed. Usually the trace of a density matrix is required to be 1, but we use a generalized form of density matrices according to Selinger in order to deal with partial computation.

Definition 2. *A matrix A is a density matrix if A is positive hermitian and $\text{tr}(A) \leq 1$ holds. The set of density matrices in $\mathbb{C}^{2 \times 2}$ is denoted by $\mathbb{Q}$. The set of diagonal density matrices in $\mathbb{C}^{2 \times 2}$ is denoted by $\mathbb{B}$.*

Since $\mathbb{B}$ can be naturally considered a subset of $\mathbb{R}^2$, $\mathbb{B}$ is a domain for bit. For a typing context $b_1 : \text{bit}, \ldots, b_m : \text{bit}, q_1 : \text{qbit}, \ldots, q_n : \text{qbit}$, we consider the domain $\mathbb{B}^m \otimes \mathbb{Q}^n$ where $\otimes$ means the tensor product on $\mathbb{R}$-modules and X^{n+1} and X^0 respectively mean $X^n \otimes X$ and the unit of $\otimes$. A program is interpreted as a superoperator on the domains which correspond to its typing contexts. The formal semantics follows Selinger.

Definition 3. *Define $[\![\text{bit}]\!] = \mathbb{B}$, $[\![\text{qbit}]\!] = \mathbb{Q}$, and $[\![x_1 : T_1, \ldots, x_n : T_n]\!] = [\![T_1]\!] \otimes \cdots \otimes [\![T_n]\!]$. $[\![\langle \Gamma \rangle \ P \ \langle \Delta \rangle]\!]$ is a function from $[\![\Gamma]\!]$ to $[\![\Delta]\!]$ defined in Table 2, where $[\![\Gamma]\!] \cong [\![\Gamma']\!]$ is the isomorphism induced from $\Gamma \cong \Gamma'$.*

In the above definition, in fact, $[\![-]\!]$ is defined on not typing judgments but derivations of typing judgments. One can see easily that $\cong$ commutes with typing rules and $[\![\langle \Gamma \rangle \ P \ \langle \Delta \rangle]\!]$ is well-defined. We may write $[\![P]\!]$ for $[\![\langle \Gamma \rangle \ P \ \langle \Delta \rangle]\!]$ if contexts are trivial.

Table 2. Semantics of QPL

$[\![\langle \Gamma \rangle \; \texttt{skip} \; \langle \Gamma \rangle]\!](A) = A$

$[\![\langle \Gamma \rangle \; P \; ; \; Q \; \langle \Delta \rangle]\!](A) = [\![\langle \Theta \rangle \; Q \; \langle \Delta \rangle]\!]([\![\langle \Gamma \rangle \; P \; \langle \Theta \rangle]\!](A))$

$[\![\langle \Gamma \rangle \; \texttt{bit} \; b \; \langle b : \texttt{bit}, \Gamma \rangle]\!](A) = \mathrm{E}_0 \otimes A$

$[\![\langle \Gamma \rangle \; \texttt{qbit} \; q \; \langle q : \texttt{qbit}, \Gamma \rangle]\!](A) = \mathrm{E}_0 \otimes A$

$[\![\langle x : t, \Gamma \rangle \; \texttt{discard} \; x \; \langle \Gamma \rangle]\!](A) = (e_0^\dagger \otimes \mathrm{I})A(e_0 \otimes \mathrm{I}) + (e_1^\dagger \otimes \mathrm{I})A(e_1 \otimes \mathrm{I})$

$[\![\langle b : \texttt{bit}, \Gamma \rangle \; b := 0 \; \langle b : \texttt{bit}, \Gamma \rangle]\!](A) = \pi_0(A) + \nu(\pi_1(A))$

$[\![\langle b : \texttt{bit}, \Gamma \rangle \; b := 1 \; \langle b : \texttt{bit}, \Gamma \rangle]\!](A) = \nu(\pi_0(A)) + \pi_1(A)$

$[\![\langle \overrightarrow{q} : \texttt{qbit}, \Gamma \rangle \; \overrightarrow{q} \mathrel{*=} U \; \langle \overrightarrow{q} : \texttt{qbit}, \Gamma \rangle]\!](A) = (U \otimes \mathrm{I})A(U^\dagger \otimes \mathrm{I})$

$[\![\langle b : \texttt{bit}, \Gamma \rangle \; \texttt{if} \; b \; \texttt{then} \; P_1 \; \texttt{else} \; P_0 \; \langle \Delta \rangle]\!](A)$
$\quad = [\![\langle b : \texttt{bit}, \Gamma \rangle \; P_0 \; \langle \Delta \rangle]\!](\pi_0(A)) + [\![\langle b : \texttt{bit}, \Gamma \rangle \; P_1 \; \langle \Delta \rangle]\!](\pi_1(A))$

$[\![\langle b : \texttt{bit}, \Gamma \rangle \; \texttt{while} \; b \; \texttt{do} \; P \; \langle b : \texttt{bit}, \Gamma \rangle]\!](A)$
$$= \sum_{n=0}^{\infty} \pi_0(([\![\langle b : \texttt{bit}, \Gamma \rangle \; P \; \langle b : \texttt{bit}, \Gamma \rangle]\!] \circ \pi_1)^n(A))$$

$[\![\langle q : \texttt{qbit}, \Gamma \rangle \; \texttt{measure} \; q \; \texttt{then} \; P_1 \; \texttt{else} \; P_0 \; \langle \Delta \rangle]\!](A)$
$\quad = [\![\langle \Gamma, q : \texttt{qbit} \rangle \; P_0 \; \langle \Delta \rangle]\!](\pi_0(A)) + [\![\langle \Gamma, q : \texttt{qbit} \rangle \; P_1 \; \langle \Delta \rangle]\!](\pi_1(A))$

$[\![\langle \Gamma \rangle \; P \; \langle \Delta \rangle]\!] = \cong \circ [\![\langle \Gamma' \rangle \; P \; \langle \Delta' \rangle]\!] \circ \cong \; \text{if} \; \Gamma \cong \Gamma' \; \text{and} \; \Delta \cong \Delta'$

$\pi_i(A) = (\mathrm{E}_i \otimes \mathrm{I})A(\mathrm{E}_i \otimes \mathrm{I})$

$\nu(A) = (\mathrm{N} \otimes \mathrm{I})A(\mathrm{N} \otimes \mathrm{I})$

4 Formulae for Quantum Computation

Before defining a Hoare-style logic, we have to define formulae and their semantics. Formulae in QHL includes first-order formulae with special terms whose values are decided probabilistically.

Definition 4. *Formulae of the quantum Hoare logic is defined in the following.*

$$c ::= r \mid \alpha \mid f(c, \ldots, c)$$
$$t ::= c \mid \mathrm{pr}\,(\rho) \mid f(t, \ldots, t)$$
$$\Phi ::= t \leq t \mid \mathrm{int}\,(t) \mid t\Phi \mid \Phi \oplus \Phi \mid {}^{x, \ldots, x}M\Phi \mid \neg\Phi \mid \Phi \wedge \Phi \mid \forall\alpha.\ \Phi$$

where r, f, M, α, and ρ range over $\mathbb{R}$, functions on $\mathbb{R}$, matrices over $\mathbb{C}$, predicate variables, and conditions on $\overline{x}$'s and α's, respectively. We also assume that the dimension of M is $2^n \times 2^n$ when ${}^{x_1, \ldots, x_n}M\Phi$ is a formula. For a formula Φ, $\mathrm{fv}\,(\Phi)$ denotes the set of all free variables occurring in Φ, and $\mathrm{pv}\,(\Phi)$ denotes the set of all program variables occurring in Φ. We write $\Phi_1 \vee \Phi_2$ for $\neg(\neg\Phi_1 \wedge \neg\Phi_2)$, $\Phi \supset \Psi$ for $\neg\Phi \vee \Psi$, and $\exists\alpha.\ \Phi$ for $\neg(\forall\alpha.\ \neg\Phi)$. The predicates $\geq$, $=$, $<$, and $>$ are defined as syntax sugar.

In the definition of formulae, ρ is not defined formally because it is out of our logic. When an assignment of program variables to 0 or 1 and an assignment of predicate variables to real numbers are fixed, it must be deterministic whether ρ is true or false. Usually, the first-order predicate is enough for describing ρ, and we also use it in this paper. If ρ is valid, we write just $\mathrm{pr}\,()$ for $\mathrm{pr}\,(\rho)$.

The semantics of formulae is given as in the first-order predicate logic on real numbers except the forms $t\Phi$, $\Phi_1 \oplus \Phi_2$, and $\vec{x}M\Phi$. The syntactic forms $t\Phi$ and $\Phi_1 \oplus \Phi_2$ are borrowed from den Hartog's probabilistic logic [5]. The form $\vec{x}M\Phi$ is a natural extension of his logic with unitary operations. A formal model consists of $\mathbb{R}$ and a typing context introduced in the previous section. The interpretation of a formula depends on a quantum state on a context.

Definition 5. *For a formula Φ, a typing context Γ which covers $\mathrm{pv}\,(\Phi)$, a function v from predicate variables to $\mathbb{R}$, and a density matrix $A \in [\![\Gamma]\!]$, a statement*

$$\langle \Gamma \rangle, A, v \models \Phi$$

is defined in Table 3, where t° is defined by

$$\alpha^{\circ} = v(\alpha)$$
$$r^{\circ} = r$$
$$(f(t_1,\ldots,t_n))^{\circ} = f(t_1^{\circ},\ldots,t_n^{\circ})$$
$$(\mathrm{pr}\,(\rho))^{\circ} = \sum \{\, u^{\dagger}Au \mid \exists i_1,\ldots,i_n \in \{0,1\} \quad u = e_{i_1} \otimes \cdots \otimes e_{i_n}$$
$$\text{and } \rho[i_1/\overline{x_1},\ldots,i_n/\overline{x_n}] \text{ is true under } v \,\}$$

when $\Gamma = x_1 : T_1,\ldots,x_n : T_n$.

A term $\mathrm{pr}\,(\rho)$ means the probability that ρ holds after measurement of all bits. For example, $(\mathrm{pr}\,(\overline{\mathsf{q}} = 0))^{\circ}$ is $1/2$ under $\Gamma = \mathsf{q} : \mathtt{qbit}$ and $A = \mathrm{HE_0H}$. Unlike the

Table 3. Semantics of formulae in QHL

$\langle \Gamma \rangle, A, v \models t_1 \le t_2$ iff $t_1^{\circ} \le t_2^{\circ}$

$\langle \Gamma \rangle, A, v \models \mathrm{int}\,(t)$ iff $t^{\circ} \in \mathbb{Z}$

$\langle \Gamma \rangle, A, v \models t\Phi$ iff $\exists A'\ \ A = t^{\circ}A'$ and $\langle \Gamma \rangle, A', v \models \Phi$

$\langle \Gamma \rangle, A, v \models \Phi_1 \oplus \Phi_2$
  iff $\exists A_1\ \exists A_2\ \ A = A_1 + A_2$ and $\langle \Gamma \rangle, A_1, v \models \Phi_1$ and $\langle \Gamma \rangle, A_2, v \models \Phi_2$

$\langle \Gamma \rangle, A, v \models {}^{x_1,\ldots,x_n}M\Phi$
  iff $\exists \Gamma'\ \exists A'\ \ \Gamma \cong x_1 : T_1,\ldots,x_n : T_n, \Gamma'$ and $A \cong (M \otimes \mathrm{I})A'(M^{\dagger} \otimes \mathrm{I})$
  and $\langle x_1 : T_1,\ldots,x_n : T_n, \Gamma' \rangle, A', v \models \Phi$

$\langle \Gamma \rangle, A, v \models \neg\Phi$ iff not $\langle \Gamma \rangle, A, v \models \Phi$

$\langle \Gamma \rangle, A, v \models \Phi_1 \wedge \Phi_2$ iff $\langle \Gamma \rangle, A, v \models \Phi_1$ and $\langle \Gamma \rangle, A, v \models \Phi_2$

$\langle \Gamma \rangle, A, v \models \forall \alpha.\ \Phi$ iff $\forall r \in \mathbb{R}\ \langle \Gamma \rangle, A, v\{\alpha \mapsto r\} \models \Phi$

logic in [12], we cannot describe a state of a quantum bit directly. We describe only a property on probability through measurement. Note that $(\mathrm{pr}\,())^\circ$ is just the trace of A, that is, the whole probability of the world represented by A.

For a unitary matrix U, $\vec{q}U^\dagger\Phi$ is true at a quantum state if and only if Φ is true after the unitary transformation represented by U. The formula $\mathfrak{E}_i\Phi$ is true at a quantum state if and only if the state is obtained by the measurement of q from a state at which Φ holds. Such interpretation is helpful for QHL defined in the next section.

Our theory can be considered naturally an extension of den Hartog's probabilistic logic: if we restrict contexts to `bit` only, our semantics essentially coincides with the probabilistic one.

We use also the following notation in the Hoare-style logic. In the case that X is finite, $X \models \Psi$ is equivalent to $\bigoplus X \models \Psi$.

Definition 6. *For a set of formulae* $X = \{\,\Phi_j \mid j \in J\,\}$, *we write* $X \models \Psi$ *if the following condition is satisfied: if*

$$\mathrm{tr}(\sum_{j\in J} A_j) \leq 1 \quad and \quad \langle\Gamma\rangle, A_j, v \models \Phi_j \ for \ j \in J$$

hold, then

$$\langle\Gamma\rangle, \sum_{j\in J} A_j, v \models \Psi$$

holds.

The following examples of the $\models$ relation are used in later sections:

$$\vec{x}M_2\,\vec{x}M_1\Phi \models \vec{x}M_2M_1\Phi \qquad \Phi \models {}^b\mathrm{E}_0\Phi \oplus {}^b\mathrm{E}_1\Phi$$
$$r(\mathrm{pr}\,(\rho)=1) \models \mathrm{pr}\,(\rho)=r \qquad (\mathrm{pr}\,()=r) \oplus (\mathrm{pr}\,()=1-r) \models \mathrm{pr}\,()=1.$$

5   Quantum Hoare Logic

We give a Hoare-style logic in this section. An assertion, which is sometimes called a Hoare triple, forms

$$\{\Phi\}\ P\ \{\Psi\}$$

as usual. Intuitively, this assertion means that if Φ holds, Ψ holds after the execution of P.

Definition 7. *The quantum Hoare logic is defined in Table 4 and Table 5.*

Our quantum Hoare logic is sound in the following sense. While the original Hoare logic proves only correctness in the case that a program terminates, our logic can derive correctness on termination of a program in the same sense as den Hartog's probabilistic logic.

Table 4. Derivation rules of QHL

$$\frac{}{\{\Phi\}\ \texttt{skip}\ \{\Phi\}}\ (\text{skip}) \qquad \frac{\{\Phi\}\ P\ \{\Upsilon\} \qquad \{\Upsilon\}\ Q\ \{\Psi\}}{\{\Phi\}\ P\ ;\ Q\ \{\Psi\}}\ (\text{seq})$$

$$\frac{}{\{\,(\mathrm{pr}\,()=1)\wedge\Phi\,\}\ \texttt{bit}\ b\ \{\,(\mathrm{pr}\,(\overline{b}=0)=1)\wedge\Phi\,\}}\ (\text{new-bit})$$

$$\frac{}{\{\,(\mathrm{pr}\,()=1)\wedge\Phi\,\}\ \texttt{qbit}\ q\ \{\,(\mathrm{pr}\,(\overline{q}=0)=1)\wedge\Phi\,\}}\ (\text{new-qbit})$$

$$\frac{x\notin\mathrm{pv}\,(\Phi)}{\{\Phi\}\ \texttt{discard}\ x\ \{\Phi\}}\ (\text{discard})$$

$$\frac{}{\{\Phi\}\ b\ \texttt{:= 0}\ \{\,{}^b\mathrm{E}_0\Phi\oplus{}^b\mathrm{NE}_1\Phi\,\}}\ (\text{assign}_0) \qquad \frac{}{\{\Phi\}\ b\ \texttt{:= 1}\ \{\,{}^b\mathrm{NE}_0\Phi\oplus{}^b\mathrm{E}_1\Phi\,\}}\ (\text{assign}_1)$$

$$\frac{}{\{\,\overrightarrow{{}^qU^\dagger}\Phi\,\}\ \overrightarrow{q}\ \texttt{*=}\ U\ \{\Phi\}}\ (\text{unitary})$$

$$\frac{\{\,{}^b\mathrm{E}_0\Phi\,\}\ P_0\ \{\Psi_0\} \qquad \{\,{}^b\mathrm{E}_1\Phi\,\}\ P_1\ \{\Psi_1\}}{\{\Phi\}\ \texttt{if}\ b\ \texttt{then}\ P_1\ \texttt{else}\ P_0\ \{\Psi_0\oplus\Psi_1\}}\ (\text{if})$$

$$\frac{\{\,{}^b\mathrm{E}_1\Phi_n\,\}\ P\ \{\Phi_{n+1}\}\ \text{for}\ n\in\mathbb{N} \qquad \{\,{}^b\mathrm{E}_0\Phi_n\mid n\in\mathbb{N}\,\}\models\Psi}{\{\Phi_o\}\ \texttt{while}\ b\ \texttt{do}\ P\ \{\Psi\}}\ (\text{while})$$

$$\frac{\{\,{}^q\mathrm{E}_0\Phi\,\}\ P_0\ \{\Psi_0\} \qquad \{\,{}^q\mathrm{E}_1\Phi\,\}\ P_1\ \{\Psi_1\}}{\{\Phi\}\ \texttt{measure}\ q\ \texttt{then}\ P_1\ \texttt{else}\ P_0\ \{\Psi_0\oplus\Psi_1\}}\ (\text{measure})$$

$$\frac{\{\Phi\}\ P\ \{\Psi\}}{\{c\Phi\}\ P\ \{c\Psi\}}\ (\text{times}) \qquad \frac{\{\Phi_0\}\ P\ \{\Psi_0\} \qquad \{\Phi_1\}\ P\ \{\Psi_1\}}{\{\Phi_0\oplus\Phi_1\}\ P\ \{\Psi_0\oplus\Psi_1\}}\ (\text{plus})$$

Table 5. Logical derivation rules of QHL

$$\frac{\Phi\models\Phi' \qquad \{\Phi'\}\ P\ \{\Psi'\} \qquad \Psi'\models\Psi}{\{\Phi\}\ P\ \{\Psi\}}\ (\text{logic}) \qquad \frac{\{\Psi\}\ P\ \{\Phi\}}{\{\Psi[c/\alpha]\}\ P\ \{\Phi[c/\alpha]\}}\ (\text{subst})$$

$$\frac{\{\Phi\}\ P\ \{\Psi_1\} \qquad \{\Phi\}\ P\ \{\Psi_2\}}{\{\Phi\}\ P\ \{\Psi_1\wedge\Psi_2\}}\ (\text{and}) \qquad \frac{\{\Phi_1\}\ P\ \{\Psi\} \qquad \{\Phi_2\}\ P\ \{\Psi\}}{\{\Phi_1\vee\Phi_2\}\ P\ \{\Psi\}}\ (\text{or})$$

$$\frac{\{\Phi\}\ P\ \{\Psi\} \qquad \alpha\notin\mathrm{fv}\,(\Phi)}{\{\Phi\}\ P\ \{\forall\alpha.\ \Psi\}}\ (\text{all}) \qquad \frac{\{\Phi\}\ P\ \{\Psi\} \qquad \alpha\notin\mathrm{fv}\,(\Psi)}{\{\exists\alpha.\ \Phi\}\ P\ \{\Psi\}}\ (\text{exist})$$

Theorem 1. *If*

$$\langle\Gamma\rangle\ P\ \langle\Delta\rangle \qquad and \qquad \{\Phi\}\ P\ \{\Psi\}$$

hold,

$$\langle\Gamma\rangle, A, v\models\Phi \qquad implies \qquad \langle\Delta\rangle, [\![P]\!](A), v\models\Psi.$$

We discuss each rule in the rest of this section instead of showing the proof.

The logical rules can be justified as in classical Hoare logics. The rule (subst) is redundant in this formulation, but useful for verification under a condition that some assertions are valid.

The rules (times) and (plus) hold because any program is linear in the semantic interpretation.

Though $\mathrm{pr}\,() = 1$ is required in (bit) and (qbit), we can derive from (times)

$$\overline{\{\,(\mathrm{pr}\,() = r) \wedge \Phi\,\}\ \mathtt{qbit}\ q\ \{\,(\mathrm{pr}\,(\overline{q} = 0) = r) \wedge \Phi\,\}}$$

for any $r \in \mathbb{R}$.

The rule (unitary) is equivalent to the rule

$$\overline{\{\,\Phi\,\}\ \overrightarrow{q}\ \mathtt{*=}\ U\ \{\,\overrightarrow{q}U\Phi\,\}}$$

which is more useful in some cases.

Our (if) rule is essentially the same as den Hartog's. The rule (measure) is similar to (if) because quantum measurement and classical branching have the same semantics.

Because our logic can verify a probabilistic assertion, the rule (while) is not an invariance condition unlike the original Hoare logic. Instead, we give a sufficient condition for formalizing the `while` rule as invariance.

Lemma 1. *If the conditions*

1. *$p\Phi \oplus (1-p)\Phi \models \Phi$ holds for any $p \in \mathbb{R}$ such that $0 \leq p \leq 1$.*
2. *${}^{b}\mathrm{E}_i\Phi \models \frac{\mathrm{pr}\,(\overline{b}=i)}{\mathrm{pr}\,()}\Phi$ holds.*
3. *$[\![\mathtt{while}\ b\ \mathtt{do}\ P]\!]$ preserves traces of density matrices.*

are satisfied,

$$\frac{\{\,(\mathrm{pr}\,(\overline{b} = 1) = 1) \wedge \Phi\,\}\ P\ \{\,\Phi\,\}}{\{\,(\mathrm{pr}\,() = 1) \wedge \Phi\,\}\ \mathtt{while}\ b\ \mathtt{do}\ P\ \{\,(\mathrm{pr}\,(\overline{b} = 0) = 1) \wedge \Phi\,\}}$$

is derivable.

When Φ does not contain $\neg$ (nor $\vee$, $\exists$), the first condition is always satisfied. The second condition holds if Φ implies that b is independent of other program variables. The third condition just says that the program always terminates. Hence, the lemma is useful in many practical cases.

6   Examples

We show some examples of derivations in the quantum Hoare logic.

First, we introduce syntax sugar for convenience:

$$\texttt{bit } b_1, \ldots, b_n \equiv \texttt{bit } b_1 \ ; \ \cdots \ ; \ \texttt{bit } b_n$$
$$\texttt{qbit } q_1, \ldots, q_n \equiv \texttt{qbit } q_1 \ ; \ \cdots \ ; \ \texttt{qbit } q_n$$
$$\texttt{discard } x_1, \ldots, x_n \equiv \texttt{discard } x_1 \ ; \ \cdots \ ; \ \texttt{discard } x_n$$
$$b_1, \ldots, b_n := i \equiv b_1 := i[1] \ ; \ \cdots \ ; \ b_n := i[n]$$
$$b := \texttt{measure } q \equiv \texttt{measure } q \texttt{ then } (b := 1) \texttt{ else } (b := 0)$$
$$b_1, \ldots, b_n := \texttt{measure } q_1, \ldots, q_n$$
$$\equiv b_1 := \texttt{measure } q_1 \ ; \ \cdots \ ; \ b_n := \texttt{measure } q_n$$
$$b := \texttt{rnd}$$
$$\equiv \texttt{qbit q ; q *= H ;}$$
$$\quad \texttt{measure q then } (b := 1) \texttt{ else } (b := 0) \ ; \ \texttt{discard q}$$
$$b_1, \ldots, b_n := \texttt{rnd} \equiv b_1 := \texttt{rnd} \ ; \ \cdots \ ; \ b_n := \texttt{rnd}$$
$$\texttt{bit } b[m\texttt{-}n] \equiv \texttt{bit } b[m], \ldots, b[n]$$
$$\texttt{qbit } q[m\texttt{-}n] \equiv \texttt{qbit } q[m], \ldots, q[n]$$
$$x[] \equiv x[1], \ldots, x[n]$$

where $i[n]$ means the n-th bit of i. Note that $\texttt{q[1]}$ is a long single program variable and '[' and ']' are not meta symbols. We can use the syntax $x[]$ for multi-bits. The syntax $\texttt{rnd}$ makes a random bit.

In this section, we use a short representation

$$\{\varPhi_1\} \ P_1 \ \{\varPhi_2\} \ P_2 \ \{\varPhi_3\} \ \cdots \ \{\varPhi_n\} \ P_n \ \{\varPhi_{n+1}\}$$

for

$$\frac{\{\varPhi_1\} \ P_1 \ \{\varPhi_2\} \qquad \cdots \qquad \{\varPhi_n\} \ P_n \ \{\varPhi_{n+1}\}}{\{\varPhi_1\} \ P_1 \ ; \ \cdots \ ; \ P_n \ \{\varPhi_{n+1}\}}$$

and may omit the program code $\texttt{skip}$.

6.1   Quantum Teleportation

We formalize the quantum teleportation protocol [6]. In the algorithm, a state of a quantum bit is teleported to another quantum bit by sending classical less information. First, we entangles two bits $\texttt{q}$ and $\texttt{qb}$ as an EPR pair. Then, Alice brings $\texttt{q}$ with her and Bob brings $\texttt{qb}$. If Alice want to send the state of $\texttt{qa}$ to Bob, she measures $\texttt{q}$ and $\texttt{qa}$ on the Bell basis and sends the obtained information to Bob. It is important that the sent message is only two classical bits which have less information than a quantum bit has.

Since QPL does not have syntax for general measurement, we have to rotate the basis before the measurement in order to simulate the measurement on the Bell basis. The verification of the teleportation algorithm in our logic is the following:

$\{\,\mathrm{pr}\,() = 1\,\}$

qbit q, qa, qb

$\{\,(\mathrm{pr}\,(\overline{\mathsf{qa}} = 0) = 1) \wedge (\mathrm{pr}\,(\overline{\mathsf{qb}} = 0) = 1) \wedge (\mathrm{pr}\,(\overline{\mathsf{q}} = 0) = 1)\,\}$

qa *= U

$\{\,^{\mathsf{qa}}U(\mathrm{pr}\,(\overline{\mathsf{qa}} = 0) = 1) \wedge (\mathrm{pr}\,(\overline{\mathsf{qb}} = 0) = 1) \wedge (\mathrm{pr}\,(\overline{\mathsf{q}} = 0) = 1)\,\}$

q, qb *= X

$\{\,^{\mathsf{q,qb}}X(^{\mathsf{qa}}U(\mathrm{pr}\,(\overline{\mathsf{qa}} = 0) = 1) \wedge (\mathrm{pr}\,(\overline{\mathsf{qb}} = 0) = 1) \wedge (\mathrm{pr}\,(\overline{\mathsf{q}} = 0) = 1))\,\}$

qa, q *= $X^{\dagger}$

$\{\,^{\mathsf{qa,q}}X^{\dagger,\mathsf{q,qb}}X(^{\mathsf{qa}}U(\mathrm{pr}\,(\overline{\mathsf{qa}} = 0) = 1) \wedge (\mathrm{pr}\,(\overline{\mathsf{qb}} = 0) = 1) \wedge (\mathrm{pr}\,(\overline{\mathsf{q}} = 0) = 1))\,\}$

measure q then (measure qa then (qb *= NV^2N) else (qb *= V^2))

   else (measure qa then (qb *= N) else skip)

$\{\,^{\mathsf{qb}}U(\mathrm{pr}\,(\overline{\mathsf{qb}} = 0) = 1)\,\}$

where X is $\begin{pmatrix} N & N \\ -I & I \end{pmatrix}$. In order to derive the last step, we need the four assertions:

$$\{\,^{\mathsf{qa}}\mathbb{E}_0{}^{\mathsf{q}}\mathbb{E}_0\varPhi\,\}\ \text{skip}\ \{\,r_{00}{}^{\mathsf{qb}}U(\mathrm{pr}\,(\overline{\mathsf{qb}} = 0) = 1)\,\}$$
$$\{\,^{\mathsf{qa}}\mathbb{E}_0{}^{\mathsf{q}}\mathbb{E}_1\varPhi\,\}\ \text{qb *= } V^2\ \{\,r_{01}{}^{\mathsf{qb}}U(\mathrm{pr}\,(\overline{\mathsf{qb}} = 0) = 1)\,\}$$
$$\{\,^{\mathsf{qa}}\mathbb{E}_1{}^{\mathsf{q}}\mathbb{E}_0\varPhi\,\}\ \text{qb *= N}\ \{\,r_{10}{}^{\mathsf{qb}}U(\mathrm{pr}\,(\overline{\mathsf{qb}} = 0) = 1)\,\}$$
$$\{\,^{\mathsf{qa}}\mathbb{E}_1{}^{\mathsf{q}}\mathbb{E}_1\varPhi\,\}\ \text{qb *= } NV^2N\ \{\,r_{11}{}^{\mathsf{qb}}U(\mathrm{pr}\,(\overline{\mathsf{qb}} = 0) = 1)\,\}$$

can be derived, where $\varPhi$ is the pre-condition and r_{ij} is the probability of $\overline{\mathsf{qa}} = i$ and $\overline{\mathsf{q}} = j$ by the measurement. Since $r_{00} + r_{01} + r_{10} + r_{11}$ is 1, $^{\mathsf{qb}}U(\mathrm{pr}\,(\overline{\mathsf{qb}} = 0) = 1)$ holds at the last state.

The above formulation claims that qb after the teleportation has the same state as qa before the teleportation has. Consequently, if a formula $\varPhi[\mathsf{qa}]$ without q or qb is true before the teleportation, $\varPhi[\mathsf{qb}]$ is true after the teleportation.

6.2   Shor's Prime Factorization

We verify Shor's prime factorization algorithm in this subsection. Shor provides a polynomial time algorithm for prime factorization in [7]. Since a classical algorithm to factorize numbers in polynomial time is not known, Shor's algorithm is considered to be important for comparison of quantum computation with classical computation.

The essential part of the algorithm is to find the order of a given number in a residue class group. We verify in the quantum Hoare logic that this part is indeed to find the order. Let n, m, and x be natural numbers such that $n^2 \leq 2^m < 2n^2$, $1 < x < n$. Let $=_n$ be the modulo equivalence w.r.t. n and r be the order of x in $\mathbb{N}/=_n$, that is, $x^r =_n 1$ and $x^k \neq_n 1$ for $k < r$. The claim is that the program finds r with large probability.

$\{\,\mathrm{pr}\,() = 1\,\}$
bit c[1-m] ; bit r[1-$\lfloor m/2 \rfloor$] ; qbit q1[1-m] ; qbit q2[1-m]
$\{\,(\mathrm{pr}\,(\overline{\mathtt{q1}} = 0) = 1) \wedge (\mathrm{pr}\,(\overline{\mathtt{q2}} = 0) = 1)\,\}$
q1[] *= H$_m$
$\{\,{}^{\mathtt{q1}}\mathrm{H}_m\,(\mathrm{pr}\,(\overline{\mathtt{q1}} = 0) = 1) \wedge (\mathrm{pr}\,(\overline{\mathtt{q2}} = 0) = 1)\,\}$
Exp (q1[], q2[])
$\{\,{}^{\mathtt{q1}}\mathrm{H}_m\,(\mathrm{pr}\,(\overline{\mathtt{q1}} = 0) = 1) \wedge (\mathrm{pr}\,(\overline{\mathtt{q2}} =_n x^{\overline{\mathtt{q1}}}) = 1)\,\}$
q1[] *= F$_m$
$\{\,{}^{\mathtt{q1}}\mathrm{F}_m\,({}^{\mathtt{q1}}\mathrm{H}_m\,(\mathrm{pr}\,(\overline{\mathtt{q1}} = 0) = 1) \wedge (\mathrm{pr}\,(\overline{\mathtt{q2}} =_n x^{\overline{\mathtt{q1}}}) = 1))\,\}$
c[] := measure q1[]
$\{\,\forall \alpha.\ \mathrm{int}\,(\alpha) \supset (\mathrm{pr}\,(\overline{\mathtt{c}} = \alpha) = f(\alpha))\,\}$
$\{\,\mathrm{pr}\,(\exists k \in \mathbb{N}.\ (r\overline{\mathtt{c}} =_{2^m} k) \wedge (-r/2 \leq k \leq r/2)) > 1/3\,\}$
$\{\,\mathrm{pr}\,(\exists d \in \mathbb{N}.\ |(\overline{\mathtt{c}}/2^m) - (d/r)| \leq 1/2^{m+1}) > 1/3\,\}$
Frac (c[], r[])
$\{\,\exists \delta.\ \mathrm{pr}\,(\overline{\mathtt{r}} = r) > \delta/(\log\log r)\,\}$

where f satisfies $f(u) = \sum_{k=0}^{r-1} \left| \sum_{d:x^d =_n x^k} e^{2\pi i du/2^m}/2^m \right|^2$, and $\mathrm{F}_m \in \mathbb{C}^{2^m \times 2^m}$ is the Fourier transformation. In Exp, q2 is set to the power of x to q1 modulo n. Exp can be defined as unitary operations. Frac, which finds r by a fraction expansion, is purely classical and deterministic. Details of Exp and Frac are found in [7].

In the above formulation, n and x are given out of the program. However, it is easy to introduce program variables for n and x in the program. Since we have the rule (while) and Lemma 1, it is also possible to formulate iteration of finding the order and the whole of Shor's algorithm.

6.3   Deutsch Problem

The Deutsch problem [15] is a problem to check whether a function on booleans is a constant function or not. In classical computation, a function has to be called at least twice. However, we can check a function with once evaluation in quantum computation.

The algorithm proposed in [8] by Cleve *et al.* is quite simple, but we have to verify four different cases. Let U_f be a given unitary transformation such that $U_f\,|x, y\rangle = |x, y\ \mathtt{xor}\ f(x)\rangle$. The case of $f(0) = f(1) = 1$, *i.e.*, $U_f = \mathrm{I} \otimes \mathrm{N}$, is

$\{\,\mathrm{pr}\,() = 1\,\}$
bit b ; qbit q1, q2
$\{\,(\mathrm{pr}\,(\overline{\mathtt{q1}} = 0) = 1) \wedge (\mathrm{pr}\,(\overline{\mathtt{q2}} = 0) = 1)\,\}$
q2 *= HN ; q1 *= H ; q1, q2 *= U_f ; q1 *= H
$\{\,{}^{\mathtt{q1,q2}}(\mathrm{H} \otimes \mathrm{I})U_f(\mathrm{H} \otimes \mathrm{HN})((\mathrm{pr}\,(\overline{\mathtt{q1}} = 0) = 1) \wedge (\mathrm{pr}\,(\overline{\mathtt{q2}} = 0) = 1))\,\}$

$\{\,\mathrm{pr}\,(\overline{\mathtt{q1}} = 0) = 1\,\}$
b := measure q1
$\{\,\mathrm{pr}\,(\overline{\mathtt{b}} = 0) = 1\,\}.$

Other cases can be proved in a similar way. Note that the last formula is $\mathrm{pr}\,(\overline{\mathtt{b}} = 1) = 1$ when f is a non-constant function.

It is also possible to verify the algorithm for the more general Deutsch-Jozsa problem [16] in our Hoare logic. In the Deutsch-Jozsa problem, the input domain of functions is generalized to n boolean bits. Let V_f be a unitary transformation satisfying $V_f\,|i\rangle = (-1)^{f(i)}\,|i\rangle$, which can be simulated by a program with U_f. This V_f gives an answer of the problem. If f is a balanced function,

$$\{\,\mathrm{pr}\,() = 1\,\}$$
$$\mathtt{bit\ b}[n]\ ;\ \mathtt{qbit\ q}[n]$$
$$\{\,\mathrm{pr}\,(\overline{\mathtt{q}} = 0) = 1\,\}$$
$$\mathtt{q[]\ *=\ H}_n\ ;\ \mathtt{q[]\ *=}\ V_f\ ;\ \mathtt{q[]\ *=\ H}_n$$
$$\{\,\mathfrak{H}_n V_f \mathrm{H}_n (\mathrm{pr}\,(\overline{\mathtt{q}} = 0) = 1)\,\}$$
$$\{\,(\mathrm{pr}\,(\overline{\mathtt{q}} = 0) = 0) \wedge (\mathrm{pr}\,() = 1)\,\}$$
$$\mathtt{b[]\ :=\ measure\ q[]}$$
$$\{\,(\mathrm{pr}\,(\overline{\mathtt{b}} = 0) = 0) \wedge (\mathrm{pr}\,() = 1)\,\}$$
$$\{\,\mathrm{pr}\,(\overline{\mathtt{b}} \neq 0) = 1\,\}.$$

In the constant cases, $\{\,\mathrm{pr}\,(\overline{\mathtt{b}} = 0) = 1\,\}$ is derived with easier calculation.

6.4   Quantum Coin Tossing

The quantum coin tossing protocol was proposed by Bennet and Brassard in [9]. This is the oldest quantum bit commitment protocol, and is important in the field of quantum cryptography. The aim of the protocol is that two remote persons, Alice and Bob, share a random bit. Alice and Bob cannot decide the bit alone but can communicate with each other.

In this paper, we show that Bob cannot decide head or tail. For simplicity, we consider the case that the length of the random sequence is just 1:

$\{\,\mathrm{pr}\,() = 1\,\}$
bit a, b, ra, rb, rc ; qbit q
$\{\,(\mathrm{pr}\,(\overline{\mathtt{q}} = 0)) = 1\,\}$
a, ra, rc := rnd
$\{\,((\mathrm{pr}\,(\overline{\mathtt{q}} = 0)) = 1) \wedge \mathrm{rnd}\,(\mathtt{a}, \mathtt{ra}, \mathtt{rc})\,\}$
if ra then (q *= N) else skip ;
if a then (q *= H) else skip ;
if rc then (q *= H) else skip

$\{ (\mathrm{pr}\,((\bar{a}=0) \wedge (\bar{q}=0)) = 1/4) \wedge (\mathrm{pr}\,((\bar{a}=0) \wedge (\bar{q}=1)) = 1/4) \wedge \cdots \}$

rb := measure q

$\{\,\mathrm{rnd}\,(a, rb)\,\}$

Bob (rb, b)

$\{\,\mathrm{pr}\,(\bar{a}=\bar{b}) = 1/2\,\}$

where $\mathrm{rnd}\,(b_1, \ldots, b_n)$ is the formula that means $b_1, \ldots, b_n$ are independently random, and Bob is the procedure that Bob decides the value of b. Whatever Bob's operation is, the conclusion holds because Bob does not touch a.

Unfortunately, it is known that Alice can cheat Bob with EPR pairs. Alice, however, cannot cheat Bob if she sends right quantum bits following the protocol. This property also can be verified in our logic.

In [9], Bennet and Brassard proposed also a key distribution protocol, which is called BB84. The security of BB84 has been proved by Mayers in [17], but the proof is too long for a non-expert reader. We expect our Hoare logic to help us to verify such a complicated proof.

7   Concluding Remarks

We have proposed a Hoare-style logic for quantum computation in this paper. Our quantum Hoare logic (QHL) is an extension of den Hartog's probabilistic Hoare logic [5], which is used in cryptographic verification. The target programming language of QHL is Selinger's QPL [4], which has clear syntax and semantics. It is shown that the quantum Hoare logic is sound for the semantics. It still remains to find a complete axiomatization of the logic. The formulation of the rule for while programs is one of contributions of this work. We have provided a sufficient condition for formalizing the rule as invariance.

In this paper, we have shown also how the quantum Hoare logic proves properties of well-known algorithms: quantum teleportation, Shor's prime factorization, a solution of the Deutsch problem, and quantum coin tossing. It is expected to verify more complicated algorithms or protocols used in quantum cryptography.

Implementing the quantum Hoare logic is an interesting future work. We need more studies on the proof system in order to automate derivations. There is a possibility to apply studies [13] and [18] on weakest preconditions to our Hoare logic. It may be helpful to cover other programming languages like [19].

Selinger provides a flowchart system equivalent to QPL in [4]. It is another possible work to analyze that flowchart system as Floyd does for classical computation in [20]. It is also challenging to characterize the logic along the line of Bloom and Ésik [21].

References

1. Hoare, C.A.R.: An axiomatic basis for computer programming. Communications of ACM 12, 576–580 (1969)
2. Cook, S.A.: Soundness and completeness of an axiom system for program verification. SIAM Journal on Computing 7(1), 70–78 (1978)

3. Harel, D., Kozen, D., Tiuryn, J.: Dynamic logic. In: Handbook of Philosophical Logic, pp. 497–604. MIT Press, Cambridge (1984)
4. Selinger, P.: Towards a quantum programming language. Mathematical Structures in Computer Science 14(4), 527–586 (2004)
5. den Hartog, J.I.: Verifying probabilistic programs using a Hoare-like logic. In: Thiagarajan, P.S., Yap, R.H.C. (eds.) ASIAN 1999. LNCS, vol. 1742, pp. 113–125. Springer, Heidelberg (1999)
6. Bennet, C.H., Brassard, G., Crépeau, C., Jozsa, R., Peres, A., Wootters, W.K.: Teleporting an unknown quantum state via dual classical and Einstein-Podolski-Rosen channels. Physical Review Letters 70, 1895–1899 (1993)
7. Shor, P.W.: Algorithms for quantum computation. In: Foundations of Computer Science, pp. 124–134. IEEE Computer Society Press, Los Alamitos (1994)
8. Cleve, R., Ekert, A.K., Macchiavello, C., Mosca, M.: Quantum algorithms revised. Proceedings of Royal Society London A 454, 339–354 (1998)
9. Bennet, C.H., Brassard, G.: Quantum cryptography: public key distribution and coin tossing. In: Computers, Systems and Signal Processing, pp. 175–179. IEEE Computer Society, Los Alamitos (1984)
10. Baltag, A., Smets, S.: LQP: the dynamic logic of quantum information. Mathematical Structures in Computer Science 16(3), 491–525 (2006)
11. Brunet, O., Jorrand, P.: Dynamic quantum logic for quantum programs. International Journal of Quantum Information 2(1) (2004)
12. Chadha, R., Mateus, P., Sernadas, A.: Reasoning about imperative quantum programs. In: Mathematical Foundations of Programming Semantics. ENTCS, vol. 158, pp. 19–39. Elsevier, Amsterdam (2006)
13. D'Hondt, E., Panangaden, P.: Quantum weakest preconditions. Mathematical Structures in Computer Science 16(3), 429–451 (2006)
14. Ying, M.S.: Hoare logic for quantum programs (2009) arXiv:0906.4586v1
15. Deutsch, D.: Quantum theory, the Church-Turing principle and the universal quantum computer. Proceedings of Royal Society London A 400, 97–117 (1985)
16. Deutsch, D., Jozsa, R.: Rapid solution of problems by quantum computation. Proceedings of Royal Society London A 439, 553–558 (1992)
17. Mayers, D.: Unconditional security in quantum cryptography. Journal of ACM 48(3), 351–406 (2001)
18. Feng, Y., Duan, R.Y., Ji, Z.F., Ying, M.S.: Proof rules for the correctness of quantum programs. Theoretical Computer Science 386(1,2), 151–166 (2007)
19. Altenkirch, T., Grattage, J.: A functional quantum programming language. In: Logic in Computer Science, pp. 249–258. IEEE Computer Society, Los Alamitos (2005)
20. Floyd, R.W.: Assigning meanings to programs. In: Applied Mathematics, AMS, pp. 19–32 (1967)
21. Bloom, S., Ésik, Z.: Floyd-Hoare logic in iteration theories. Journal of ACM 38(4), 887–934 (1991)

Reducing Equational Theories
for the Decision of Static Equivalence[*]

Steve Kremer[1], Antoine Mercier[1], and Ralf Treinen[2]

[1] LSV, ENS Cachan, CNRS, INRIA, France
[2] PPS, Université Paris Diderot, CNRS, France

Abstract. Static equivalence is a well established notion of indistinguishability of sequences of terms which is useful in the symbolic analysis of cryptographic protocols. Static equivalence modulo equational theories allows a more accurate representation of cryptographic primitives by modelling properties of operators by equational axioms. We develop a method that allows in some cases to simplify the task of deciding static equivalence in a multi-sorted setting, by removing a symbol from the term signature and reducing the problem to several simpler equational theories. We illustrate our technique at hand of bilinear pairings.

1 Introduction

Many formal models for analyzing cryptographic protocols have been developed over the last thirty years. Among them we find logical or symbolic models, based on the seminal ideas of Dolev and Yao [11], which represent cryptographic primitives in an abstract way. This is justified by the so-called *perfect cryptography assumption* which states that the intruder has no means to break the cryptographic primitives themselves, and that he can hence break security only by exploiting logical flaws in the protocol.

In symbolic models, messages of the protocol are represented by terms in an abstract algebra. The motivation this abstraction was the simplification and even automation of the analysis and the proof of security protocols. Since the assumption of perfect cryptography is not always realistic, some properties of cryptographic primitives (a survey can be found in [10]) have been taken into account in logical models by the means of equational theories on the terms.

In this paper we concentrate on *static equivalence*, a standard notion of indistinguishability of sequences of terms originating from the applied pi calculus [3]. Intuitively static equivalence asks whether or not an attacker can distinguish between two sequences of messages, later called *frames*, by exhibiting a relation which holds on one sequence but not on the other. Static equivalence provides an elegant means to express security properties on pieces of data, for instance those observed by a passive attacker during the run of a protocol. In the context of active attackers, static equivalence has also been used to characterize process equivalences [3] and off-line guessing attacks [9,5]. There now exist exact [2],

---

[*] This work has been partially supported by the ANR-07-SESU-002 project AVOTÉ.

A. Datta (Ed.): ASIAN 2009, LNCS 5913, pp. 94–108, 2009.

and approximate [1] algorithms to decide static equivalence for a large family of equational theories.

Our ultimate goal is to develop combination methods for deciding static equivalence, that is to develop means to algorithmically reduce a static equivalence problem modulo some equational theory to some other static equivalence problems modulo simpler equational theories.

Contribution of this paper. We exhibit criteria on equational theories allowing simplifications for the decision of static equivalence. The kind of simplification we describe is the removal of a particular symbol which we call a *valve*. More precisely, given a sorted signature, and two sorts r and s, a valve from r to s is a symbol expecting arguments of sort r and producing a term of another sort s. Moreover, it is the only function symbol which allows to build terms of sort s out of terms of sort r. Signatures of this kind occur when representing cryptographic primitives using elements of two distinct algebraic structures and a mapping function from one structure to the other. A concrete example occurs in the bilinear pairing operation [7,12,14]. We will use this operation as a running example throughout the paper.

We show that under some conditions a valve can be removed from the terms in the frames on which we want to decide the static equivalence, and from the equational theory. Hence our purpose is dual. First we show that deciding static equivalence of a pair of frames involving a given valve can be reduced to the decision of the static equivalence of pairs of frames without this symbol. Second, we show that deciding static equivalence on a pair of frames, not involving a given valve f, in the presence of an equational theory involving f, can be done in the presence of two other, generally simpler equational theories without f. Obviously this cannot be done in general and the first step of this work consists in identifying sufficient conditions on equational theories for which this kind of reduction is possible. The result is illustrated by reducing the decision of static equivalence for an equational theory modelling bilinear pairings between two groups to the decision of static equivalence on groups, yielding a new decidability result.

A completely different combination problem for deciding static equivalence was studied in [4], namely the combination of *disjoint* equational theories. On the one hand we do not require the two simpler signatures obtained by the reduction to be disjoint, on the other hand we are working in a well-sorted setting.

Structure of the paper. In Section 2 we introduce our formal model. Section 3 presents the running example used throughout the paper. In Section 4 we introduce the concepts of *valve* and *reducibility*. Section 5 is dedicated to the presentation of our reduction results. We give a first syntactic criterion for the applicability of our reduction results in Section 6, and conclude in Section 7. Exhaustive versions of some of the proofs are given in [15].

2   Model

2.1   Sorted Term Algebras

A *sorted signature* $(\mathcal{S},\mathcal{F})$ is defined by a set of *sorts* $\mathcal{S} = \{s, s_1, s_2, \dots\}$ and a set of function symbols $\mathcal{F} = \{f, f_1, f_2, \dots\}$ with arities of the form $\mathsf{arity}(f) = s_1 \times \dots \times s_k \to s$ where $k \geq 0$. If $k = 0$ the symbol is called a *constant* and its arity is simply written s. We fix an $\mathcal{S}$-indexed family of sorted *names* $\mathcal{N} = (\mathcal{N}_s)_{s \in \mathcal{S}}$ where $\mathcal{N}_s = \{n_{s1}, n_{s2}, \dots\}$ and an infinite ordered set of sorted *variables* $\mathcal{X}$.

The set of *terms of sort s* is defined inductively by :

t ::=   term of sort s
| x variable x of sort s
| n name n of sort s
| $f(t_1, \dots, t_k)$ application of symbol $f \in \mathcal{F}$

where each t_i is a term of sort s_i and $\mathsf{arity}(f) = s_1 \times \dots \times s_k \to s$. The set of terms $T(\mathcal{F}, \mathcal{N}, \mathcal{X})$ is the union of the sets of terms of sort s for every $s \in \mathcal{S}$. We denote by $\mathsf{sort}(t)$ the sort of term t. We write $\mathsf{var}(t)$ and $\mathsf{names}(t)$ for the set of variables and names occurring in t, respectively. A term t is *ground* iff $\mathsf{var}(t) = \emptyset$. The set of ground terms is denoted by $T(\mathcal{F}, \mathcal{N})$.

We extend the notion of arity to terms as follows. If t is a ground term of sort s then $\mathsf{arity}(t) = s$, otherwise $\mathsf{arity}(t) = s_1 \times \dots \times s_n \to s$ if the ordered sequence $x_1, \dots, x_n$ of variables of t are of sort $s_1, \dots, s_n$ respectively.

We write $|t|$ for the *size* of t, i.e. the number of symbols of t.

A *context* C is a term with distinguished variables sometimes called *holes*. It can be formalized as a lambda-term of the form $\lambda x_1. \dots. \lambda x_n . t_C$ where the x_i may appear or not in t_C. For the sake of simplicity, in most cases we simply write $C[x_1, \dots, x_n]$ instead of $\lambda x_1. \dots. \lambda x_n . t_C$ as well as $C[t_1, \dots, t_n]$ instead of $(\dots (\lambda x_1. \dots. \lambda x_n . t_C) t_1 \dots) t_n$. Hence $C[t_1, \dots, t_n]$ is simply the result of replacing each x_i by t_i. A context is *public* if it does not involve any name.

The *positions* $Pos(t)$ of a term t are defined as usual by $Pos(u) = \{\Lambda\}$ when $u \in \mathcal{N} \cup \mathcal{X}$ and $Pos(f(t_1, \dots, t_n)) = \{\Lambda\} \cup \{i \cdot \pi \mid 1 \leq i \leq n, \pi \in Pos(t_i)\}$ otherwise. The subterm of t at position p is written $t|_p$, and the replacement in t at position p by u is written $t[u]_p$.

A *substitution* σ written $\sigma = \{x_1 \mapsto t_1, \dots, x_n \mapsto t_n\}$ with domain $\mathsf{dom}(\sigma) = \{x_1, \dots, x_n\}$ is a mapping from $\{x_1, \dots, x_n\} \subseteq \mathcal{X}$ to $T(\mathcal{F}, \mathcal{N}, \mathcal{X})$. We only consider *well sorted* substitutions in which x_i and t_i have the same sort. A substitution σ is *ground* if all t_i are ground. The *application* of a substitution σ to a term t is written $t\sigma$.

2.2   Equational Theories and Rewriting Systems

An *equation* is an equality $t = u$ where t and u are two terms of the same sort. An *equational theory* E is a finite set of equations. We denote by $=_E$ the smallest congruence relation on $T(\mathcal{F}, \mathcal{N}, \mathcal{X})$ such that $t\sigma =_E u\sigma$ for any $t = u \in E$ and for any substitution σ. We say that a symbol f is *free* in E if f does not occur in E.

A *term rewriting system* $\mathcal{R}$ is a finite set of *rewrite rules* $l \to r$ where $l \in T(\mathcal{F}, \mathcal{N}, \mathcal{X})$ and $r \in T(\mathcal{F}, \mathcal{N}, \mathsf{var}(l))$. A term $u \in T(\mathcal{F}, \mathcal{N}, \mathcal{X})$ rewrites to v by $\mathcal{R}$, denoted $u \to_{\mathcal{R}} v$ if there is a rewrite rule $l \to r \in \mathcal{R}$, a position p and a substitution σ such that $u|_p = l\sigma$ and $v = u[r\sigma]_p$. We write $\to^*$ for the transitive and reflexive closure of $\to$. Given a set of equations E, u rewrites modulo E by $\mathcal{R}$ to v, denoted $u \to_{\mathcal{R}/E} v$, if $u =_E t[l\sigma]_p$ and $t[r\sigma]_p =_E v$ for some context t, position p in t, rule $l \to r$ in $\mathcal{R}$, and substitution σ. $\mathcal{R}$ is *E-terminating* if there are no infinite chains $t_1 \to_{\mathcal{R}/E} t_2 \to_{\mathcal{R}/E} \dots$. $\mathcal{R}$ is *E-confluent* iff whenever $t \to_{\mathcal{R}/E} u$ and $t \to_{\mathcal{R}/E} v$, there exist u', v' such that $u \to^*_{\mathcal{R}/E} u'$, $v \to^*_{\mathcal{R}/E} v'$, and $u' =_E v'$. $\mathcal{R}$ is *E-convergent* if it is *E-terminating* and *E-confluent*. A term t is in *normal form* with respect to $(\mathcal{R}/E)$ if there is no term s such that $t \to_{\mathcal{R}/E} s$. If $t \to^*_{\mathcal{R}/E} s$ and s is in normal form, we say that s is a normal form of t. When this normal form is unique (up to E) we write $s = t \downarrow_{\mathcal{R}/E}$.

2.3 Substitutions and Frames

A *frame* is an expression $\phi = \nu\tilde{n}_\phi.\sigma_\phi$ where $\tilde{n}_\phi$ is a set of *bound names*, and σ_ϕ is a substitution. $|\phi|$ is the size of ϕ, i.e. the number of elements in $\mathrm{dom}(\sigma_\phi)$. σ_ϕ is called the *underlying substitution* of ϕ. We extend the notation *dom* to frames by $\mathrm{dom}(\nu\tilde{n}.\sigma) = \mathrm{dom}(\sigma)$. We write $\phi =_\alpha \psi$ when the frames ϕ and ψ are equal up to alpha-conversion of bound names. For two frames $\phi = \nu\tilde{n}_\phi.\sigma_\phi$ and $\psi = \nu\tilde{n}_\psi.\sigma_\psi$ with $\mathrm{dom}(\phi) \cap \mathrm{dom}(\psi) = \emptyset$ and $\tilde{n}_\phi \cap \tilde{n}_\psi = \emptyset$ we write $\phi\psi$ for the *disjoint composition* of ϕ and ψ defined as $\phi\psi = \nu(\tilde{n}_\phi \cup \tilde{n}_\psi).\sigma_\phi\sigma_\psi$. Note that $\tilde{n}_\phi \cap \tilde{n}_\psi = \emptyset$ is always possible by alpha-conversion of the bound names of ϕ and ψ. The sort of a frame ϕ is the set $S = \{\mathsf{sort}(x) | x \in \mathrm{dom}(\phi)\}$, and we say that ϕ is *S-sorted*.

For simplicity, we only consider frames $\phi = \nu\tilde{n}\{x_1 \mapsto t_1, \dots, x_n \mapsto t_n\}$ that restrict every name in use, that is, for which $\tilde{n} = \mathsf{names}(t_1, \dots, t_n)$. A name a may still be disclosed explicitly by adding a mapping $x_a \mapsto a$ to the frame.

2.4 Static Equivalence

Definition 1 (equality in a frame [2]). *We say that two terms M and N are equal in a frame ϕ for the equational theory E, and write $(M =_E N)\phi$, if and only if $\phi =_\alpha \nu\tilde{n}.\sigma$, $M\sigma =_E N\sigma$, and $\{\tilde{n}\} \cap (\mathsf{names}(M) \cup \mathsf{names}(N)) = \emptyset$.*

Definition 2 (static equivalence [2]). *Two frames ϕ and ψ are statically equivalent for the equational theory E, written $\phi \approx_E \psi$, iff $\mathrm{dom}(\phi) = \mathrm{dom}(\psi)$, and for all terms M and N, we have $(M =_E N)\phi$ if and only if $(M =_E N)\psi$.*

For two frames ϕ and ψ, two terms M, N such that $(M =_E N)\phi$ and $(M \neq_E N)\psi$ are called *distinguishers* of ϕ and ψ.

3 Running Example

We will illustrate our specific definitions and lemmas by a running example involving two distinct algebraic groups $\mathbb{G}_1$ and $\mathbb{G}_2$ and a pairing operation e

mapping two elements of $\mathbb{G}_1$ to an element of $\mathbb{G}_2$. A concrete cryptographic definition can be found in [7]. In general, a pairing operation maps elements of an additive group to elements of a multiplicative group in the following way.

$$e : \quad \mathbb{G}_1 \times \mathbb{G}_1 \to \mathbb{G}_2$$
$$e(ag_1, bg_2) = e(g_1, g_2)^{ab}$$

In some protocols, e.g. [12], one has in fact $g_1 = g_2$. We use this assumption in order to simplify our notations. Moreover, we use a multiplicative notation to represent elements of $\mathbb{G}_1$, e.g. we write $exp_1(x)$ for both xg_1 and xg_2.

Let $\mathcal{S}_{BP}$ be the set of sorts $\{R, G_1, G_2\}$, R is the sort of the exponents of a chosen generator of the $\mathbb{G}_i$, and G_1 (resp. G_2) are the sorts of the elements of the groups $\mathbb{G}_1$ (resp. $\mathbb{G}_2$). Let $\mathcal{F}_{BP}$ be the following set of symbols:

$$
\begin{array}{lll}
+, \cdot : R \times R \to R & & \text{add, mult} \\
- : R \to R & & \text{inverse} \\
0_R, 1_R : R & & \text{constants} \\
exp_i : R \to G_i & i \in \{1, 2\} & \text{exponentiation} \\
*_i : G_i \times G_i \to G_i & i \in \{1, 2\} & \text{mult in } \mathbb{G}_i \\
e : G_1 \times G_1 \to G_2 & & \text{pairing}
\end{array}
$$

We will write $*$ instead of $*_i$, the sort of $*$ being always clear from the context. As a convenient shortcut we sometimes write t^i for $\underbrace{t * \ldots * t}_{i \times}$. The properties of these function symbols are defined by the following equational theory E_{BP}.

$$
\begin{array}{ll}
x + y = y + x & 0_R + x = x \\
(x + y) + z = x + (y + z) & x + (-x) = 0_R \\
x \cdot y = y \cdot x & x \cdot (y + z) = (x \cdot y) + (x \cdot z) \\
(x \cdot y) \cdot z = x \cdot (y \cdot z) & 1_R \cdot x = x
\end{array}
$$

$$
\begin{array}{ll}
exp_i(x) *_i exp_i(y) = exp_i(x + y) & i \in \{1, 2\} \\
e(exp_1(x), exp_1(y)) = exp_2(x \cdot y) &
\end{array}
$$

This signature and this equational theory represent operations realized in protocols where the exchanged messages are elements of the groups $\mathbb{G}_i$. The symbol e represents a pairing operation.

Example 1. Bilinear pairing is a central primitive of the Joux protocol [12], a three participant variation of the Diffie-Hellman protocol. It implicitly relies on the decisional Bilinear Diffie-Hellman Assumption (BDH) which can be formally modelled using static equivalence as follows:

$$\nu a, b, c, r.\{x_1 \mapsto exp_1(a), x_2 \mapsto exp_1(b), x_3 \mapsto exp_1(c), y_1 \mapsto exp_2(a \cdot b \cdot c)\}$$
$$\approx_{E_{BP}}$$
$$\nu a, b, c, r.\{x_1 \mapsto exp_1(a), x_2 \mapsto exp_1(b), x_3 \mapsto exp_1(c), y_1 \mapsto exp_2(r)\}$$

4   Valves and Reducibility

The main result of our paper concerns signatures involving a special function symbol which we call a *valve*. Intuitively, as it is suggested by the name "valve", a valve f is a symbol such that applying f on terms of sort r, we obtain a term t of sort s and such that t cannot be a subterm of a term of sort r.

We borrow here some useful notions from graph theory.

Definition 3 (Signature graph). *Let $(\mathcal{S}, \mathcal{F})$ be a sorted signature. The graph $\mathcal{G}(\mathcal{S}, \mathcal{F})$ is the directed labelled graph (V, E) where $V = \mathcal{S}$, $E \subseteq V \times V \times \mathcal{F}$ and $(r, s, f) \in E$ iff $\mathsf{sort}(f) = s_1 \times \cdots \times s_n \to s$ and $s_i = r$ for some i.*

We recall that a *path* in a graph is a sequence of edges such that for two consecutive edges (r, s, f) and (r', s', f') we have $s = r'$.

Definition 4 (valve). *A symbol f of arity $\cdots \times r \times \cdots \to s$ is a* valve *from r to s iff every path from r to s in $\mathcal{G}(\mathcal{S}, \mathcal{F})$ contains (r, s, f) and there is no path from s to r.*

Example 2 (continued). Let us consider the sorted signature $(\mathcal{S}_{\mathsf{BP}}, \mathcal{F}_{\mathsf{BP}})$ introduced in our running example in Section 3. $\mathcal{G}(\mathcal{S}_{\mathsf{BP}}, \mathcal{F}_{\mathsf{BP}})$ is given in Figure 1.

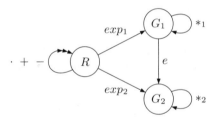

Fig. 1. $\mathcal{G}(\mathcal{S}_{\mathsf{BP}}, \mathcal{F}_{\mathsf{BP}})$

In the signature of Figure 1, e is a valve from G_1 to G_2 as (G_1, G_2, e) lies on every path from G_1 and G_2, and since no path leads from G_2 to G_1. We also have that exp_1 is a valve from R to G_1. However, exp_2 is not a valve from R to G_2 as the sequence $(R, G_1, exp_1), (G_1, G_2, e)$ is a path from R to G_2.

We are now able to present the central notion of reducibility.

Definition 5 (reducible). *Let r and s be two sorts and f a valve from r to s. An equational theory E is reducible for f iff for every $n \geq 0$ there exist m public contexts $T_1[x_1, \ldots, x_n], \ldots, T_m[x_1, \ldots, x_n]$ of arity $r \times \cdots \times r \to s$ such that for all public contexts $C_1[x_1, \ldots, x_n], \ldots, C_k[x_1, \ldots, x_n]$ of arity $r \times \cdots \times r \to r$ there exists a public context $D[y_1, \ldots, y_m]$ of arity $s \times \cdots \times s \to s$ such that for any ground terms $t_1, \ldots, t_n$ of sort r*

$$f(C_1, \ldots, C_k)[t_1, \ldots, t_n] =_E D[T_1, \ldots, T_m][t_1, \ldots, t_n]$$

Intuitively, reducibility for a valve f means that given a cardinality n of sets of ground terms of sort r, we can construct in a uniform way a set of terms such that any sequence of operations performed before applying f, there will be a way to reproduce these operations on the terms obtained with the context T_i. The uniformity lies in the fact that the contexts T_i depend only on the number n but *not* on the contexts C_i. We illustrate this notion by showing the reducibility for e of the theory of our running example E_{BP} in case $\mathcal{N}_{G_1} = \emptyset$.

Proposition 1. E_{BP} *is reducible for* e *if* $\mathcal{N}_{G_1} = \emptyset$.

Proof. Let n be an integer. We define $m = n + \frac{n*(n+1)}{2}$ contexts

$$T_i = \lambda x_1.\ldots.\lambda x_n.e(x_i, exp_1(1_R)) \text{ for } 1 \le i \le n$$
$$T_{ij} = \lambda x_1.\ldots.\lambda x_n.e(x_i, x_j) \qquad \text{for } 1 \le i \le j \le n$$

Every public context $C_i[x_1, \ldots, x_n]$ of arity $G_1 \times \cdots \times G_1 \to G_1$ is of the form $\lambda x_1.\ldots.\lambda x_n.x_1^{e_{i1}} * \cdots * x_n^{e_{in}} * exp_1(p_i)$ where $p_i =_{E_{\mathsf{BP}}} 1_R + \cdots + 1_R$ (l_i times). Hence $exp_1(p_i) =_{E_{\mathsf{BP}}} exp_1(1_R)^{l_i}$.

Let us show by induction on the size of the contexts C_i that there exists a context D such that for any sequence of ground terms $t_1, \ldots, t_n$

$$e(C_1, C_2)[t_1, \ldots t_n] =_{E_{\mathsf{BP}}} D[T_1, \ldots, T_n, T_{11}, \ldots, T_{nn}][t_1, \ldots, t_n]$$

Base case. We distinguish four cases:

1. $C_1 = \lambda x_1.\ldots.\lambda x_n.x_i$ and $C_2 = \lambda x_1.\ldots.\lambda x_n.x_j$
   For any sequence of terms $t_1, \ldots, t_n$ we have that $e(C_1, C_2)[t_1, \ldots, t_n] = e(t_i, t_j)$. As $\mathcal{N}_{G_1} = \emptyset$ there exist terms t'_i and t'_j of sort R such that $t_i =_{E_{\mathsf{BP}}} exp_1(t'_i)$ and $t_j =_{E_{\mathsf{BP}}} exp_1(t'_j)$. Hence

$$e(C_1, C_2)[t_1, \ldots, t_n] =_{E_{\mathsf{BP}}} e(exp_1(t'_i), exp_1(t'_j))$$
$$=_{E_{\mathsf{BP}}} exp_2(t'_i \cdot t'_j) =_{E_{\mathsf{BP}}} T_{ij}[t_1, \ldots, t_n]$$

   Let $D = \lambda y_1.\ldots.\lambda y_n.\lambda y_{11}.\ldots.\lambda y_{nn}.y_{ij}$. We have that $e(C_i, C_j)[t_1, \ldots, t_n] =_{E_{\mathsf{BP}}} D[T_1, \ldots, T_n, T_{11}, \ldots, T_{nn}][t_1, \ldots, t_n]$.

2. $C_1 = \lambda x_1.\ldots.\lambda x_n.x_i$ and $C_2 = exp_1(1_R)^l$
   For any sequence of terms $t_1, \ldots, t_n$ we have that $e(C_1, C_2)[t_1, \ldots, t_n] = e(t_i, exp(1_R)^l)$. As $\mathcal{N}_{G_1} = \emptyset$ there exists a term t'_i of sort R such that $t_i =_{E_{\mathsf{BP}}} exp_1(t'_i)$. Hence

$$e(C_1, C_2)[t_1, \ldots, t_n] =_{E_{\mathsf{BP}}} e(exp_1(t'_i), exp_1(\underbrace{1_R + \cdots + 1_R}_{l\times}))$$
$$=_{E_{\mathsf{BP}}} exp_2(t'_i \cdot (\underbrace{1_R + \cdots + 1_R}_{l\times}))$$
$$=_{E_{\mathsf{BP}}} exp_2(t'_i)^l =_{E_{\mathsf{BP}}} (T_i[t_1, \ldots, t_n])^l$$

   Let $D = \lambda y_1.\ldots.\lambda y_n.\lambda y_{11}.\ldots.\lambda y_{nn}.y_i^l$. We have that $e(C_i, C_j)[t_1, \ldots, t_n] =_{E_{\mathsf{BP}}} D[T_1, \ldots, T_n, T_{11}, \ldots, T_{nn}][t_1, \ldots, t_n]$.

3. $C_1 = exp_1(1_R)^l$ and $C_2 = \lambda x_1.\dots.\lambda x_n.x_i$

As $C_1 * C_2 =_{E_{BP}} C_2 * C_1$ this case is similar to case 2.

4. $C_1 = exp_1(1_R)^{l_1}$ and $C_2 = exp_1(1_R)^{l_2}$

We immediately conclude by defining $D = exp_2(1_R)^{l_1 \cdot l_2}$.

Inductive case : $C_i = C_{i1} * C_{i2}$. Let $i = 1$. The case where $i = 2$ is similar. We note that every term of sort R can be written as a sum of products of names of sort R. More formally for any contexts $C_{11}[x_1, \dots, x_n]$, $C_{12}[x_1, \dots, x_n]$, $C_2[x_1, \dots, x_n]$, for any term $t_1, \dots t_n$ we have that $C_{11}[t_1, \dots t_n] = exp_1(p_{11})$, $C_{12}[t_1, \dots t_n] = exp_1(p_{12})$ and $C_2[t_1, \dots t_n] = exp_1(p_2)$, for some elements of sort R described as above. We note that the equational theory implies that $e(C_{11} * C_{12}, C_2) = e(C_{11}, C_2) * e(C_{12}, C_2)$.

By induction there are D_1 and D_2 such that $e(C_{11} * C_2)[t_1, \dots, t_n] =_E D_1[T_1, \dots, T_m][t_1, \dots, t_n]$ and $e(C_{12} * C_2)[t_1, \dots, t_n] =_E D_2[T_1, \dots, T_m][t_1, \dots, t_n]$. Hence defining D as $D_1 * D_2$ we conclude. $\square$

Example 3. For $n = 2$ we have that

$$T_1 = e(x_1, exp_1(1)) \qquad T_2 = e(x_2, exp_1(1))$$
$$T_{1,1} = e(x_1, x_1) \quad T_{1,2} = e(x_1, x_2) \quad T_{2,2} = e(x_2, x_2)$$

Let $C_1 = \lambda x_1 \lambda x_2.x_1$ and $C_2 = \lambda x_1 \lambda x_2.x_2 * x_2 * exp_1(1+1)$. We define

$$D = \lambda y_1 \lambda y_2 \lambda y_{1,1} \lambda y_{1,2} \lambda y_{2,2}.y_{1,2} * y_{1,2} * y_1 * y_1$$

since $e(t_1, t_2 * t_2 * exp_1(1+1)) = e(t_1, t_2) * e(t_1, t_2) * e(t_1, exp_1(1)) * e(t_1, exp_1(1))$ for any *ground* terms t_1, t_2.

Remark 1. Proposition 1 requires that we do not have names of sort G_1. We argue that this is not restrictive in the context of protocols. As we expect that terms of sort G_1 represent the elements of a group with a given generator each element of the group G_1 can indeed be written as $exp_1(r)$ for some element of R.

One might have expected reducibility for a symbol f to be related to being *sufficiently complete w.r.t.* f as defined in [8].

Definition 6 (sufficiently complete). *E is a* sufficiently complete *equational theory with respect to $f \in \mathcal{F}$ if for every ground term $t \in T(\mathcal{F}, \mathcal{N})$ there exists a ground term $u \in T(\mathcal{F} \setminus \{f\}, \mathcal{N})$ such that $t =_E u$.*

The next two lemmas show, however, that these two notions are in fact independent of each other.

Lemma 1. *Reducibility of an equational theory E for a symbol f does not imply sufficient completeness of E w.r.t. f.*

Proof. Let $\mathcal{S} = \{r, s\}$ and $\mathcal{F} = \{f\}$, with $\mathsf{sort}(f) = r \to s$, and $E = \emptyset$. We show that E is reducible for f but not sufficiently complete w.r.t. f. Consider an integer n and the contexts $T_1 = \lambda x_1.\dots.\lambda x_n.f(x_1), \dots, T_n = \lambda x_1.\dots.\lambda x_n.f(x_n)$.

As the only ground terms t_i of sort r are names n_i, we consider w.l.o.g. that any sequence of terms $t_1, \ldots, t_n$ is equal to $n_1, \ldots, n_n$, and as the only possible contexts C of sort r are of the form $\lambda x_1 \ldots \lambda x_n . x_i$, we have $f(C[t_1, \ldots, t_n]) = f(n_i)$. Hence we only have to verify that for any i there exists a context D such that $f(n_i) =_E D[T_1, \ldots, T_n][n_1, \ldots, n_n]$. We choose $D = \lambda y_1 \ldots \lambda y_n . y_i$.

To show that E is not sufficiently complete w.r.t. f, we note that as f is free, for any i the term $f(n_i)$ is not equivalent to a term without f.   □

Lemma 2. *Sufficient completeness of E w.r.t. a symbol f does not imply reducibility of E for f.*

Proof. We define a signature with two sorts r and s, no names, and the function symbols $0_r : r$, $s_r : r \to r$, $f : r \to s$, $0_s : s$, $s_s : s \to s$. The function symbol f is the valve. We have the following equational theory:

$$f(s_r(x), y)) = s_s(f(x, y)) \qquad f(0_r, s_r(y)) = f(s_r(y), y) \qquad f(0_r, 0_r) = 0_s$$

Identifying any ground term of sort r or s with a natural number, the function f satisfies $f(n, m) = n + \frac{m*(m+1)}{2}$. Since there are no names E is sufficiently complete for f. The fact that f has a quadratic growth contradicts reducibility. A detailed proof can be found in [15].   □

5   Getting Rid of Reducible Symbols

We now present the central result of our work and show that if an equational theory E is *reducible* for f then it is possible to get rid of f when deciding static equivalence.

First, we show that deciding static equivalence on $\{r, s\}$-sorted frames in the presence of a valve from r to s can be reduced to deciding two equivalences, one on r-sorted frames and one on s-sorted frames (Lemma 4).

Second, we show that under some conditions on the equational theory, deciding static equivalence for a given equational theory can be reduced to deciding static equivalence for an equational theory that does not involve a reducible symbol (Theorem 1). As a corollary we get the possibility of splitting the equational theory into simpler equational theories.

Definition 7 (reduction). *Let the equational theory E be reducible for f, where f is a valve from r to s, and let $\phi = \nu\tilde{n}\{x_1 \mapsto t_1, \ldots, x_n \mapsto t_n\}$ be a frame of sort $\{r\}$. The reduction of ϕ is defined as $\overline{\phi} = \nu\tilde{n}\{y_1 \mapsto T_1[t_1, \ldots t_n], \ldots, y_m \mapsto T_m[t_1, \ldots t_n]\}$ where T_i are contexts as defined in Definition 5.*

We note that $\overline{\phi}$ is $\{s\}$-sorted. Before giving an example illustrating the construction of $\overline{\phi}$ we define the following useful notation.

Definition 8 (s-restriction). *Let $\phi = \nu\tilde{n}.\sigma_\phi$ be an $\{s_1, \ldots, s_n\}$-sorted frame. The s_i-restriction of ϕ, denoted $\phi_{|s_i}$ is the frame $\nu\tilde{n}.\sigma_{\phi_{|s_i}}$ where $\sigma_{\phi_{|s_i}}$ is the substitution σ_ϕ restricted to the variables of sort s_i.*

Example 4. Let ϕ_{BDH} be the G_1-restriction of the frames presented in Example 1 : $\phi_{BDH} = \nu a, b, c, r.\{x_1 \mapsto exp_1(a), x_2 \mapsto exp_1(b), x_3 \mapsto exp_1(c)\}$. Using the set of terms T_i and T_{ij} defined in the proof of Proposition 1, we get

$$\overline{\phi}_{BDH} = \nu a, b, c, r.\{ \; y_1 \mapsto e(exp_1(a), exp_1(1)), \; y_{12} \mapsto e(exp_1(a), exp_1(b)),$$
$$y_2 \mapsto e(exp_1(b), exp_1(1)), \; y_{13} \mapsto e(exp_1(a), exp_1(c)),$$
$$y_3 \mapsto e(exp_1(c), exp_1(1)), \; y_{23} \mapsto e(exp_1(b), exp_1(c)) \; \}$$

We now prove a technical lemma which will be used to transfer tests on a frame to tests on its reduction.

Lemma 3. *Let $(\mathcal{S}, \mathcal{F})$ be a signature such that $f \in \mathcal{F}$ is a valve from r to s, and E an equational theory that is reducible for f. For any integer n, and for any public context M of sort s there exists a public context M' such that for any $\{r, s\}$-sorted frame ϕ of size n, $M\phi =_E M'\overline{\phi_{|r}}\phi_{|s}$.*

Proof. Let us show this by induction on the height of M. If M is a variable or a constant then we define $M' = M$. If $M = y \in \mathcal{X}$ then $y(\overline{\phi_{|r}}\phi_{|s}) = y\phi$ since the sort of y is s. If $M = c$ is a constant then $M\phi =_E M'\overline{\phi_{|r}}\phi_{|s}$ holds trivially.

If the height of M is non-null then the top symbol of M can be the valve f, or some function symbol $f' \neq f$.

If $M = f(C_1[x_1, \ldots, x_n], \ldots, C_k[x_1, \ldots, x_n])$ then all variables of M are of sort r, and hence $M\phi = M\phi_{|r}$ where $\phi_{|r} = \{x_1 \mapsto t_1, \ldots, x_{n'} \mapsto t_{n'}\}$. As E is reducible for f, we can define $\overline{\phi_{|r}}$ as $\{y_1 \mapsto T_1[t_1, \ldots t_{n'}], \ldots, y_m \mapsto T_m[t_1, \ldots t_{n'}]\}$. By Definition 5 there exists a public context $D[y_1, \ldots, y_m]$ such that

$$f(C_1, \ldots, C_k)[t_1, \ldots, t_{n'}] = D[T_1, \ldots, T_m][t_1, \ldots, t_{n'}]$$

With $M' = D$ we have that $M\phi_{|r} =_E M'\overline{\phi_{|r}}$, and hence $M\phi =_E M'\overline{\phi_{|r}}\phi_{|s}$.

If $M = f'(C_1[x_1, \ldots, x_n, y_1, \ldots, y_m], \ldots, C_{k'}[x_1, \ldots, x_n, y_1, \ldots, y_m])$ with $f' \neq f$ then $\mathsf{sort}(C_i) = s$. By induction there exist public contexts $M_1 \ldots M_{k'}$ such that for any $\{r, s\}$-sorted frame ϕ of size n, $C_{i'}\phi =_E M_{i'}\overline{\phi_{|r}}\phi_{|s}$. We define $M' = f'(M_1 \ldots M_{k'})$, and obtain $M\phi =_E M'\overline{\phi_{|r}}\phi_{|s}$. $\qquad\square$

The following lemma allows us to split the decision of static equivalence of $\{r, s\}$-sorted frames into two equivalences on r-sorted frames and s-sorted frames.

Lemma 4. *For any $\{r, s\}$-sorted frames ϕ_1 and ϕ_2 built on $(\mathcal{S}, \mathcal{F})$, and for a valve f from r to s, if E is a reducible equational theory for f then $\phi_1 \approx_E \phi_2$ iff $\phi_{1|r} \approx_E \phi_{2|r}$ and $\overline{\phi_{1|r}}\phi_{1|s} \approx_E \overline{\phi_{2|r}}\phi_{2|s}$.*

Proof (Sketch). We prove the two directions of the equivalence separately.

$(\Rightarrow)$ If $\phi_1 \approx_E \phi_2$, then $\phi_{1|r} \approx_E \phi_{2|r}$ and $\overline{\phi_{1|r}}\phi_{1|s} \approx_E \overline{\phi_{2|r}}\phi_{2|s}$. The proof is done by contraposition. We obviously have that $\phi_{1|r} \not\approx_E \phi_{2|r}$ implies $\phi_1 \not\approx_E \phi_2$ as $M\phi_{i|r} = M\phi_i$ for any term M having only variables of sort r. Furthermore, we have that $\overline{\phi_{1|r}}\phi_{1|s} \not\approx_E \overline{\phi_{2|r}}\phi_{2|s}$ implies $\phi_1 \not\approx_E \phi_2$. The proof uses the fact that the elements $\overline{\phi_{i|r}}$ are obtained by some fixed contexts T_i in order to build distinguishers for ϕ_1 and ϕ_2.

$(\Leftarrow)$ If $\phi_{1|r} \approx_E \phi_{2|r}$ and $\overline{\phi_{1|r}}\phi_{1|s} \approx_E \overline{\phi_{2|r}}\phi_{2|s}$ then $\phi_1 \approx_E \phi_2$. The proof is done by contraposition. Suppose that $\phi_1 \not\approx_E \phi_2$ and consider the two possibilities for the sorts of the distinguishers M and N. If $\mathsf{sort}(M) = r$, by the fact that f is a valve, we have that M and N distinguish $\phi_{1|r}$ and $\phi_{2|r}$. If $\mathsf{sort}(M) = s$, by invoking Lemma 3, we infer the existence of distinguishers for $\overline{\phi_{1|r}}\phi_{1|s}$ and $\overline{\phi_{2|r}}\phi_{2|s}$. $\qquad\square$

A detailed proof can be found in [15].

By the following definition we identify a sufficient condition to get rid of the symbol f for deciding static equivalence between frames that do not involve this symbol. In the following section we exhibit a syntactic condition that is sufficient to obtain such a theory.

Definition 9 (sufficient equational theory). *Let $(\mathcal{S}, \mathcal{F} \uplus \{f\})$ be a sorted signature and E an equational theory. An equational theory E' is sufficient for E without f iff for any terms $u, v \in T(\mathcal{F}, \mathcal{N})$, $u =_E v$ iff $u =_{E'} v$ and E' does not involve f.*

Theorem 1. *Let E be an equational theory on the sorted signature $(\mathcal{S}, \mathcal{F} \uplus \{f\})$ such that*
  – f is a valve,
  – E is a reducible equational theory for f,
  – E is sufficiently complete w.r.t. $\{f\}$.

If there exists an equational theory E' sufficient for E without f then for any $\{r, s\}$-sorted frames ϕ_1 and ϕ_2, we have that $\phi_1 \approx_E \phi_2$ iff $\phi_{1|r} \approx_{E'} \phi_{2|r}$ and $\overline{\phi_{1|r}}\phi_{1|s} \approx_{E'} \overline{\phi_{2|r}}\phi_{2|s}$.

The proof of Theorem 1 relies on Lemma 5.

Lemma 5. *Let ϕ_1 and ϕ_2 be two $\{r\}$-sorted frames, E an equational theory, and f a valve from r to a distinct sort s, which is free in E. If for any two terms M, N of sort r $(M =_E N)\phi_1$ iff $(M =_E N)\phi_2$, then for any two terms M and N of sort s, $(M =_E N)\phi_1$ iff $(M =_E N)\phi_2$.*

Proof (sketch). We will exhibit two replacements functions σ_1 (resp. σ_2) defined on pairs (α, p) where α identifies M or N and p is a position in $M\phi_1$ or $N\phi_1$ (resp. $M\phi_2, N\phi_2$) such that $M\phi_1|_p$ or $N\phi_1|_p$ is headed by f. The co-domain of σ_1 (resp. σ_2) is a set of fresh names w.r.t. ϕ_1 (resp. ϕ_2). We show the two following assertions

  1. $M\phi_1\sigma_1 =_E M\phi_2\sigma_2$ and $N\phi_1\sigma_1 =_E N\phi_2\sigma_2$,
  2. $M\phi_i =_E N\phi_i$ iff $M\phi_i\sigma_i =_E N\phi_i\sigma_i$ for $i \in \{1, 2\}$.

Their conjunction implies that for any two terms M, N of sort s, $(M =_E N)\phi_1$ iff $(M =_E N)\phi_2$.

   To show that $M\phi_1\sigma_1 =_E M\phi_2\sigma_2$ and $N\phi_1\sigma_1 =_E N\phi_2\sigma_2$ we rely on the hypothesis that for any two terms M, N of sort r we have that $(M =_E N)\phi_1$ iff $(M =_E N)\phi_2$ as well as the construction of σ_1 and σ_2.

To show that $M\phi_i =_E N\phi_i$ implies $M\phi_i\sigma_i =_E N\phi_i\sigma_i$, we use the notion of *cut function* introduced in [6]. Showing that σ_1 (resp. σ_2) corresponds to a sequence of applications of a cut function allows us to conclude using Lemma 15 of [6]. To show that $M\phi_i\sigma_i =_E N\phi_i\sigma_i$ implies $M\phi_i =_E N\phi_i$ we use the fact that σ_1 and σ_2 are bijective.   □

A complete proof is given in in [15].

Proof (of Theorem 1). We suppose that $\phi_1 \approx_E \phi_2$. By Lemma 4 we have that $\phi_{1|r} \approx_E \phi_{2|r}$ and $\overline{\phi_{1|r}}\phi_{1|s} \approx_E \overline{\phi_{2|r}}\phi_{2|s}$.

We will show that

$$\phi_{1|r} \approx_E \phi_{2|r}(p) \wedge \overline{\phi_{1|r}}\phi_{1|s} \approx_E \overline{\phi_{2|r}}\phi_{2|s}(q)$$
$$\Leftrightarrow$$
$$\phi_{1|r} \approx_{E'} \phi_{2|r}(p_1) \wedge \overline{\phi_{1|r}}\phi_{1|s} \approx_{E'} \overline{\phi_{2|r}}\phi_{2|s}(q_1)$$

We will prove the three following assertions separately :

$$(1)\neg q \Leftrightarrow \neg q_1 \qquad (2)\neg p \Rightarrow \neg p_1 \vee \neg q_1 \qquad (3)\neg p_1 \Rightarrow \neg p$$

The conjunction of these three assertions implies the fact that $(p \wedge q) \Leftrightarrow (p_1 \wedge q_1)$.

(1) $\overline{\phi_{1|r}}\phi_{1|s} \not\approx_E \overline{\phi_{2|r}}\phi_{2|s}$ iff $\overline{\phi_{1|r}}\phi_{1|s} \not\approx_{E'} \overline{\phi_{2|r}}\phi_{2|s}$

As $\overline{\phi_{1|r}}\phi_{1|s} \not\approx_E \overline{\phi_{2|r}}\phi_{2|s}$ there exist two terms M and N distinguishing $\overline{\phi_{1|r}}\phi_{1|s}$ and $\overline{\phi_{2|r}}\phi_{2|s}$. As f is a valve, there exist M and N that do not involve any symbol f. As E is sufficiently complete w.r.t. $\{f\}$ we can suppose that frames $\overline{\phi_{1|r}}\phi_{1|s}$ and $\overline{\phi_{2|r}}\phi_{2|s}$ do not involve f. Hence $M\overline{\phi_{i|r}}\phi_{i|s}$ and $N\overline{\phi_{i|r}}\phi_{i|s}$ also do not involve f. As E' is sufficient for E without f we have that $M\overline{\phi_{i|r}}\phi_{i|s} =_E N\overline{\phi_{i|r}}\phi_{i|s}$ iff $M\overline{\phi_{i|r}}\phi_{i|s} =_{E'} N\overline{\phi_{i|r}}\phi_{i|s}$. Hence $\overline{\phi_{1|r}}\phi_{1|s} \not\approx_{E'} \overline{\phi_{2|r}}\phi_{2|s}$.

(2) if $\phi_{1|r} \not\approx_E \phi_{2|r}$ then $\phi_{1|r} \not\approx_{E'} \phi_{2|r}$ or $\overline{\phi_{1|r}}\phi_{1|s} \not\approx_{E'} \overline{\phi_{2|r}}\phi_{2|s}$

Let M and N be two terms distinguishing $\phi_{1|r}$ and $\phi_{2|r}$.

If M is of sort r, as f is a valve, we can suppose w.l.o.g. that M, N, $\phi_{1|r}$ and $\phi_{2|r}$ do not involve any f. Hence $M\phi_{i|r}$ and $N\phi_{i|r}$ do not involve f. As E' is sufficient for E without f we have that $M\phi_{i|r} =_E N\phi_{i|r}$ iff $M\phi_{i|r} =_{E'} N\phi_{i|r}$. Hence $\phi_{1|r} \not\approx_{E'} \phi_{2|r}$.

If M is of sort s, by Lemma 3 there exist terms M' and N' such that $M\phi_{i|r} =_E M'\overline{\phi_{i|r}}$ and $N\phi_{i|r} =_E N'\overline{\phi_{i|r}}$. As f is a valve, M' and N' do not involve any symbol f. By sufficient completeness of E w.r.t. $\{f\}$, we can consider frames $\overline{\phi_{1|r}}$ and $\overline{\phi_{2|r}}$ that do not involve f, $M'\overline{\phi_{i|r}}$ and $N'\overline{\phi_{i|r}}$ do not involve f either. As E' is sufficient without f we have that $M'\overline{\phi_{i|r}} =_E N'\overline{\phi_{i|r}}$ iff $M'\overline{\phi_{i|r}} =_{E'} N'\overline{\phi_{i|r}}$. Hence $\overline{\phi_{1|r}} \not\approx_{E'} \overline{\phi_{2|r}}$ and $\overline{\phi_{1|r}}\phi_{1|s} \not\approx_{E'} \overline{\phi_{2|r}}\phi_{2|s}$.

(3) if $\phi_{1|r} \not\approx_{E'} \phi_{2|r}$ then $\phi_{1|r} \not\approx_E \phi_{2|r}$

As $\phi_{1|r} \not\approx_{E'} \phi_{2|r}$ there exist terms M and N distinguishing $\phi_{1|r}$ and $\phi_{2|r}$. If there are no terms M and N of sort r distinguishing $\phi_{1|r}$ and $\phi_{2|r}$, by Lemma 5 there are no terms of sort s distinguishing $\phi_{1|r}$ and $\phi_{2|r}$. Hence if $\phi_{1|r} \not\approx_{E'} \phi_{2|r}$ then there are terms M and N distinguishing $\phi_{1|r}$ and $\phi_{2|r}$ of sort r.

If M is of sort r, as f is a valve, M, N, $\phi_{1|r}$ and $\phi_{2|r}$ do not involve any f. Hence $M\phi_{i|r}$ and $N\phi_{i|r}$ do not involve f. As E' is sufficient without f we have that $M\phi_{i|r} =_{E'} N\phi_{i|r}$ iff $M\phi_{i|r} =_E N\phi_{i|r}$. Hence $\phi_{1|r} \not\approx_E \phi_{2|r}$.   □

We denote by E^{-r} the equational theory E without equations of sort r.

Corollary 1. *Let E be an equational theory on the sorted signature $(\mathcal{S}, \mathcal{F} \cup \{f\})$ such that (i) f is a valve, (ii) E is a reducible equational theory for f, and (iii) E is sufficiently complete w.r.t. $\{f\}$. If there exists an equational theory E' sufficient for E without f then for any $\{r, s\}$-sorted frames ϕ_1 and ϕ_2, we have that $\phi_1 \approx_E \phi_2$ iff $\phi_{1|r} \approx_{E'^{-s}} \phi_{2|r}$ and $\overline{\phi_{1|r}}\phi_{1|s} \approx_{E'^{-r}} \overline{\phi_{2|r}}\phi_{2|s}$.*

Proof. By Theorem 1, we have $\phi_1 \approx_E \phi_2$ iff $\phi_{1|r} \approx_{E'} \phi_{2|r}$ and $\overline{\phi_{1|r}}\phi_{1|s} \approx_{E'} \overline{\phi_{2|r}}\phi_{2|s}$.

By Lemma 5, we have that if for any two terms M and N of sort r $(M =_E N)\phi_1$ iff $(M =_E N)\phi_2$, then for any two terms M and N of sort s, $(M =_E N)\phi_1$ iff $(M =_E N)\phi_2$. Hence it is sufficient to consider terms of sort r to decide static equivalence between $\phi_{1|r}$ and $\phi_{2|r}$. As f is a valve for any term M, no subterms of M are of sort s. We can consider only E'^{-r} to decide static equivalence between $\phi_{1|r}$ and $\phi_{2|r}$.

Let us show that $\overline{\phi_{1|r}}\phi_{1|s} \approx_{E'} \overline{\phi_{2|r}}\phi_{2|s}$ iff $\overline{\phi_{1|r}}\phi_{1|s} \approx_{E'^{-r}} \overline{\phi_{2|r}}\phi_{2|s}$.

$\overline{\phi_{1|r}}\phi_{1|s} \not\approx_{E'} \overline{\phi_{2|r}}\phi_{2|s}$ iff there are two terms M and N distinguishing $\overline{\phi_{1|r}}\phi_{1|s}$ and $\overline{\phi_{2|r}}\phi_{2|s}$. As f is a valve, there exist M and N that do not involve any symbol f. As E is sufficiently complete w.r.t. $\{f\}$ we can suppose that frames $\overline{\phi_{1|r}}\phi_{1|s}$ and $\overline{\phi_{2|r}}\phi_{2|s}$ do not involve f. Hence $M\overline{\phi_{i|r}}\phi_{i|s}$ and $N\overline{\phi_{i|r}}\phi_{i|s}$ do not involve f either. As f is a valve $M\overline{\phi_{i|r}}\phi_{i|s}$ and $N\overline{\phi_{i|r}}\phi_{i|s}$ do not involve subterms of sort r we have that $M\overline{\phi_{i|r}} =_{E'} N'\overline{\phi_{i|r}}$ iff $M\overline{\phi_{i|r}}\phi_{i|s} =_{E'^{-r}} N\overline{\phi_{i|r}}\phi_{i|s}$. Hence $\overline{\phi_{1|r}}\phi_{1|s} \not\approx_{E'^{-r}} \overline{\phi_{2|r}}\phi_{2|s}$.   □

6   A Criterion for Sufficient Equational Theories

In this section we make a first attempt to find sufficient criteria for applying Theorem 1. Future work includes finding broader criteria. We also briefly explain how our running example fits this criterion.

Definition 10 (decomposition). *A pair $(\mathcal{R}, E')$ is a decomposition of an equational theory E iff*

- *E' is an equational theory,*
- *$\mathcal{R}$ is a rewriting system convergent modulo E',*
- *for any terms u and v $u =_E v$ iff $u \downarrow_{\mathcal{R}/E'} = v \downarrow_{\mathcal{R}/E'}$.*

Definition 11 (exclusively define). *Let $(\mathcal{S}, \mathcal{F} \uplus \{f\})$ be a sorted signature. A rewriting system $\mathcal{R}$ exclusively defines f if any term in normal form modulo $\mathcal{R}/E'$ is in $T(\mathcal{F}, \mathcal{N})$ and if for any rewrite rule $l \to r \in \mathcal{R}$, f appears in l.*

Lemma 6. *Let $(\mathcal{S}, \mathcal{F} \uplus \{f\})$ be a signature. If a theory E on this signature has a decomposition $(\mathcal{R}, E')$ and if $\mathcal{R}$ exclusively defines f then E' is sufficient for E without f.*

Proof. Let u and v be two terms not involving f. As $\mathcal{R}$ exclusively defines f and as u and v do not involve any f symbol, no rule of $\mathcal{R}$ can be applied. Hence $u =_E v$ iff $u =_{E'} v$. □

Example 5 (continued). We define $\mathcal{R}_{\mathsf{BP}}$ to be the rewriting system obtained by orienting the rule $e(exp_1(x), exp_1(y)) = exp_2(x \cdot y)$ from left to right, and E'_{BP} the equational theory E_{BP} without this rule. We remark that $(\mathcal{R}, E'_{\mathsf{BP}})$ is a decomposition of E_{BP} and it is easy to see that $\mathcal{R}$ exclusively defines e.

Corollary 2. *If the set of names of sorts G_1 and G_2 are empty, static equivalence for E_{BP} is decidable for $\{G_1, G_2\}$-sorted frames.*

Proof. As $\mathcal{R}_{\mathsf{BP}}$ exclusively defines e, by Lemma 6, we have that E'_{BP} is sufficient for E_{BP} without e. By Proposition 1 we have that E_{BP} is reducible for f. Finally, as the set of names of sorts G_1 and G_2 is empty, E_{BP} is sufficiently complete for e. Hence by Corollary 1, for two frames ϕ_1 and ϕ_2, $\phi_1 \approx_E \phi_2$ iff $\phi_{1|G_1} \approx_{E'^{-G_2}_{\mathsf{BP}}} \phi_{2|G_1}$ and $\overline{\phi_{1|G_1}} \phi_{1|G_2} \approx_{E'^{-G_1}_{\mathsf{BP}}} \overline{\phi_{2|G_1}} \phi_{2|G_2}$.

As $E'^{-G_2}_{\mathsf{BP}}$ and $E'^{-G_1}_{\mathsf{BP}}$ correspond both to the classical equational theory modelling Diffie-Hellman, which is known to be decidable [13] for frames whose only names are of sort R we have that static equivalence is decidable for E_{BP} on $\{G_1, G_2\}$-sorted frames. □

7   Conclusion and Future Work

In this paper we have defined the notions of valve and reducibility which allow to simplify equational theories for the decision of static equivalence. This constitutes a first step towards finding generic criteria. Our results apply to the case of bilinear pairing. We believe that this result may apply to other situations where several algebraic structures are used in the model of the same cryptographic operator. In the short term we are investigating the following directions:

(1) We are trying to identify criteria for reducibility which are easier to decide. Even on our quite simple example, proving reducibility is a bit technical. Hence we are trying to determine either syntactic criteria on the equational theory, or more classical properties as a constrained form of sufficient completeness, that would imply reducibility.

(2) In this paper we have analyzed the case where there is only one reducible valve in an equational theory. Extending reducibility to the case where several valves belong to the theory seems possible. However it requires defining a priority order on the reductions of the different valves.

(3) We are also trying to widen the notion of valve. In the definition we propose here, a valve is defined from a given sort to another. Yet cases where

a valve takes as argument terms of different sorts can be considered. We think that such a notion could give rise to a wider notion of reducibility than the one we have analyzed. It seems that we need conditions on the links between the arguments of such valves.

References

1. Abadi, M., Blanchet, B., Fournet, C.: Verification of selected equivalences for security protocols. Journal of Logic and Algebraic Programming 75(1), 3–51 (2008)
2. Abadi, M., Cortier, V.: Deciding knowledge in security protocols under equational theories. Theoretical Computer Science 367(1), 2–32 (2006)
3. Abadi, M., Fournet, C.: Mobile values, new names, and secure communication. In: Proceedings of the 28th ACM SIGPLAN-SIGACT Symposium on Principles of Programming Languages(POPL 2001), pp. 104–115. ACM Press, New York (2001)
4. Arnaud, M., Cortier, V., Delaune, S.: Combining algorithms for deciding knowledge in security protocols. In: Konev, B., Wolter, F. (eds.) FroCos 2007. LNCS (LNAI), vol. 4720, pp. 103–117. Springer, Heidelberg (2007)
5. Baudet, M.: Deciding security of protocols against off-line guessing attacks. In: Proceedings of the 12th ACM Conference on Computer and Communications Security (CCS 2005), pp. 16–25. ACM Press, New York (2005)
6. Baudet, M., Cortier, V., Kremer, S.: Computationally sound implementations of equational theories against passive adversaries. Information and Computation 207(4), 496–520 (2009)
7. Boneh, D., Franklin, M.: Identity-based encryption from the Weil pairing. In: Kilian, J. (ed.) CRYPTO 2001. LNCS, vol. 2139, pp. 213–229. Springer, Heidelberg (2001)
8. Common, H.: Inductionless induction. In: Handbook of Automated Reasoning, Elsevier, Amsterdam (2001)
9. Ricardo, C., Jeroen, D., Sandro, E.: Analysing password protocol security against off-line dictionary attacks. In: Proceedings of the 2nd International Workshop on Security Issues with Petri Nets and other Computational Models (WISP 2004). ENTCS, vol. 121, pp. 47–63. Elsevier, Amsterdam (2004)
10. Cortier, V., Delaune, S., Lafourcade, P.: A survey of algebraic properties used in cryptographic protocols. Journal of Computer Security 14(1), 1–43 (2006)
11. Dolev, D., Yao, A.C.: On the security of public key protocols. IEEE Transactions on Information Theory 29(2), 198–208 (1983)
12. Joux, A.: A one round protocol for tripartite Diffie-Hellman. In: Bosma, W. (ed.) ANTS 2000. LNCS, vol. 1838, pp. 385–394. Springer, Heidelberg (2000)
13. Kremer, S., Mazaré, L.: Adaptive soundness of static equivalence. In: Biskup, J., López, J. (eds.) ESORICS 2007. LNCS, vol. 4734, pp. 610–625. Springer, Heidelberg (2007)
14. Kremer, S., Mazaré, L.: Computationally sound analysis of protocols using bilinear pairings. Journal of Computer Security (to appear, 2009)
15. Kremer, S., Mercier, A., Treinen, R.: Reducing equational theories for the decision of static equivalence. Research Report LSV-09-19, LSV, ENS Cachan, France (May 2009)

A Simulation-Based Treatment of Authenticated Message Exchange[*]

Klaas Ole Kürtz, Henning Schnoor, and Thomas Wilke

Christian-Albrechts-Universität zu Kiel, 24098 Kiel, Germany
{kuertz,schnoor,wilke}@ti.informatik.uni-kiel.de

Abstract. Simulation-based security notions for cryptographic protocols are regarded as highly desirable, primarily because they admit strong composability and, consequently, a modular design. In this paper, we give a simulation-based security definition for two-round authenticated message exchange and show that a concrete protocol, 2AMEX-1, satisfies our security property, that is, we provide an ideal functionality for two-round authenticated message exchange and show that 2AMEX-1 realizes it securely. To model the involved public-key infrastructure adequately, we use a joint-state approach.

1 Introduction

Simulation-based security definitions for cryptographic protocols, see, for instance, [1,2,3,4], are attracting much attention, the reasons being that such security definitions "guarantee security even when a secure protocol [. . .] is used as a component of an arbitrary system" [1] and that they enable "modular proofs of security" [2]. As a consequence, a variety of cryptographic primitives such as asymmetric encryption and digital signatures have been treated following the simulation-based approach. There are, however, only few complex cryptographic protocols that have been tackled within the simulation-based framework. We are aware of [5,6,7,8,9], where, for instance, Kerberos and the Yahalom protocol are treated.

In this paper, we deal with two-round authenticated message exchange protocols following the simulation-based approach. We (i) provide an ideal functionality for two-round authenticated message exchange protocols, $\mathcal{F}_{2AM}$, (ii) provide an implementation, $\mathcal{P}_{2AMEX-1}$, corresponding to a particular such protocol, 2AMEX-1, and (iii) prove the implementation of 2AMEX-1 to be secure, that is, prove that $\mathcal{P}_{2AMEX-1}$ securely realizes the ideal functionality, in symbols $\mathcal{P}_{2AMEX-1} \leq^{BB} \mathcal{F}_{2AM}$. (The superscript stands for black-box simulatability.)

The protocol 2AMEX-1, see [10], which is a generic protocol for message authentication in a web service setting, is complex in several respects: it distinguishes between short-lived clients and long-lived servers; it uses digital signatures and therefore makes use of a public-key infrastructure; it requires only bounded memory; it uses nonces and timestamps to counter replay attacks; each client and each

---

[*] This work was partially supported by the DFG under grant KU 1434/4-2.

A. Datta (Ed.): ASIAN 2009, LNCS 5913, pp. 109–123, 2009.

server has its own local clock. In [10], 2AMEX-1 was proved to be secure in the Bellare-Rogaway framework as presented in [11].

Several simulation-based approaches have been developed over the last decade (see above). We could have used any of these approaches, but we have adopted the one by Küsters, see [4], because it provides a very flexible addressing mechanism and easy-to-use joint-state theorems, see [12]. The latter is especially useful in the analysis of 2AMEX-1, because it allows us to show with only little effort that 2AMEX-1 works securely with a simple, but realistic public-key infrastructure. Although Küsters' setting comes in handy in many respects, it also has some shortcomings, which become evident from our analysis and are discussed in this paper.

Due to the space limit, we can only provide a high-level account of Küsters' model, provide a brief description of the functionalities we have developed, and give a short sketch of the proof of our main result. A full version of this paper can be found in [13]. We start with the sketch of Küsters' model in Section 2, go on with a description of the setting and the ideal functionalities in Section 3 and a description of the implementation for 2AMEX-1 in Section 4, and conclude with our main result and a discussion in Sections 5 and 6.

We are grateful to Max Tuengerthal for helpful comments.

2   Simulation-Based Security

In this section, we give a high-level description of the simulation-based framework from [4], which is referred to as the *IITM framework*, where IITM stands for *inexhaustible interactive Turing machine*.

In the IITM framework cryptographic protocols and the environment they are run in (including the adversary) are modeled as concurrent, polynomial-time, probabilistic, interactive, replicable Turing machines. Here, "concurrent" refers to an interleaving semantics, that is, only one IITM is active at a time and there is a mechanism that determines which IITM is activated next; "replicable" refers to a mechanism which allows certain machines, the so-called banged machines, to be instantiated several times (and run concurrently); "interactive" means that the machines can communicate by sharing tapes, more precisely: an output tape of one machine can be the input tape of another machine. From a security point of view, it is important that systems of IITM's can be simulated in polynomial time. To achieve this, it is, however, not enough to require that the individual IITM's are polynomial-time, because two IITM's "playing ping pong" could double their outputs on each activation, leading to an overall exponential running time. For that reason the IITM framework imposes certain restrictions on how machines are interconnected, based on a partition of tapes into consuming and enriching. Roughly speaking, the overall length of the output of one IITM up to a certain point may be polynomial in the overall length of the input on enriching tapes up to the same point, but there must not be any cycle of enriching tapes. This is less restrictive than requiring that each IITM runs in time polynomial in the security parameter; it allows to process inputs of arbitrary size.

To illustrate the IITM framework consider Figure 1 and first focus on the box labeled $\mathcal{F}_{2\mathrm{AM}}$. This box represents a model of two-round authenticated message exchange protocols (details follow in the next section); it contains four machines which represent an actual protocol: C, S, EI, and NG, of which the first three are banged (can be replicated), and the last one is not. Every instance of machine C is connected with machine NG, in both directions. The corresponding input tape of NG is enriching, while the input tape of C is not.

There are two types of connections crossing the borders of $\mathcal{F}_{2\mathrm{AM}}$: solid connections representing tapes classified as I/O tapes and dashed connections representing tapes classified as network tapes. I/O tapes should roughly be thought of as tapes communicating with "users" of the system, whereas network tapes are tapes where the adversary can interfere.

In Figure 1, the adversary, represented by an IITM denoted $\mathcal{A}$, is not connected directly with $\mathcal{F}_{2\mathrm{AM}}$. Rather, there is a mediator between $\mathcal{A}$ and $\mathcal{F}_{2\mathrm{AM}}$, namely an IITM $\mathcal{S}$ called simulator. The situation is typical for simulation-based security: a simulator "translates" network traffic to make a system (in this case $\mathcal{F}_{2\mathrm{AM}}$) seem equivalent to another one (usually a "real" system $\mathcal{P}$, see below) to an outside observer consisting of an environment machine $\mathcal{E}$ (taking over the role of all users) and an adversary $\mathcal{A}$.

Another feature of Figure 1 not discussed yet has to do with how different instances of the same machine are addressed. Underlining the name of a machine indicates the usage of a generic addressing mechanism provided by the IITM framework, which works by using prefixes of messages as identifiers for instances.

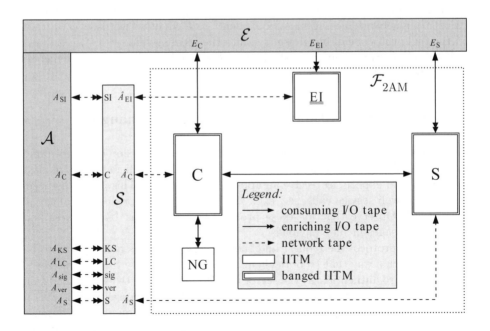

Fig. 1. Ideal functionality for two-round message authentication

In Figure 1 the machine EI is underlined twice, which adds two prefixes for addressing, that is, a hierarchical addressing mechanism is used. We use it to model multi-user multi-session instances.

The formal way to specify the system represented by the box $\mathcal{F}_{2\text{AM}}$ in Figure 1 is by the expression

$$\mathcal{F}_{2\text{AM}} = !\mathcal{F}_{\text{C}} \mid !\mathcal{F}_{\text{S}} \mid \mathcal{F}_{\text{NG}} \mid !\underline{\underline{\mathcal{F}_{\text{EI}}}} \ , \tag{1}$$

where $\mathcal{F}_{\text{C}}$, $\mathcal{F}_{\text{S}}$, $\mathcal{F}_{\text{NG}}$, and $\mathcal{F}_{\text{EI}}$ denote (descriptions of) the underlying IITM's, and $\mid$ denotes an operator for composing machines.

In the IITM framework, security of a protocol is defined as follows. First, one describes a system of IITM's, $\mathcal{F}$, which works in an ideal fashion in every setting where an environment and an adversary are connected to it, that is, how one would expect a perfect protocol to work. Such a system is called an ideal functionality. Then, given a real protocol, one describes a system of IITM's, $\mathcal{P}$, which works just the way the real protocol would work in every setting where an environment and an adversary are connected to it. Now, $\mathcal{P}$ is considered secure if there is a simulator IITM $\mathcal{S}$ with the following property. For every environment machine $\mathcal{E}$ and every adversary machine $\mathcal{A}$, the system composed of $\mathcal{P}$, $\mathcal{E}$, and $\mathcal{A}$ is computationally indistinguishable from the system composed of $\mathcal{F}$, $\mathcal{E}$, $\mathcal{A}$, and $\mathcal{S}$. As explained above communication between these machines is restricted as follows: all external network connections of $\mathcal{F}$ are handled by the simulator $\mathcal{S}$; the adversary may only communicate with $\mathcal{F}$ using the network interface provided by the simulator; and the environment may only communicate with $\mathcal{F}$ using I/O connections. Hence, the system composed of $\mathcal{F}$ and the simulator (translating network messages) is "equivalent" to $\mathcal{P}$. In other words, every attack on the real protocol can be transferred into the ideal system.

If the above condition is satisfied, then $\mathcal{P}$ securely realizes (or implements) $\mathcal{F}$, denoted by $\mathcal{P} \leq^{\text{BB}} \mathcal{F}$ (for *black-box simulation*).

3   Two-Round Authenticated Message Exchange

We start with a description of the general scenario. In a session of a two-round authenticated message exchange protocol (2AM protocol) a client sends a request to a server and expects to receive an appropriate response. This is, for instance, the case for web service calls, see, e.g., [14,15] and remote procedure calls, see, e.g. [16,17]. Observe that for these protocols to make sense the request and response messages include payloads.

In a 2AM protocol the request and the response messages are required to be secured in such a way that (i) both client and server can verify that the messages they receive are authentic, (ii) the server accepts no message twice (payloads, on the contrary, may be received twice, but only in different messages), and (iii) if the client receives a response, it can be sure which of his requests the response refers to. Note that the same client may have multiple sessions with the same or different servers in parallel, but each session has only two rounds.

Tapes: C $\longleftrightarrow E_C$, C $\dashleftarrow\dashrightarrow \hat{A}_C$, C $\longleftrightarrow$ S, C $\longleftrightarrow\!\!\!\to$ NG
Initialization: $c = s = r = \varepsilon$, $n = 0$, $state = $ Init, $cor = $ false
Steps: loop
    Send a request to the server:
    if $(c', (\text{Client}, s'), \text{Init})$ received from E_C
        Let $state = $ OK, $c = c'$ and $s = s'$.
        Send $(c, (\text{Client}, s), \text{GetNonce})$ to NG.
        Recv $(c, (\text{Client}, s), \text{Nonce}, r')$ from NG, let $r = r'$.
        Send $(c, (\text{Client}, s, r), \text{Nonce}, r)$ to E_C.
        Recv $(c, (\text{Client}, s, r), \text{Request}, p_c, 1^{n'})$ from E_C, let $n = n'$.
        Send $(c, (\text{Client}, s, r), \text{Request}, p_c, n)$ to $\hat{A}_C$.
        Recv $(c, (\text{Client}, s, r), \text{Request}, \text{Send})$ from $\hat{A}_C$.
        Send $(c, (\text{Client}, s, r), \text{Request}, p_c)$ to S.
    Receive and process a response from the server:
    if $(s, (\text{Server}, c, r), \text{Response}, p_s)$ received from S
        If $state \neq $ OK or $|p_s| > n$, abort.
        Let $state = $ Stopped.
        Send $(c, (\text{Client}, s, r), \text{Response}, p_s)$ to E_C.
Corruption: $\text{Corr}(cor, \text{true}, state \neq \text{Init}, \varepsilon, \hat{A}_C, \{E_C\}, E_C)$
CheckAddress: Accept the initialization message only once. Check for c, s, and r as soon as each
    one has been set.

Fig. 2. The client functionality $\mathcal{F}_C$

3.1 Overview of the Ideal Functionality

Our model of the ideal functionality for 2AM protocols consists of four function-alities, see Figure 1: a client $\mathcal{F}_C$ (defined in Figure 2), a server $\mathcal{F}_S$ (defined in Figure 3), a nonce generator $\mathcal{F}_{NG}$, and an enriching input functionality $\mathcal{F}_{EI}$. The ideal functionality $\mathcal{F}_{2AM}$ is the composition of these functionalities, as defined in (1).

One instance of the client functionality handles exactly one session between a client identity and a server, i. e., after initialization it basically (i) receives a request from the environment and encapsulates it in a message to a server, and (ii) receives a response from the server and forwards its contents to the environment. One instance of the server functionality also handles exactly one session; as with the client, it consists of receiving a request and sending a response. The nonce generator generates globally unique session identifiers (numbers used once, nonces) to distinguish multiple sessions between two parties. The enriching input functionality passes bits from an enriching input tape to the adversary. These bits are necessary to give the adversary additional capabilities as explained in Section 4.3.

3.2 Ideal Client Functionality

When the environment wants to start a new session, it provides the client with the identity of a server the client is supposed to communicate with. The client then responds with a nonce, which can be viewed as a handle, i. e., it allows the environment to distinguish different sessions this client is involved in.

The environment can now pass the payload of the request message to the client as well as enough resources to process a possible response from the server. The client then notifies the adversary that a message is ready to be sent. If the

Tapes: $S \longleftrightarrow E_S$, $S \leftarrow\text{--}\rightarrow \hat{A}_S$, $S \longleftrightarrow C$
Initialization: $s = c = r = p_s = \varepsilon$, $n = 0$, $state = \mathsf{Init}_0$, $cor = \mathsf{false}$
Steps: loop
    Initialization by the environment:
    if $(s', (\mathsf{Server}), \mathsf{Init}, 1^{n'})$ received from E_S
        If $state \neq \mathsf{Init}_0$, abort. Let $s = s'$ and $n = n'$.
        Send $(s, (\mathsf{Server}), \mathsf{Init}, n)$ to $\hat{A}_S$.
        Recv $(s, (\mathsf{Server}), \mathsf{Init}, \mathsf{OK})$ from $\hat{A}_S$.
        Let $state = \mathsf{Init}_1$.
    Receive and process a request from the client:
    if $(c', (\mathsf{Client}, s, r'), \mathsf{Request}, p_c)$ received from C
        If $state \neq \mathsf{Init}_1$ or $|p_c| > n$, abort. Let $state = \mathsf{OK}$, $c = c'$, and $r = r'$.
        Send $(s, (\mathsf{Server}, c, r), \mathsf{Request}, p_c)$ to E_S.
    Receive a response payload from the environment:
    if $(s, (\mathsf{Server}, c, r), \mathsf{Response}, p)$ received from E_S
        Let $p_s = p$. Send $(s, (\mathsf{Server}, c, r), \mathsf{Response}, p_s)$ to $\hat{A}_S$.
    Deliver a response to the client:
    if $(s, (\mathsf{Server}, c, r), \mathsf{Response}, \mathsf{Send})$ received from $\hat{A}_S$ and not cor
        If $state \neq \mathsf{OK}$, abort. Let $state = \mathsf{Stopped}$.
        Send $(s, (\mathsf{Server}, c, r), \mathsf{Response}, p_s)$ to C.
    Send an error message to the environment:
    if $(s, (\mathsf{Server}, c, r), \mathsf{Response}, \mathsf{Error})$ received from $\hat{A}_S$
        Send $(s, (\mathsf{Server}, c, r), \mathsf{Response}, \mathsf{Error})$ to E_S.
Corruption: $\mathsf{Corr}(cor, \mathsf{true}, state \neq \mathsf{Init}_0, \varepsilon, \hat{A}_S, \{E_S\}, E_S, s)$
CheckAddress: Accept the initialization message only once. Check for s, c, and r as soon as each one has been set.

Fig. 3. The server functionality $\mathcal{F}_S$

adversary (ever) allows the transfer, the message is written to the incoming tape of the server. This models the adversary's ability to delay or drop messages on the network.

When the server transfers a response (which is not too large), the client simply unwraps it and forwards the contents to the environment. The details are spelled out in Figure 2.

A special mode of computation of IITM's, CheckAddress, is used in the last line of IITM definitions like Figure 2 to determine whether an incoming message is addressed to the current instance of the client IITM. If a message is rejected by all running instances, a new instance of the client IITM is started since the client IITM is banged in $\mathcal{F}_{2\mathrm{AM}}$. In addition, we use the corruption macro Corr from [12] (with a slightly extended addressing mechanism) to allow a uniform treatment of corruption of clients and servers in both the ideal and the real world, see Appendix A.

3.3 Ideal Server Functionality

To start a session on the server side, the environment sends a message to the server with the identity it is supposed to receive messages for and the maximal length of an incoming request message.

Upon receiving a request from a client, the server unwraps it and forwards the request payload to the environment. Now the environment can respond by passing a response payload to the server functionality. The server asks the adversary, who has three options: It can either approve the sending of the payload, in which case the server delivers the message directly to the client. Secondly, the adversary can ignore the response, in which case the server sends no message at all. Thirdly, the adversary can also explicitly deny processing the payload, which results in an error message being sent to the environment.

The first two options again model that the adversary may intercept and delay network traffic. The third type of reaction models that in our implementation the server may reject messages due to bounded memory and notify the environment of the rejection.

4   Implementation of the 2AMEX-1 Protocol

In this section, we describe a system of IITM's implementing the 2AMEX-1 protocol, which is a 2AM protocol in the above sense and described in detail in [10]. First, we give an informal introduction into the protocol.

4.1   The Protocol 2AMEX-1

In 2AMEX-1, an authenticated message exchange between a client with identity c and a server with identity s works roughly as follows.

 1. a) c is asked by the environment to send the request p_c
  b) c sends $\{(\mathsf{From}\colon c, \mathsf{To}\colon s, \mathsf{MsgID}\colon r, \mathsf{Time}\colon t, \mathsf{Body}\colon p_c)\}_{sk_c}$ to s
  c) s checks whether the message is admissible and if not, stops
  d) s forwards the request (r, p_c) to the environment

 2. a) s receives a response (r, p_s) from the environment
  b) s checks whether the response is admissible and if not, stops
  c) s sends $\{(\mathsf{From}\colon s, \mathsf{To}\colon c, \mathsf{Ref}\colon r, \mathsf{Body}\colon p_s)\}_{sk_s}$ to c
  d) c checks whether the response is admissible and if not, stops
  e) c forwards the response p_s to the environment

Here, r is the nonce as described in the previous section, which is also used as a handle by the server (see steps 1. d) and 2. a)), t is the value of a local clock of the client, p_c is the payload the client sends, p_s is the payload the server returns, and $\{\cdot\}_{sk_c}$ and $\{\cdot\}_{sk_s}$ stand for signing the message by the client and server, respectively. Repeating the message id of the request allows the client to verify that p_s is indeed a response to the request p_c.

The interesting parts are steps 1. c) and 2. b). We assume that there is a constant $\mathrm{cap}_s > 0$, the so-called capacity of the server, and a constant tol_s^+ that indicates its tolerance with respect to inaccurate clocks. At all times the server keeps a time $t_s^{\min}$ and a finite list L of triples (t, r, c) of pending and handled requests. At the beginning or after a reset, $t^{\min}$ is set to $t_s + \mathrm{tol}_s^+$, where t_s is a timestamp retrieved from the local clock functionality, and L is set to the empty list.

 Step 1. c). Upon receiving a message as above, the server s rejects if $t \notin \left[t_s^{\min} + 1, t_s + \mathrm{tol}_s^+\right]$ or if $(t', r, c') \in L$ for some t' and c', and otherwise proceeds as follows: If L contains less than cap_s elements, it inserts (t, r, c) into L. Otherwise, the server deletes all tuples containing the oldest timestamp from L, until L contains less than cap_s tuples. Then it sets $t_s^{\min}$ to the timestamp contained in the last tuple deleted from L, and finally inserts (t, r, c) into L.

Step 2. b). When asked to send a payload p_s with message handle r, the server rejects if there is no triple $(t, r, c) \in L$ with $c \neq \varepsilon$. If it does not reject, it updates L by overwriting c with ε in the tuple (t, r, c) to ensure that the service cannot respond to the same message twice.

4.2 Implementation in the IITM Model

We will now describe the system of IITM's defined by

$$\mathcal{P}_{2\mathrm{AMEX}-1} = !\mathcal{P}_\mathrm{C} \mid !\mathcal{P}_\mathrm{S} \mid !\underline{\mathcal{F}_{\mathrm{Sig}}} \mid !\underline{\mathcal{P}_{\mathrm{SI}}} \mid !\underline{\mathcal{F}_{\mathrm{KS}}} \mid !\underline{\mathcal{F}_{\mathrm{LC}}} \tag{2}$$

and illustrated in Figure 4, which implements the 2AMEX-1 protocol.

In (2), $\mathcal{P}_\mathrm{C}$ is the client-side part of the protocol (defined in Figure 5), $\mathcal{P}_\mathrm{S}$ is the server-side part of the protocol (defined in Appendix B), $\mathcal{F}_{\mathrm{Sig}}$ is the signature functionality as defined in [18], $\mathcal{P}_{\mathrm{SI}}$ is an interface which allows the adversary to access the signature functionality with few restrictions, $\mathcal{F}_{\mathrm{KS}}$ is an ideal functionality of a trusted key store, and $\mathcal{F}_{\mathrm{LC}}$ models a local clock which is controlled by the adversary, i.e. not synchronized with the clocks of other parties and not even monotone.

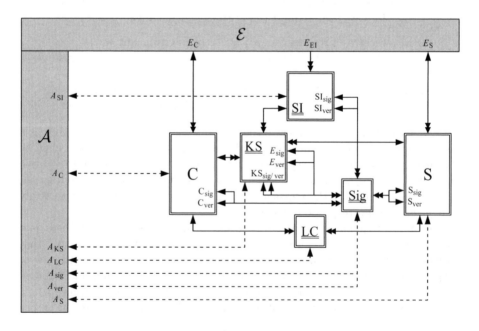

Fig. 4. Overview of 2AMEX-1 protocol implementation

4.3   Signatures and the Public Key Infrastructure

We model the digital signatures that 2AMEX-1 uses by the ideal functionality $\mathcal{F}_{\mathrm{Sig}}$ from [18], which was proved to be securely implementable using any existentially unforgeable signature scheme.

We give the adversary access to the signature scheme and allow him to sign any bit string that does not have the format of a 2AMEX-1 message. This models that our protocol does not have exclusive access to the keys used to sign the messages. For example, the same key can be used to sign a 2AMEX-1 message and parts of the payload contained in that message. This is realized by the signature interface functionality $\mathcal{P}_{\mathrm{SI}}$, which accepts requests from the adversary to (i) sign messages that do not have the format of 2AMEX-1 messages and (ii) verify arbitrary signatures. In $\mathcal{P}_{2\mathrm{AMEX}-1}$, the signature interface functionality is banged in the multi-user multi-session version, effectively meaning that the adversary has access to all keys used in the protocol.

As the signature interface needs resources from the environment to sign messages for the adversary, it has an enriching input tape E_{EI}. Its counterpart in the ideal system is a tape in the enriching input functionality EI.

To coordinate how different IITM's access a single instance of the signature functionality, we define the ideal functionality of a key store, $\mathcal{F}_{\mathrm{KS}}$, which allows clients, servers, and the signature interface functionality to retrieve trusted keys as well as the corruption status of that key. To be able to distribute the public key, $\mathcal{F}_{\mathrm{KS}}$ also initializes the instances of the signature functionality. The particular form of this functionality is due to the fact that we want to use $\mathcal{F}_{\mathrm{Sig}}$ from [18] as is. Nevertheless, one can implement $\mathcal{F}_{\mathrm{KS}}$ using standard techniques for building a public key infrastructure.

4.4   Client Implementation

The client protocol $\mathcal{P}_{\mathrm{C}}$ (see Figure 5) is a direct implementation of the ideal functionality $\mathcal{F}_{\mathrm{C}}$ with the following changes:

- The messages are transferred over the network (rather than exchanged directly between client and server). This is modeled by writing the messages on an external network tape.
- To secure the request message, the client signs it using a digital signature obtained from an instance of $\mathcal{F}_{\mathrm{Sig}}$ for this session. The server will be able to obtain the public key from the according key store and verify the signature.
- When receiving a response from the server, the signature of that message is verified by the client in the same way.
- The nonces are not generated by a centralized entity, but randomly chosen locally by each client. While this does not guarantee that the numbers are unique, the probability of a collision is negligible if the length of the nonces grows linearly with the security parameter.
- The request message is additionally secured by a timestamp. The client uses the local clock functionality $\mathcal{F}_{\mathrm{LC}}$ to obtain a timestamp.

Tapes: $C \longleftrightarrow E_C$, $C \longleftrightarrow A_C$, $C \longleftrightarrow KS$, $C \longleftrightarrow LC$, $C_{sig} \longleftrightarrow Sig$, $C_{ver} \longleftrightarrow Sig$
Initialization: $c = s = r = \varepsilon$, $n = 0$, $state = $ Init, $cor = $ false
Steps: loop

    Send a request to the server:
    if $(c', (\text{Client}, s'), \text{Init})$ received from E_C
        If $state \neq$ Init, abort. Let $c = c'$ and $s = s'$.
        Generate an η-bit nonce r randomly, where η is the security parameter.
        Send $(c, (\text{Client}, s, r), \text{Nonce}, r)$ to E_C.
        Recv $(c, (\text{Client}, s, r), \text{Request}, p_c, 1^{n'})$ from E_C, let $n = n'$.
        Send $(c, (\text{Client}, s, r), \text{GetKey})$ to KS.
        Recv $(c, (\text{Client}, s, r), \text{PublicKey}, k_c)$ from KS.
        Send $(c, (\text{Client}, s, r), \text{GetTime})$ to LC.
        Recv $(c, (\text{Client}, s, r), \text{Time}, t)$ from LC.
        Send $(c, (\text{Client}, s, r), \text{Corrupted?})$ to KS.
        Recv $(c, (\text{Client}, s, r), \text{Corrupted}, cor')$ from KS. If cor', abort.
        Let $m_c = (\text{From: } c, \text{To: } s, \text{MsgID: } r, \text{Time: } t, \text{Body: } p_c)$.
        Send $(c, (\text{Client}, s, r), \text{Sign}, m_c)$ on C_{sig}.
        Recv $(c, (\text{Client}, s, r), \text{Signature}, \sigma_c)$ on C_{sig}. Let $state = $ OK.
        Send (m_c, σ_c) to A_C.
    Receive and process a response from the server:
    if (m_s, σ_s) received from A_C with $m_s = (\text{From: } c, \text{To: } s, \text{Ref: } r, \text{Body: } p_s)$
        If $state \neq$ OK or cor or $|p_s| > n$, abort.
        Let $n = n - |p_s|$.
        Send $(s, (\text{Server}, c, r), \text{GetKey})$ to KS.
        Recv $(s, (\text{Server}, c, r), \text{PublicKey}, k_s)$ from KS.
        Send $(s, (\text{Server}, c, r), \text{Client}, \text{Init})$ on C_{ver}.
        Recv $(s, (\text{Server}, c, r), \text{Client}, \text{Init})$ on C_{ver}.
        Send $(s, (\text{Server}, c, r), \text{Client}, \text{Corrupted?})$ to KS.
        Recv $(s, (\text{Server}, c, r), \text{Client}, \text{Corrupted}, cor')$ from KS. If cor', abort.
        Send $(s, (\text{Server}, c, r), \text{Client}, \text{Verify}, m_s, \sigma_s, k_s)$ on C_{ver}.
        Recv $(s, (\text{Server}, c, r), \text{Client}, \text{Verified}, b)$ from on C_{ver}, if $b \neq 1$, stop.
        Let $state = $ Stopped and send $(c, (\text{Client}, s, r), \text{Response}, p_s)$ to E_C.
Corruption: $\text{Corr}(cor, \text{true}, state \neq \text{Init}, \varepsilon, A_C, \{E_C\}, E_C, c, (\text{Client}, s, r))$
CheckAddress: Check for c, s, and r as soon as each one has been set.

Fig. 5. The client protocol $\mathcal{P}_C$

- Before using a signature functionality to sign or verify a message, the client checks if the signature or the verification functionality is corrupted. If either one is, the client aborts.

4.5 Server Implementation

The implementation $\mathcal{P}_S$ of the server functionality (see Appendix B) is more complicated than the client. To be able to counteract replay attacks, one single IITM handles all sessions. That is, for each identity s all communication of that identity in the server role is handled by one single instance of $\mathcal{P}_S$.

Therefore, the server maintains two lists: R stores resources passed by the environment (corresponding to the fact that in the ideal system, each session of the server is started by the environment), while L (corresponding to L described in Section 4.1) is used to store information from request messages received so far by this server. During initialization, i.e., when receiving the first message, the server asks the adversary to provide values for two parameters of the 2AMEX-1 protocol, namely the capacity cap_s and the tolerance tol_s^+.

When receiving a message from the client, the server (i) tries to retrieve the client's key, (ii) obtains the current time from $\mathcal{F}_{LC}$ (and checks for monotonicity of the clock), (iii) verifies the signature, (iv) checks if a message with the same nonce has already been accepted (i. e. the nonce is in L), (v) checks if the timestamp is in order (i. e. not too old and not too new), and (vi) forwards the message to the environment if everything is in order. If some step fails, the server simply drops the message.

When the environment wants to reply to a message, the server first checks if the nonce is valid (i. e. occurs in L), else it sends an error message to the environment. This is important as the nonce may have been removed from L due to capacity reasons without notification to the environment. Then, the server initializes its instance of the signature scheme for this session, signs the message, and writes it on an external network tape.

Note that during the steps to process a request or a response, the control may be passed to the adversary by some of the ideal functionalities the server uses. Hence, the execution of the steps when processing a request or response may be interrupted by the adversary (e. g., by sending another incoming message to this server). As soon as a message is received that is not related to processing the current message, the processing of the current message is aborted by the server and cannot be resumed later.

5   Results

Our result states that our protocol securely realizes the ideal functionality $\mathcal{F}_{2AM}$. The formal statement of the theorem is as follows:

Theorem 1

$$!\mathcal{F}_C \mid !\mathcal{F}_S \mid \mathcal{F}_{NG} \mid !\underline{\mathcal{F}_{EI}} \geq^{BB} !\mathcal{P}_C \mid !\mathcal{P}_S \mid !\underline{\mathcal{P}_{SI}} \mid !\underline{\mathcal{F}_{KS}} \mid !\underline{\mathcal{F}_{Sig}} \mid !\underline{\mathcal{F}_{LC}} \qquad (3)$$

$$\geq^{BB} !\mathcal{P}_C \mid !\mathcal{P}_S \mid !\underline{\mathcal{P}_{SI}} \mid !\underline{\mathcal{F}_{KS}} \mid !\mathcal{P}_{Sig}^{JS} \mid !\underline{\mathcal{F}_{Sig}} \mid !\underline{\mathcal{F}_{LC}} \qquad (4)$$

The first of these inequalities states that the IITM realization of our protocol, when using an ideal signature functionality, realizes the system consisting of the ideal functionalities for $\mathcal{F}_{2AM}$. The main part of the proof is the construction of the simulator, which essentially simulates our concrete protocol. It keeps track of the internal state of all involved parties and "translates" problems that can occur in the real protocol (e. g., the server running out of memory and therefore being unable to respond to old messages) into attacks on the ideal functionalities (the simulator may, e. g., prevent the ideal server functionality from responding to an old message).

Due to the way in which the ideal signature functionality is used, the realization of the protocol as stated in the first inequality is unrealistic, because for each message sent a new key for the signature scheme is generated. This can be avoided by applying a joint-state theorem [12,18] allowing different sessions to use the same key. Essentially, a "wrapper" $\mathcal{P}_{\mathrm{Sig}}^{\mathrm{JS}}$ managing different sessions is used to access the signature functionalities. The second inequality in Theorem 1 (which follows directly from [18]) makes use of this wrapper, so that instead of one key per party and per session ($!\mathcal{F}_{\mathrm{Sig}}$), there is only a single key for each party ($!\underline{\underline{\mathcal{F}}}_{\mathrm{Sig}}$), as in a realistic public-key infrastructure.

Theorem 1 gives a security treatment of a complex protocol in a simulation-based security setting: Our protocol features a long-lived server role, uses time-stamps to prevent replay attacks, and accesses a public-key infrastructure for digital signatures. It is easy to see that long-livedness and timestamps are required to realize our ideal functionality with bounded memory (see [10]). It is interesting to note that while our ideal server functionality is short-lived, a realization necessarily needs to be long-lived; this is a particular property of authenticated message exchange with only two rounds.

6   Discussion

Simulation-based security clearly has the advantage that it leads to an easier statement of security than an individual, trace-based definition, and moreover, allows to treat protocols for very different tasks in a single model. The security properties obtained by such an analysis are quite strong and hold (via composition) in an arbitrary context. The IITM framework (and related frameworks) is designed to support modular protocol analysis.

However, these advantages come with a price when considering a concrete complex protocol. In [10], we presented a customized model (based on the seminal work by Bellare and Rogaway [11]) for proving security of 2AMEX-1. A comparison between that work and the current paper gives insights into the advantages and disadvantages of both approaches.

The formulation of both ideal functionalities and concrete implementations for authenticated message exchange in the current paper is rather long and unintuitive (the latter are significantly more complex than their counterparts in [10]). Both feature unnatural communication (bit strings to provide computing resources, status and activation messages exchanged sent to and received from the adversary and the environment), which are necessary due to how resources and activation are handled. Intuitively, one would like the environment to only access the "service" provided by the functionalities, but in the IITM framework, the environment additionally needs to provide resources for the involved parties that allow them to process the input.

Furthermore, the handling of corruption in the IITM framework is more complex and seems less natural than in the Bellare-Rogaway based model. Also, for the analysis of our protocol, the modular approach provided by the IITM framework does not simplify the security analysis, compared to the proof in [10]. Finally, the use of the joint-state theorem to enable realistic treatment of signatures results in a slightly different protocol from the one originally stated in [10] and from a realistic implementation.

It would be very interesting to know whether the IITM framework can be adapted to remove the above-mentioned difficulties.

References

1. Canetti, R.: Universally composable security: A new paradigm for cryptographic protocols. In: FOCS, pp. 136–145 (2001)
2. Pfitzmann, B., Waidner, M.: A model for asynchronous reactive systems and its application to secure message transmission. In: IEEE Symposium on Security and Privacy, pp. 184–201 (2001)
3. Backes, M., Pfitzmann, B., Waidner, M.: A general composition theorem for secure reactive systems. In: Naor, M. (ed.) TCC 2004. LNCS, vol. 2951, pp. 336–354. Springer, Heidelberg (2004)
4. Küsters, R.: Simulation-based security with inexhaustible interactive Turing machines. In: CSFW, pp. 309–320. IEEE Computer Society, Los Alamitos (2006)
5. Canetti, R., Krawczyk, H.: Universally composable notions of key exchange and secure channels. In: Knudsen, L.R. (ed.) EUROCRYPT 2002. LNCS, vol. 2332, pp. 337–351. Springer, Heidelberg (2002)
6. Moran, T., Naor, M.: Receipt-free universally-verifiable voting with everlasting privacy. In: Dwork, C. (ed.) CRYPTO 2006. LNCS, vol. 4117, pp. 373–392. Springer, Heidelberg (2006)
7. Backes, M., Cervesato, I., Jaggard, A.D., Scedrov, A., Tsay, J.K.: Cryptographically sound security proofs for basic and public-key Kerberos. In: Gollmann, D., Meier, J., Sabelfeld, A. (eds.) ESORICS 2006. LNCS, vol. 4189, pp. 362–383. Springer, Heidelberg (2006)
8. Backes, M., Pfitzmann, B.: On the cryptographic key secrecy of the strengthened Yahalom protocol. In: Fischer-Hübner, S., Rannenberg, K., Yngström, L., Lindskog, S. (eds.) SEC. IFIP, vol. 201, pp. 233–245. Springer, Heidelberg (2006)
9. Gajek, S., Manulis, M., Pereira, O., Sadeghi, A.R., Schwenk, J.: Universally composable security analysis of TLS. In: Baek, J., Bao, F., Chen, K., Lai, X. (eds.) ProvSec 2008. LNCS, vol. 5324, pp. 313–327. Springer, Heidelberg (2008)
10. Kürtz, K.O., Schnoor, H., Wilke, T.: Computationally secure two-round authenticated message exchange. Cryptology ePrint Archive, Report 2009/262 (2009), http://eprint.iacr.org/
11. Bellare, M., Rogaway, P.: Entity authentication and key distribution. In: Stinson, D.R. (ed.) CRYPTO 1993. LNCS, vol. 773, pp. 232–249. Springer, Heidelberg (1994)
12. Küsters, R., Tuengerthal, M.: Joint state theorems for public-key encryption and digital signature functionalities with local computation. In: CSF, pp. 270–284. IEEE Computer Society, Los Alamitos (2008)
13. Kürtz, K.O., Schnoor, H., Wilke, T.: A simulation-based treatment of authenticated message exchange. Cryptology ePrint Archive, Report 2009/368 (2009), http://eprint.iacr.org/
14. Mitra, N., Lafon, Y.: SOAP version 1.2 part 0: Primer (second edition). Technical report, W3C (2007), http://www.w3.org/TR/soap12-part0/

15. Liu, C.K., Booth, D.: Web services description language (WSDL) version 2.0 part 0: Primer. W3C recommendation, W3C (2007),
    http://www.w3.org/TR/wsdl20-primer
16. Sun Microsystems: RPC: Remote procedure call protocol specification version 2. IETF RFC 1057, Informational (1998)
17. Winer, D.: XML-RPC specification (1999),
    http://www.xmlrpc.com/spec
18. Küsters, R., Tuengerthal, M.: Joint state theorems for public-key encryption and digital signature functionalities with local computation. Cryptology ePrint Archive, Report 2008/006 (2008),
    http://eprint.iacr.org/

A   Corruption

Both in the ideal functionality $\mathcal{F}_{2AM}$ and in the implementation $\mathcal{P}_{2AMEX-1}$ we model corruption by using the corruption macro from [12] in a slightly modified variant, in which we add parameters for an addressing mechanism. Details can be found in [13].

Using the corruption macro we allow the adversary to corrupt our clients and servers, while the environment can check the corruption status of each instance and provide resources for corrupted machines. Once corrupted, clients and servers abort their normal execution and only forward messages from and to the adversary as defined in the macro.

While the adversary can corrupt single client instances, the situation on the server side is different: If the adversary sends a corruption request to one instance of $\mathcal{F}_S$ running under identity s, this instance will accept all messages which are directed to any instance running under identity s. This reflects that in the implementation $\mathcal{P}_{2AMEX-1}$ only one (long-lived) instance of $\mathcal{P}_S$ is running per identity.

Note that the signature and verification functionality $\mathcal{F}_{Sig}$ used in $\mathcal{P}_{2AMEX-1}$ also allows corruption. But if the adversary would corrupt, e. g., a verification instance, it would have no advantage against our protocol as long as it does not also corrupt the server or client using that particular instance of the verifier. In addition, in $\mathcal{P}_{2AMEX-1}$ the environment would have to pass resources to that verification instance, while in $\mathcal{F}_{2AM}$ no signature scheme is available to receive the resources—but adding a mechanism to $\mathcal{F}_{2AM}$ which receives the resources and passes them on to the simulator would result in a rather unnatural ideal functionality.

Therefore, even though we technically allow the adversary to corrupt instances of the signature scheme (or its verifiers) in $\mathcal{P}_{2AMEX-1}$, we make it rather useless: Before $\mathcal{P}_C$ and $\mathcal{P}_S$ use any signature or verification functionality, they check the functionalities' corruption status and abort if it is corrupted. Note that the adversary may still get complete control over the input and output of a client or server by simply corrupting that client or server instance.

B   The Server Protocol $\mathcal{P}_S$

Tapes: $S \longleftrightarrow E_S$, $S \longleftarrow\cdots\rightarrow A_S$, $S \longleftrightarrow\!\!\!\twoheadrightarrow KS$, $S \longleftrightarrow\!\!\!\twoheadrightarrow LC$, $S_{sig} \longleftrightarrow\!\!\!\twoheadrightarrow Sig$, $S_{ver} \longleftrightarrow Sig$

Initialization: $s = \text{cap}_s = \text{tol}_s^+ = m_c = \sigma_c = k_c = \varepsilon$, $R = L = [\,]$, $t_s = t^{\min} = 0$, $state = \mathsf{Init}$, $cor = \mathsf{false}$

Steps: loop

Initialize a new buffer:
if $(s', (\mathsf{Server}), \mathsf{Init}, 1^n)$ received from E_S
>If $state = \mathsf{Init}$,
>>Send $(s', (\mathsf{Server}), \mathsf{GetParameters})$ to A_S.
>>Recv $(s', (\mathsf{Server}), \mathsf{Parameters}, \text{cap}, \text{tol}^+)$ from A_S.
>>Let $s = s'$. If $\text{cap} \leq 0$ or $\text{tol}^+ \leq 0$, abort.
>>Send $(s, (\mathsf{Server}, c, r), \mathsf{GetTime})$ to LC.
>>Recv $(s, (\mathsf{Server}, c, r), \mathsf{Time}, t)$ from LC.
>>Let $state = \mathsf{OK}$, $\text{cap}_s = \text{cap}$, $\text{tol}_s^+ = \text{tol}^+$, $t_s = t$, $t^{\min} = t_s + \text{tol}_s^+$.
>>Append n to R.

Receive and process a request: Request the client's key:
if (m, σ) received from A_S with $m = (\mathsf{From}\colon c, \mathsf{To}\colon s, \mathsf{MsgID}\colon r, \mathsf{Time}\colon t, \mathsf{Body}\colon p_c)$
>If $state = \mathsf{Init}$ or cor, abort.
>Let n be the first item of R. If $|p_c| > n$, abort. Remove n from R.
>Let $state = \mathsf{WaitingForKey}_c$, $m_c = m$, and $\sigma_c = \sigma$.
>Send $(c, (\mathsf{Client}, s, r), \mathsf{GetKey})$ to KS.

Receive and process a request: Receive the key, request time:
if $(c, (\mathsf{Client}, s, r), \mathsf{PublicKey}, k)$ received from KS
>If $state \neq \mathsf{WaitingForKey}_c$ or cor, abort. Let $state = \mathsf{WaitingForTime}$ and $k_c = k$.
>Send $(s, (\mathsf{Server}, c, r), \mathsf{GetTime})$ to LC.

Receive and process a request: Receive time, initialize the verifier:
if $(s, (\mathsf{Server}, c, r), \mathsf{Time}, t)$ received from LC
>If $state \neq \mathsf{WaitingForTime}$ or cor, abort.
>If $t \geq t_s$, let $t_s = t$. Let $state = \mathsf{WaitingForVerifier}$.
>Send $(c, (\mathsf{Client}, s, r), \mathsf{Server}, \mathsf{Init})$ on S_{ver}.

Receive and process a request: Execute 2AMEX-1 protocol steps, relay request:
if $(c, (\mathsf{Client}, s, r), \mathsf{Server}, \mathsf{Init})$ received on S_{ver}
>If $state \neq \mathsf{WaitingForVerifier}$ or cor, abort. Let $state = \mathsf{OK}$.
>Send $(c, (\mathsf{Client}, s, r), \mathsf{Server}, \mathsf{Corrupted?})$ to KS.
>Recv $(c, (\mathsf{Client}, s, r), \mathsf{Server}, \mathsf{Corrupted}, cor')$ from KS. If cor', abort.
>Send $(c, (\mathsf{Client}, s, r), \mathsf{Server}, \mathsf{Verify}, m_c, \sigma_c, k_c)$ on S_{ver}.
>Recv $(c, (\mathsf{Client}, s, r), \mathsf{Server}, \mathsf{Verified}, b)$ on S_{ver}.
>If $b \neq 1$, $t \leq t^{\min}$ or $t > t_s + \text{tol}_s^+$, or $(t', r, c') \in L$ for some t', c', abort.
>While $|L| \geq \text{cap}_s$:
>>Let $t^{\min} = \min\{t' \mid (t', r', c') \in L\}$ and $L = \{(t', r', c') \in L \mid t' > t^{\min}\}$.
>Insert (t, r, c) into L and send $(s, (\mathsf{Server}, c, r), \mathsf{Request}, p_c)$ to E_S.

Receive and process a response: Receive response payload, request key:
if $(s, (\mathsf{Server}, c, r), \mathsf{Response}, p_s)$ received from E_S
>If $state = \mathsf{Init}$ or cor, abort.
>If $(t', r, c) \notin L$ for any t':
>>Let $state = \mathsf{OK}$, send $(s, (\mathsf{Server}, c, r), \mathsf{Response}, \mathsf{Error})$ to E_S, and abort.
>Let $state = \mathsf{WaitingForKey}_s$ and send $(s, (\mathsf{Server}, c, r), \mathsf{GetKey})$ to KS.

Receive and process a response: Construct, sign, and send response message:
if $(s, (\mathsf{Server}, c, r), \mathsf{PublicKey}, k)$ received from KS
>If $state \neq \mathsf{WaitingForKey}_s$ or cor, abort. Let $state = \mathsf{OK}$.
>Send $(s, (\mathsf{Server}, c, r), \mathsf{Corrupted?})$ to KS.
>Recv $(s, (\mathsf{Server}, c, r), \mathsf{Corrupted}, cor')$ from KS. If cor', abort.
>Let $m_s = (\mathsf{From}\colon c, \mathsf{To}\colon s, \mathsf{Ref}\colon r, \mathsf{Body}\colon p_s)$.
>Send $(s, (\mathsf{Server}, c, r), \mathsf{Sign}, m_s)$ on S_{sig}.
>Recv $(s, (\mathsf{Server}, c, r), \mathsf{Signature}, \sigma_s)$ on S_{sig}.
>Update (t, r, c) to $(t, r, *)$ in L and send (m_s, σ_s) to A_S.

Reset the server:
if (s, Reset) received from A_S
>If $state = \mathsf{Init}$ or cor, abort.
>Send $(s, \mathsf{Server}, \mathsf{GetTime})$ to LC.
>Recv $(s, \mathsf{Server}, \mathsf{Time}, t)$ from LC.
>If $t \geq t_s$, let $t_s = t$.
>Let $t^{\min} = t_s + \text{tol}_s^+$, $R = L = [\,]$, and $state = \mathsf{OK}$.

Corruption: $\mathrm{Corr}(cor, \mathsf{true}, state \neq \mathsf{Init}, \varepsilon, A_S, \{E_S\}, E_S, s)$

CheckAddress: Check for s as soon as it has been set.

Trusted Deployment of Virtual Execution Environment in Grid Systems[*]

Deqing Zou, Jinjiu Long, and Hai Jin

Services Computing Technology and System Lab
Cluster and Grid Computing Lab
School of Computer Science and Technology
Huazhong University of Science and Technology, Wuhan, 430074, China
hjin@hust.edu.cn

Abstract. Grids are constructed to integrate different kinds of resources and services in distributed computing environments. Grid users may transfer their applications and data to remote grid nodes which are easy to be compromised. In this paper, we utilize trusted computing and virtualization technologies to construct trusted execution environments in grid systems. Grid nodes are equipped with *Trusted Platform Module* (TPM) and secure *Virtual Machine Monitor* (VMM) in order to provide a *Trusted Computing Base* (TCB) for job execution environment. A secure *Virtual Machine* (VM) for protecting job execution can be deployed into a grid node remotely. During the VM deployment, current configuration information in a grid node is reported to a remote party for remote attestation. Furthermore, encryption technologies are used to protect grid jobs during their whole lifecycle. Experiments and analysis show our method is efficient and secure.

Keywords: Grid Computing, Virtual Machine, Trusted Computing, Trusted Execution Environment.

1 Introduction

Currently grid security technologies mainly concern secure communication, authentication and authorization, and neglect the security of job execution environments in grid nodes. It is a great challenge to guarantee the execution environment trustworthy, and grid jobs are not intruded during their whole lifecycle. A compromised execution environment makes the embedded security mechanisms invalid, and endangers the confidentiality, integrity or availability of user applications and data. In addition, grid systems need to attest to grid users that the execution environment is trustworthy in order to reduce their worries about the security risks.

VM technology is introduced [1] to support running multiple operating systems simultaneously on a single physical hardware platform. Isolation is one of the most important characteristics for VM technology. The VMM is a privileged software layer

---

[*] The work is supported by National 973 Basic Research Program of China under grant No.2007CB310900.

A. Datta (Ed.): ASIAN 2009, LNCS 5913, pp. 124–136, 2009.

running between hardware resources and operating systems, which manages all VMs running on it and keeps them isolated from each other. As the VMM is a thin software layer and its size is relatively small, it can be easily security-enhanced and is commonly regarded as a trust computing base to provide effective security protection for applications. Daoli [2] system uses a secure VMM to interpose privileged operations, isolate sensitive information and seal persistent data, thus protects a trusted process from being compromised by a compromised OS kernel and other processes. The work in this paper is conducted based on the Daoli system.

Trusted Computing (TC) technology [3] aims to improve the security of computer platforms by hardware-based security mechanism, and TPM is a hardware security chip embedded on the motherboard providing encryption functions. TPM measures the state of the platform, and records it in PCRs (*Platform Configuration Register*) located in TPM during the boot process. The measurement information can be signed by the private key of an AIK (*Attestation Identity Key*) and passed to the challenger to prove the trustworthiness of the platform, which is called remote attestation. By utilizing remote attestation mechanism, a remote challenger who might be a grid broker or a grid user can verify whether a remote execution environment is trustworthy or not.

Our solution proposed in this paper aims to implement a trusted grid platform to provide functions of deploying a secure execution environment to a grid node based on trusted computing and virtualization technologies. Grid broker needs to find suitable grid nodes for users, and such nodes are equipped with the secure VMM and TPM, and can meet the resource and security requirement of virtual machine instance deployment and job execution. Isolation mechanism provided by the VMM guarantees that virtual machine instances running on it would not affect each other. In this paper, we assume grid broker is secure and it can be protected by traditional security technologies. We focus on the security of job execution environment in grid nodes.

As the secure VMM plays a very important role for protecting user jobs from being compromised, it is necessary to leverage TC technology to provide integrity protection for the VMM. In addition, remote attestation is used to verify whether the remote VMM and the VM boot process are trustworthy as expected. A VM image, used for job execution environment, is measured and verified for integrity protection before its deployment. Our solution also allows clients to check and verify the trustworthiness of remote execution environment through grid portal to make sure that their applications and data are not intruded by malicious node.

The rest of this paper is organized as follows: we discuss the related work in section 2. In section 3, we introduce the architecture of VM based trusted execution environment in grid systems. In section 4, we discuss trusted deployment of virtual execution environment, remote attestation protocol and job security management in detail, and then analyze the performance and security of our proposed solution in section 5 and section 6. Finally, the conclusions and future work are drawn in section 7.

2   Related Work

The Virtual Workspace project [4] is developed to provide metadata defined abstraction of an execution environment that can be made available dynamically to authorized clients by using well-defined protocols. The workspace metadata file contains information needed for the deployment of a workspace. The workspace service allows remote authorized clients to deploy, pause, restart, shutdown, and inspect workspaces through a WSRF (*Web Service Resource Framework*) based protocol. Virtual workspace is implemented based on Globus Toolkit 4 [5], and one of its main features, remote deployment and lifecycle management of virtual machines, seems to be similar to the approach we propose in this paper. The major difference is that virtual workspaces focuses on dynamically constructing execution environments with distributed resources, while our approach mainly concerns how to construct trusted execution environments, and provide strong security functions to protect user applications and data. Besides, our implementation is based on another grid middleware named CGSP [6] (ChinaGrid [7] Support Platform).

Other researches about trusted execution environment also adopt trusted computing or virtualization technologies. IBM's vTPM [8] project proposes the design and implementation of virtual trusted platform module for each virtual machine, and such software TPM has been integrated into a Xen [9] hypervisor environment to make TPM functions available to virtual machines. Terra [10] is a flexible architecture for trusted computing, which uses a *trusted virtual machine monitor* (TVMM) to partition a tamper-resistant hardware platform into multiple isolated virtual machines, providing multiple boxes on a single, general purpose platform. Trusted Grub [11] extends the widely used grub with security offered by TPM to implement the trusted boot. The Integrity Measurement Architecture [12] is a security enhancement of Linux by a TPM-based Linux Security Module which aims to provide trust attestation of the software stack running on the Linux system.

There are some proposals on trusted grids that use TC technologies for grid computing. Daonity [13] is a project that aims to strengthen the grid security infrastructure by integrating TC technologies into the Globus toolkit. Cooper et al. [14] proposed trusted grid platform architecture to allow users and systems to dynamically negotiate platform trust within the grid.

The above methods are not good enough in constructing a trusted grid platform because there is no remote attestation to job execution environment and the security of grid jobs during their whole lifecycle can not be guaranteed.

3   Trusted Grid Architecture

The proposed trusted grid architecture is presented in Fig.1. The middle layer is mainly responsible for resource management based on CGSP to support the construction of grid computing environment across large numbers of Chinese universities. The WSRF-based, VM scheduling services including the VM factory service and the VM control service are hosted by the CGSP container. An authorized grid user configures remote execution environment via such services, which allows a grid client to deploy a VM-based execution environment, named VM instance, on a trusted grid node according to the deployment request specifying resource allocation, environment definition and security policy for the client. VM control operations such as VM pause, shutdown and restart can be carried out by the VM control service, and applications submitted by the client will be scheduled to VM instances by the job manager. If a grid node has no capacity to run a job continually, the corresponding VM instance will be migrated securely to another trusted node, which is transparent to the end user.

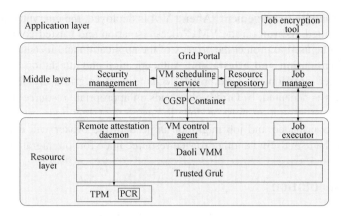

Fig. 1. Trusted grid architecture

On the resource layer, grid nodes, willing to lease computing and storage resources, register their resource information into the resource repository in grid broker, located in the middle layer. Such nodes are equipped with the secure VMM and Trusted Grub. The process isolation technology provided by the Daoli VMM is used to protect the privacy of user applications and data. Trusted Grub integrates TC technology to provide integrity protection for the secure VMM. A VM control agent installed in domain0 of a grid node has the privileged access of performing job management including the deployment and control of virtual machine instances. A remote attestation daemon runs as a process in domain 0, enabling remote attestation by signing the hash values of the Daoli VMM and VMs, and reporting them to the security management service in grid broker for trusted resource scheduling. The job executor utilizes GRS (*General Running Service*) [15] which is a program execution engine for CGSP and provides execution management and task scheduling for grid jobs on virtual machines.

The application layer of our architecture is used to conduct the preparation of grid requests, including request files construction and encrypted applications construction. The request file specifies resource allocation and job execution environment, such as deployment time, vCPU numbers, memory, CPU architecture, operating system. An application is developed by a grid user and performs specific functions. Before submitted, the application should be encrypted by encryption tools.

Following are the main features of our trusted virtual execution environment in CGSP:

(1) Resource registration and monitoring: Anyone who wants to be a resource provider should register its computing and storage resources to a resource repository through grid portal, and grid broker monitors current resource status of all grid nodes registered to the repository.

(2) Remote deployment and control of virtual machines: The VM scheduling services, including VM Factory service and VM control service, are WSRF-based services in the CGSP Container. These services provide client interfaces to manage virtual machines, such as VM deploy, pause, restart and shutdown.

(3) Job security management: After a VM is deployed, the encrypted application will be submitted and run on the VM. Process isolation and trusted computing technologies will be used to protect the privacy of the application and its data.

(4) Authentication and attestation: Authentication and attestation happen in the following three situations: a) Grid broker needs to verify a grid user's identity before a user request is accepted; b) Grid broker finds an appropriate resource node to run a user's job. Trust attestation must be done to ensure the target node trustworthy; c) If one node is overloaded and job migration is needed, the broker will exploit the attestation mechanism to find another trusted resource node for job migration.

4 Implementation

As we discussed in section 3, we leverage Daoli VMM to protect user applications from being compromised by malwares in VMs. We use Trusted Grub to protect the integrity of the VMM.

In this section, we introduce how to deploy a trusted execution environment on the grid resource nodes equipped with Daoli VMM, how to use TC technology to provide remote attestation of the execution environment, and how to implement job security management.

4.1 Trusted Deployment of Virtual Execution Environment

In order to implement trusted deployment of job execution environment in grid systems, we adopt several technologies including grid computing, trusted computing and virtualization. WSRF-based services, including VM factory service and VM control service, are implemented based on CGSP. Such services are designed and implemented with a feasible design pattern, called factory and instance pattern. Whenever a client wants to create a new virtual machine instance, it will contact the factory service, which first selects a suitable grid node which can meet the resource requirement of the client, conducts remote attestation to ensure that the target node is trustworthy, and then creates and initializes a new virtual machine. The VM control service provides remote control operations on the virtual machine such as VM start, pause, shutdown, restart, destroy and migration.

There are five stages dealing with trusted deployment of virtual execution environment: (1) Resource scheduling. The factory service accepts deployment requests from authorized grid users, and finds suitable resource nodes, registered in the resource repository, which can meet the requirement of users. (2) VMM remote attestation. Remote attestation on the VMM is conducted to confirm that the corresponding node meets the security requirement of users. (3) VM image integrity measurement and verification. Virtual machine image is measured and verified for integrity protection. (4) VM initialization and remote launch. A new virtual machine instance is initialized and remotely started. (5) VM remote attestation. Remote attestation on the new VM is conducted to verify whether the VM boot process is trustworthy as expected.

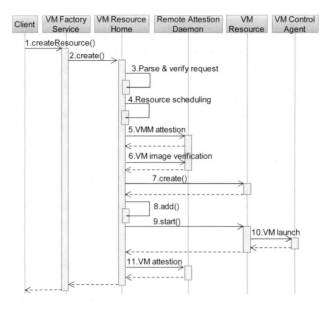

Fig. 2. Trusted deployment of virtual execution environment

These five stages consist of one or several steps. The detail is depicted in Fig.2.

(1) Resource scheduling

Step 1: With the URI of the factory service, such as http://www.daoliproject.org/wsrf/services/VirtualMachineFactoryService, the client invokes operation *createResource* to send a deployment request. The function is defined as *createResource(CreateResource request)*.

The request parameter in the function specifies the conditions of resource allocation conditions and job execution environment including domain name, deployment time, vCPU numbers, memory, CPU architecture, and operating system. The security information such as the expected VMM hash value and VM image hash value are also included. This function will finally return an endpoint reference structure that consists of the URI of the instance service and the key of the newly created virtual machine resource.

Step 2: Class *ResourceContext* is used to invoke operation *getResourceContext* to locate the VM resource home which is responsible for managing all the virtual machine resources, and require the resource home to create a new resource.

Step 3: The deployment request is parsed and verified during this step, for example, the request for configuring an execution environment with the requirement of too long lifecycle or too large memory will be denied.

Step 4: After request verification, the VM resource home tries to find suitable nodes whose resources meet the user's deployment request. Resource reservation focuses on CPU, available memory, network configuration and VM image.

(2) VMM remote attestation

Step 5: The VMM in a grid node is attested remotely on the user's behalf to make sure it is un-tampered and trustworthy. The expected VMM hash value is either from security policy made by the security manager or directly from the user's deployment request. The detailed process of remote attestation will be discussed in subsection 4.2.

(3) VM image integrity measurement and verification

Step 6: During this procedure, the virtual machine image in the target node is measured and verified for integrity protection. A digest is updated with the image's hash, signed by the private key of the platform in the node, and sent to grid broker. The encrypted digest will be decrypted by the platform's public key and compared to the expected measurement value to determine whether the VM image has been tampered or not.

(4) VM initialization and remote launch

Step 7: The resource home creates a new virtual machine resource instance and specifies resource properties, described by WSRF resource properties including domain name, current status, time-to-live, vCPU numbers, memory, network configuration. Such property information is stored in the VM resource, which is also responsible for interacting with the VM control agent in grid nodes.

Step 8: The resource home adds the new virtual machine resource instance to its internal list of resources which allow the client to access virtual machine resources according to its endpoint reference.

Step 9: Operation start is invoked to send a virtual machine launch request from the VM resource home to the VM resource.

Step 10: The VM resource communicates with the VM control agent in the target node via SSH to launch a new virtual machine which satisfies user requirements. The virtual machine will be bound with a vTPM instance which makes TPM functions available to the virtual machine. As Linux Integrity Measurement Architecture is used, the Linux kernel image and initial RAM disk are measured when loaded and the measurement will be record in PCR16 of the vTPM instance.

(5) VM remote attestation

Step 11: The VM is verified remotely to determine the integrity of the VM execution environment, which is similar to VMM remote attestation.

4.2   Remote Attestation of Execution Environment

Remote attestation of execution environment focuses on how to verify the trustworthiness of the VMM based on which the privacy of user applications and data are protected. TPM stores the hash values of configuration information in PCRs during the process of system boot. As Trusted Grub is installed, during the process of measurement, the VMM is measured and the *Stored Measurement Log* (SML) which records the measurement series is updated. The measurement result can be signed with the private key of an AIK, alias of the unique *Endorsement Key* (EK), and reported to a remote challenger in order to provide the evidence that the VMM has not been compromised. The remote attestation protocol is described in detail as follows, as depicted in Fig.3.

Step 1: The VMM is measured by Trusted Grub during the trusted boot process, the measurement information is recorded in PCR15 of TPM, and the Stored Measurement Log is updated.

Step 2: The security management service in grid broker as a challenger creates a 160 bit random nonce, initializes an attestation request for inspecting the PCR value

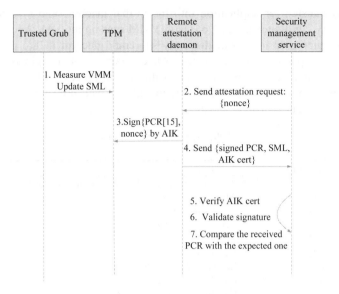

Fig. 3. Remote attestation protocol

of the VMM, and sends a piece of challenge message to the remote attestation daemon located in resource nodes.

Step 3: The remote attestation daemon loads an AIK protected by the *storage root key* (SRK), then invokes *TPM_Quote* operation to sign the PCR value of the VMM and nonce by the private key of an AIK, and gets the signed PCR value as follows:

$$Q_{TPM} = \text{Sign}_{AIK}\text{SHA1}(\text{PCR15} \parallel \text{nonce}) \tag{1}$$

The $\parallel$ operation represents a concatenation of PCR15 and nonce. SHA1 represents a kind of *Secure Hash Algorithm* that produces a 160 bit message digest for a given data stream. We get by signing the message digest with the private key of an AIK.

Step 4: The signed PCR value, along with the relevant SML entries and the AIK credential, are forwarded to the challenger.

Step 5: The credential of the AIK is verified with the relevant CA credential, as the AIK credential is signed by a privacy CA, just like grid CA.

Step 6: The challenger receives the corresponding PCR value from the SML, calculates the digest of the concatenation of the PCR value and nonce, and verifies the signed PCR by the public key of the AIK, compares it to the digest to determine whether the signature signed by the AIK is valid or not.

Step 7: The received PCR value is compared to the expected one to determine the trustworthiness of the VMM.

4.3 Job Security Management

After a grid user, assume Alice, has her trusted virtual machine deployed, she can submit her encrypted job to the virtual machine. The job management service is invoked to transfer her application into the virtual machine and a secure process using memory curtain technology of Daoli VMM runs on the VM. Alice will finally receive the encrypted job result that only she could decrypt it into plain context. Any malicious process can not access Alice's data when the job is transferred, stored or executed. There are three stages during the process of job security management. We define the related symbols in Table 1, and use them to describe the process of job security management.

Table 1. Symbol definitions

Symbol	Definition
key	Alice's symmetric AES key, as job's session key
job	Alice's grid job
result	Alice's job result
broker_pk	Grid broker's public key
broker_sk	Grid broker's private key
xen_pk	Resource node's public key
xen_sk	Resource node's private key
AES_Enc_X(Y)	Use AES algorithm to encrypt *Y* with *X*
AES_Dec_X(Y)	Use AES algorithm to decrypt *Y* with *X*
RSA_Enc_X(Y)	Use RSA algorithm to encrypt *Y* with *X*
RSA_Dec_X(Y)	Use RSA algorithm to decrypt *Y* with *X*
X ‖ Y	Concatenation of *X* and *Y*

(1) Job encryption and submission

Step 1: Alice sends an encrypted job to grid broker, where *subJob=encJob‖encKey, encJob=AES_Enc_key(job), encKey=RSA_Enc_broker_pk(key)*.

It denotes that Alice submits an encrypted job to grid broker. Before submitted, Alice's application must be encrypted with an AES session key from Alice. This key is encrypted with grid broker's public key and the encrypted AES key is appended to the end of the encrypted executable binary job.

Step 2: Grid broker sends a re-encrypted job to the resource node, where *reEncJob = encJob ‖ reEncKey, where reEncKey = RSA_Enc_xen_pk(RSA_Dec_broker_sk(encKey))*.

It denotes that grid broker re-encrypts Alice's AES key and deploys the re-encrypted job to the resource node. Grid broker uses the RSA algorithm to decrypt the encrypted AES key with its private key, and then the AES key is re-encrypted with Xen platform's public key fetched from the resource node after remote attestation. The re-encrypted AES key is appended to the end of the encrypted executable binary job again.

(2) Job trusted execution and result encryption

The job runs as a trusted process protected by Daoli VMM. The secure VMM gets the job's session key by decrypting the re-encrypted AES key with its private key located in the VMM. With the session key, the encrypted job can be decrypted and executed in the memory space where other processes cannot access. After the job is finished, with I/O sealing mechanism, the secure VMM encrypts the job result with the session key before writing it to the disk.

(3) Job result returns and decryption

Alice gets the encrypted job result after the job is finished, decrypts it with her AES key and gets the plain job result.

5 Experiments and Analysis

Our grid experiment environment consists of 5 machines connected through 100 Mbps campus LAN. The CGSP node is a Pentium 4 machine with 2.53GHz, 512MB RAM and Ubuntu7.10 installed. Grid users login grid portal through an AMD 1.6GHz PC with 1GB RAM and Ubuntu7.10 installed. There are also 3 worker nodes running Xen platform: two of them are equipped with TPM 1.2, Daoli VMM (Xen 3.02) and Trusted Grub, 1.6GHz, 1GB RAM and Fedora 8 installed; the other has almost the same configuration as the above two, which is equipped with normal Xen 3.02, not Daoli VMM. There is one Xen-based VM image involved in our experiment, with Fedora 8 OS and 750MB in size.

Although our primary concern is the security of trusted deployment of virtual machine in grid systems, which we will discuss in section 6. Due to the attestation and cryptographic technologies being used, the deployment performance should be considered. In order to show that the overhead is acceptable, we study two virtual machine deployment methods.

The first one is the traditional method that grid broker finds a suitable resource node through resource scheduling to launch a remote virtual machine. The deployment time is mainly spent on resource scheduling and launching a remote VM.

The second one is the trusted method we proposed. Except resource scheduling and VM launch, the time spent by VMM and VM remote attestation, measurement and verification of VM image should be calculated.

We conduct the experiments for the above two methods 30 times respectively. The overhead under traditional deployment is depicted in Fig.4, while the overhead under trusted deployment is depicted in Fig.5.

For each experiment in Fig.4, the overhead can be divided into two parts. The lower part shows the time that grid broker needs to find a suitable resource node through resource scheduling, and the mean time is about 2.46 seconds. The upper part shows the time to launch a remote virtual machine, about 11.88 seconds. The mean time cost under traditional deployment is about 14.34 seconds.

For each experiment in Fig.5, the overhead can be divided into five parts. From the bottom to the top, the first part shows the time for resource scheduling, and the mean time is about 2.48 seconds; the second part shows the time for VMM remote attestation, about 2.84 seconds. The third part shows the time for integrity measurement and verification of a virtual machine image, about 14.03 seconds. The fourth part shows the time for remote launch of virtual machine, about 12.29 seconds. The fifth part shows the time for VM remote attestation, about 2.06 seconds. The mean time for trusted deployment is about 33.70 seconds.

By comparison between these two deployment methods, the extra time for trusted deployment is about 19.36 seconds, of which most of the time (about 14 seconds) is spent on the measurement and verification of virtual machine image, which depends on the size of the image file and the computing capability of resource nodes. It is acceptable because it takes only about extra 19.36 seconds to gain a secure execution environment, especially for some security sensitive computing tasks. For some computing tasks running as long as several hours after the execution environment is deployed, the time cost is negligible.

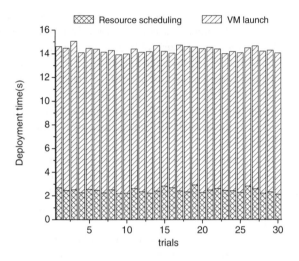

Fig. 4. Performance overhead under traditional deployment

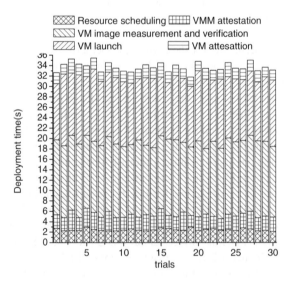

Fig. 5. Performance overhead under trusted deployment

6 Security Analysis

In this section, we will analyze the security of our proposal. Our solution aims to construct a trusted grid architecture based on trusted computing and virtualization technologies. To prove that our integration perfectly solves the security problem we described in section 1, we will review and discuss several security mechanisms we achieved, including isolation, integrity, authentication, and confidentiality protection.

(1) Isolation: Strong isolation between grid jobs is achieved by deploying them in different protected VM instances which are trusted execution environments for users in grid systems. Even in the same virtual machine, grid applications are curtained by Daoli VMM by which it is isolated from other processes.

(2) Integrity protection: Integrity protection for VMM and VM is provided. Trusted Grub provides integrity measurement and protection for the VMM during the trusted boot process, and the virtual machine image is measured and verified for integrity protection before its deployment.

(3) Authentication: Our approach enhances current *Grid Security Infrastructure* (GSI) by using TC technology, not only authenticating grid certificates submitted by users, but also verifying remote platforms to determine the trustworthiness of the execution environment.

(4) Confidentiality protection: Job session keys protected by asymmetrical keys can protect the confidentiality of user applications and data when they are transferred and stored. Job execution is protected by the secure VMM and malicious processes cannot access user data.

7 Conclusions and Future Work

A compromised execution environment in grid systems may endanger the confidentiality and integrity of user applications and data. Grid users always concern whether their execution environments are secure enough to run their jobs. To solve this problem, we propose a trusted grid platform based on trusted computing and virtualization technologies, which can deploy a VM based trusted execution environment on TPM and secure VMM enabled resource nodes, and provide grid users with remote attestation to nodes for trust establishment. The experimental results and security analysis show that our solution is efficient and secure. Our future work will focus on integrating our architecture into some grid application scenarios to meet the requirement of security sensitive applications.

References

1. Popek, G.J., Goldberg, R.P.: Formal Requirements for Virtualizable Third Generation Architectures. Communications of the ACM 17(7), 412–421 (1974)
2. Daoli project, http://www.daoliproject.org
3. Trusted Computing Group, TCG Specification Architecture Overview Version 1.2, http://www.trustedcomputinggroup.org

4. Keahey, K., Foster, I., Freeman, T., Zhang, X.: Virtual Workspaces: Achieving Quality of Service and Quality of Life in the Grid. Scientific Programming Journal, Special Issue: Dynamic Grids and Worldwide Computing 13(4), 265–276 (2005)
5. Foster, I.: Globus Toolkit Version 4: Software for Service-Oriented Systems. In: Jin, H., Reed, D., Jiang, W. (eds.) NPC 2005. LNCS, vol. 3779, pp. 2–13. Springer, Heidelberg (2005)
6. Wu, Y., Wu, S., Yu, H., Hu, C.: CGSP: An Extensible and Reconfigurable Grid Framework. In: Cao, J., Nejdl, W., Xu, M. (eds.) APPT 2005. LNCS, vol. 3756, pp. 292–300. Springer, Heidelberg (2005)
7. Jin, H.: ChinaGrid: Making Grid Computing a Reality. In: Chen, Z., Chen, H., Miao, Q., Fu, Y., Fox, E., Lim, E.-p. (eds.) ICADL 2004. LNCS, vol. 3334, pp. 13–24. Springer, Heidelberg (2004)
8. Berger, S., Caceres, R., Goldman, K.A., Perez, R., Sailer, R., van Doorn, L.: vTPM: Virtualizing the Trusted Platform Module. In: Proceedings of 15th Conference on USENIX Security Symposium, Vancouver, B. C, Canada, pp. 305–320 (2006)
9. Dragovic, B., Fraser, K., Hand, S., Harris, T., Ho, A., Pratt, I., Warfield, A., Barham, P., Neugebauer, R.: Xen and the Art of Virtualization. In: Proceedings of ACM Symposium on Operating Systems Principles, pp. 164–177 (2003)
10. Garfinkel, T., Pfaff, B., Chow, J., Rosenblum, M., Boneh, D.: Terra: a virtual machine-based platform for trusted computing. In: Proceedings of 19th ACM Symposium on Operating Systems Principles 2003 (SOSP 2003), Bolton Landing, NY, USA, pp. 193–206 (2003)
11. Trusted Grub, Applied Data Security at University of Bochum, http://www.prosec.rub.de/trustedgrub.html
12. Sailer, R., Zhang, X., Jaeger, T., van Doorn, L.: Design and implementation of a TCG-based integrity measurement architecture. In: Proceedings of USENIX Security Symposium, pp. 223–238 (2004)
13. Mao, W., Yan, F., Chen, C.: Daonity: grid security with behaviour conformity from trusted computing. In: Proceedings of 1st ACM Workshop on Scalable Trusted Computing, pp. 43–46 (2006)
14. Cooper, A., Martin, A.: Towards a secure, tamper-proof grid platform. In: Proceedings of 6th IEEE International Symposium on Cluster Computing and the Grid, Singapore, pp. 373–380 (2006)
15. Liu, L., Wu, Y., Yang, G., Ma, R., He, F.: General Running Service: An Execution Framework for Executing Legacy Program on Grid. In: Proceedings of 5th International Conference on Grid and Cooperative Computing, pp. 522–529 (2006)

A Dolev-Yao Model for Zero Knowledge*

Anguraj Baskar[1],[**], R. Ramanujam[2], and S.P. Suresh[1]

[1] Chennai Mathematical Institute, Chennai
{abaskar,spsuresh}@cmi.ac.in
[2] Institute of Mathematical Sciences, Chennai
jam@imsc.res.in

Abstract. We propose an extension of the standard Dolev-Yao model of cryptographic protocols to facilitate symbolic reasoning about zero-knowledge proofs. This is accomplished by communicating typed terms, and providing a proof amounts to certifying that a term is of a particular type. We present a proof system for term derivability, which is employed to yield a decision procedure for checking whether a given protocol meets its zero knowledge specification.

1 Introduction

Zero-knowledge proofs were introduced by [GMR89] and have since been extensively applied in a variety of security contexts including electronic voting protocols, contract signing protocols and designated verifier proofs.

On the other hand, security protocols are known to be difficult to design and hard to analyze, principally due to the concurrent execution of such protocols, leading to information transfer across many interleaved runs. Discovery of design flaws in early key distribution and authentication protocols ([Low96]) led to the advent of formal methods in verification of cryptographic protocols ([MS01], [RT03]). A key abstraction in such employment of formal methods is that of the *Dolev-Yao* model, in which cryptographic operations are idealized and proofs can be carried out without the complications relating to implementation of cryptographic primitives, random numbers and error probabilities. Symbolic abstraction has not only proved to be useful, recent research has also proved symbolic models sound with respect to underlying computational models (see, for instance, [CKKW06]) thus achieving a satisfactory two-level layering of security proofs.

The standard Dolev-Yao model offers a term algebra with operators for encryption and pairing. Many extensions exist ([CDL06], [Bau05]), and it is natural to consider Dolev-Yao models for analysis of cryptographic protocols that employ zero-knowledge proofs as well.

---

* We thank the anonymous referees for many helpful comments that helped improve the presentation immensely.
** Supported by the Council of Scientific and Industrial Research (CSIR), India, till August 2008.

A. Datta (Ed.): ASIAN 2009, LNCS 5913, pp. 137–146, 2009.

Two approaches suggest themselves. One is to symbolically represent a zero-knowledge proof as an explicit constructor in the term algebra, say zk with appropriate parameters, and study protocols using such terms in communications. Separately, one ensures that guarantees given by proofs with such symbolic abstraction are applicable to protocol implementations where the abstractions are realised by cryptographic zero-knowledge proofs. This is the line of work successfully carried out by [BMU08] and [BU08]. [BHM08] extends this line of work by considering a type system for static type-checking of protocols based using zero-knowledge proofs. They also develop a type-checker for automatic analysis of such protocols.

An alternative is to so extend the Dolev-Yao model such as to formalise aspects of cryptographic zero-knowledge proof construction as well, within the symbolic abstraction. The underlying idea is that an idealisation of the sequence of operations that constitute a cryptographic zero-knowledge proof is itself possible within such an extended Dolev-Yao model. This is in the spirit of logical studies of security protocols, where we wish to identify patterns of reasoning relating to information transfer and hiding. The advantage of such an approach is that computational soundness of underlying abstractions can be 'lifted' to the construction. This is the approach we follow in this paper.

In general, a zero-knowledge proof is a proof of a statement α. A principal A tries to convince another principal B that α is true, but in such a way that for any β such that $\beta \supset \alpha$ and $\neg(\alpha \supset \beta)$, B does not receive any new information as to whether β holds or not. In the context of Dolev-Yao models, α refers to some property of a set of terms X without revealing X itself.

How do we bring such a capability in a formal model? We employ another standard notion, that of a typed term. This is of the form $t : p$, where t is a term formed using the operations of pairing and encryption starting from atomic terms, while p is a pattern built using pairing, encryption, and disjunction starting from atomic terms, and $\square$ (denoting an unknown term). The use of disjunction is central for information hiding in this model. For example, the inference that t is either $\{0\}_k$ or $\{1\}_k$ is represented by $t : \{0\}_k + \{1\}_k$. Such a typed term would be sent by a principal who wishes to convince the recipient that the disjunction holds while keeping the recipient uncertain which of the disjuncts actually holds.

We now sketch further examples:

- If someone has provided a proof that a term t is of the form $\{t'\}_k$ (for a fixed k, and arbitrary t'), this might be represented by the typed term $t : \{\square\}_k$.
- A proof of the fact that two terms t and t' are encrypted using the same key k might be represented by $(t, t') : (\{\square\}_k, \{\square\}_k)$.
- That either t or t' is of the form r can be represented by (for instance) $(t, t') : (r, \square) + (\square, r)$.
- That t is encrypted by either k or k' can be represented by $\{t\}_k : \{t\}_{k+k'}$. If t is a term known to A (a nonce generated by A, say) and the inverse of k is also known to her, then she can in fact verify more of the structure of $\{t\}_k$ (in particular, that the given term is indeed encrypted using k and

not k'). Such considerations are important in modelling examples like the whistle blower's problem [Cla].

In general, protocols in our model communicate a typed term $t : p$ where p is a disjunctive pattern $p_1 + p_2$. The typed term should be derivable by the sender, but the receiver can in general not resolve the disjunction. Then interesting questions about "leak of knowledge" can be asked. If the protocol intends only $t : p$ to be known by an agent A, but she gets to know $t : p'$ for a "stronger pattern" p', that would constitute a leak.

Thus the central contribution of the paper is the setting up of a proof system for when a given typed term is derivable from a set of typed terms, and its use in proving the decidability of the verification problem for "information leakage". What is notable about this system is that we do nontrivial reasoning with disjunction and contradiction. In contrast, the typical proof systems that one encounters in relation to security protocols essentially reason with conjunction and some form of implication, with some algebraic rules.

Our type system shares some features with the one used in [BHM08] (the use of disjunction in the types, for example). But in their paper, they use the type system to ensure that every well-typed protocol is safe, whereas here our focus is on the decidability of our proof system.

2   The Term Model and Derivations

Fix a finite set of **agents** Ag, which includes the **intruder** I, which is an abstraction that quantifies over the malicious forces at work to compromise security. The intruder is assumed to have unbounded memory, has access to all that travels on the public channel, can forge and block messages.

Fix a countable set of **fresh secrets** $\mathcal{N}$. (This includes *random, unguessable nonces* as well as *temporary session keys*.) $\mathcal{B} = \mathcal{N} \cup Ag$ is the set of **basic terms**. The set of *keys* is $\mathcal{K} = \mathcal{N} \cup \{public(A), private(A), shared(A, B) | A, B \in Ag\}$. Here $public(A)$, $private(A)$, and $shared(A, B)$ denote the public key of A, private key of A, and (long-term) shared key between A and B, respectively. We define $inv(k)$ for every $k \in \mathcal{K}$ as follows: $inv(public(A)) = private(A)$, $inv(private(A)) = public(A)$, and $inv(k) = k$ for every other $k \in \mathcal{K}$. The set $\mathcal{T}$ of **terms** is given by the following syntax:

$$\mathcal{T} ::= m \mid (t, t') \mid \{t\}_{t'}$$

where m ranges over $\mathcal{K} \cup Ag$, and t, t' over $\mathcal{T}$. Here (t, t') denotes the pair consisting of t and t', and $\{t\}_{t'}$ denotes the term t encrypted using t'.

Given a term, its set of subterms $st(t)$ is defined as usual: $st(m) = m$; $st((t, t')) = \{(t, t')\} \cup st(t) \cup st(t')$; $st(\{t\}_{t'}) = \{\{t\}_{t'}\} \cup st(t) \cup st(t')$. The notion of **inverse** is extended to all terms t by letting $inv(t) = t$ for all $t \notin \mathcal{K}$.

Terms conform to certain **patterns**. A pattern has the same structure as a term, except for two important differences: we use a special pattern $\square$ to signify that nothing is known about the structure of a given term; and we use *disjunction*, in the form $p+p'$, to signify that a given term has either the structure specified in p or the structure specified in p'. Patterns are given by the following syntax:

$$\mathscr{P} ::= \Box \mid m \mid (p, p') \mid \{p\}_{p'} \mid p + p'$$

where $m \in \mathscr{K} \cup Ag$ and $p, p' \in \mathscr{P}$.

We extend the notion of inverse to an arbitrary basic pattern $p \in \mathscr{P}$ by letting $inv(p) = p$ if $p \notin \mathscr{K}$ and p is not of the form $p_0 + p_1$. We define $inv(p + p')$ to be $inv(p) + inv(p')$.

Given two patterns p and q, we define when p is **incompatible** with q (in symbols: $p\#q$) by the following rules:

> if $m \neq n$ then $m\#n$ for $m, n \in \mathscr{B}$; $m\#(q, q')$ and $m\#\{q\}_{q'}$ for $m \in \mathscr{B}$;
> $(p, p')\#\{q\}_{q'}$; $p\#(q + q')$ if $p\#q$ and $p\#q'$; and $p\#q$ if $q\#p$.

We say that a term t is **compatible** with a pattern p if $\neg(t\#p)$. A **typed term** is of the form $t : p$ where t is a term and p is a pattern, and it is **well-formed** if t is compatible with p.

We next describe rules that let one derive new terms from old. The rules, given in Figure 1, involve **sequents** of the form $X \vdash t : p$ where $X \cup \{t : p\}$ is a set of typed terms. We use $X, t : p$ as a shorthand for $X \cup \{t : p\}$. We use $X \vdash t : p$ to also denote the fact that the sequent $X \vdash t : p$ has a derivation. We let $\overline{X} = \{t : p \mid X \vdash t : p\}$.

Proposition 1. *If X is a set of well-formed typed terms, then any $t : p \in \overline{X}$ is well-formed.*

The proof system can be established to be *sound* in the following sense. Suppose we equip each agent with the usual construction and deconstruction abilities of a standard Dolev-Yao agent, and in addition the ability to probe terms by trying to split them, or decrypt them using available keys, and thereby deduce the structure of a term from the structure of its subterms. Then it can be seen that whenever the typing judgements in the premises can be "computed" by an agent, so can the judgement in the conclusion. The *contr* and *contr'* rules reflect the fact that there are some contradictory judgements in the assumptions, and hence anything can be derived. The disjunction elimination is primarily used to eliminate the possibility of one of the disjuncts in the typing judgement.

For an untyped term t, define the "default typing" to be the typed term $\hat{t} = t : \Box$, and for a set of untyped terms X, let $\hat{X} = \{\hat{t} \mid t \in X\}$. Let $X \vdash_{DY} t$ denote that t is derivable from X in the basic Dolev-Yao model. Then, the following proposition asserts that the system above is a conservative extension.

Proposition 2. $X \vdash_{DY} t$ *iff* $\hat{X} \vdash \hat{t}$.

The **derivability problem** asks, given a set of typed terms X and a typed term $t : p$, whether $t : p \in \overline{X}$. The following theorem is central to the application of this proof system to protocols.

Theorem 1. *The derivability problem is decidable.*

$$\frac{}{X, t{:}p \vdash t{:}p}\ Axiom \qquad\qquad \frac{X \vdash t{:}p \quad X \subseteq X' \quad p' \in \{p, \square\}}{X' \vdash t{:}p'}\ weaken$$

$$\frac{X \vdash t{:}p \quad X \vdash t'{:}p'}{X \vdash (t, t'){:}(p, p')}\ pair \qquad\qquad \frac{X \vdash (t_0, t_1){:}p}{X \vdash t_i{:}\pi^i(p)}\ split_i\ (i = 0, 1)$$

$$\frac{X \vdash t{:}p \quad X \vdash t'{:}p'}{X \vdash \{t\}_{t'}{:}\{p\}_{p'}}\ encrypt \qquad\qquad \frac{X \vdash \{t\}_{t'}{:}p \quad X \vdash inv(t'){:}inv(p')}{X \vdash t{:}\delta(p, inv(p'))}\ decrypt$$

$$\frac{X \vdash t{:}p \quad X \vdash inv(t'){:}inv(p') \quad X \vdash \{t\}_{t'}{:}\square}{X \vdash \{t\}_{t'}{:}\{p\}_{p'}}\ verifyEncrypt$$

$$\frac{X \vdash t{:}p \quad X \vdash t{:}p' \quad p\#p'}{X \vdash r{:}q}\ contr \qquad\qquad \frac{X \vdash t{:}p \quad t, p \in \mathscr{B} \quad t \neq p}{X \vdash r{:}q}\ contr'$$

$$\frac{X \vdash t{:}p + p' \quad X, t{:}p \vdash r{:}q \quad X, t{:}p' \vdash r{:}q}{X \vdash r{:}q}\ +\text{-}elim$$

Fig. 1. The derivation rules. In the $split_i$ rule, $\pi^i(p)$ is p_i if $p = (p_0, p_1)$ and $\square$ if $p = \square$. In the *decrypt* rule, $\delta(p, p')$ is p'' if $p = \{p''\}_{inv(p')}$ and is $\square$ otherwise.

3   The Protocol Model

Protocols[1] are typically given as a sequence of communications of the form $A \to B{:}[\![t]\!]$, which denotes the sending of t by A and its receipt by B. The new element in the model in this paper is that we allow typed terms in the communications.

An action is either a **send action** of the form $A!B{:}[\![(M)t{:}p]\!]$ or a **receive action** of the form $A?B{:}[\![t{:}p]\!]$, where $t{:}p$ is *a well-formed typed term*, and A and B are agent names. By an A-action, we mean $A!B{:}[\![(M)t{:}p]\!]$ or $A?B{:}[\![t{:}p]\!]$, for some B and $t{:}p$. In all the send actions, M is a set of typed terms of the form $m{:}m$ where $m \in st(t)$. These are the nonces supposed to be freshly generated as part of the send action. For an action a of the form $A!B{:}[\![(M)t{:}p]\!]$ or $A?B{:}[\![t{:}p]\!]$, $term(a)$ is defined to be $t{:}p$.

A **communication** is of the form $A \to B{:}[\![(M)t{:}p]\!]$. If $c = A \to B{:}[\![(M)t{:}p]\!]$, then $send(c) = A!B{:}[\![(M)t{:}p]\!]$, and $rec(c) = B?A{:}[\![t{:}p]\!]$.

A **protocol specification** (or **protocol**) Pr is a tuple $(const, c_1 \cdots c_\ell, P, N)$ which satisfies the following conditions:

---

[1] The model we present here is based on [RS05].

- for each $i \leq \ell$, c_i is a communication $A_i \rightarrow B_i : [\![(M_i)t_i : p_i]\!]$
- $\{t_1 : p_1, \ldots, t_\ell : p_\ell\}$ is a set of well-formed typed terms,
- $const \subseteq \mathscr{B}$ is a set of **constants** of the protocol, and
- P and N are finite sets whose elements are of the form $(A, t : p)$ for some $A \in Ag$ and some typed term $t : p$. P specifies the **positive requirements** and N the **negative requirements**.

For ease of notation, we refer to protocols using the sequence of communications. The idea is that $const(Pr)$ should be interpreted the same way throughout any run of the protocol, while the other basic terms can get different interpretations in different **sessions** of a single run of a protocol.

Given a protocol $Pr = c_1 \cdots c_\ell$, one can extract its set of roles $\{\eta_1, \ldots, \eta_n\}$ as follows: consider the sequence of actions $\eta = send(c_1) rec(c_1) \cdots send(c_\ell) rec(c_\ell)$, and for every A that is either a sender or a recipient in the protocol, consider the subsequence of all A-actions in η. This is referred to as the A-role of Pr.

A **substitution** σ is a map from $\mathscr{B}$ to $\mathscr{T}$ such that $\sigma(Ag) \subseteq Ag$ and $\sigma(I) = I$ and $\sigma(\mathscr{N}) \subseteq \mathscr{N}$. We say that a substitution σ is suitable for a protocol Pr if for every basic term m specified to be a constant of the protocol, $\sigma(m) = m$. For an arbitrary term t and pattern p, $\sigma(t)$ and $\sigma(p)$ are defined in the obvious manner. For a typed term $t : p$, $\sigma(t : p) = \sigma(t) : \sigma(p)$.

An **event** of a protocol Pr is a triple $e = (\eta, \sigma, lp)$ where η is a role of Pr, σ is a substitution suitable for Pr, and $1 \leq lp \leq |\eta|$. For events $e = (\eta, \sigma, lp)$ and $e' = (\eta', \sigma', lp')$ of Pr, we say that $e \prec e'$ (meaning that e is in the *local past* of e') if $\eta = \eta'$, $\sigma = \sigma'$, and $lp < lp'$. For an event $e = (\eta, \sigma, lp)$ of Pr, the action of e, $act(e)$ is defined to be $\sigma(a_{lp})$, where $\eta = a_1 \cdots a_k$, and $term(e) = term(act(e))$.

A **state** is a tuple $(s_A)_{A \in Ag}$, where $s_A \subseteq \mathscr{T}$ for each $A \in Ag$. The **initial state** of Pr, denoted by $initstate(Pr)$, is the tuple $(s_A)_{A \in Ag}$ such that for all $A \in Ag$,

$$s_A = \{m : m \mid m \in Ag\} \cup \{private(A) : private(A)\}$$
$$\cup \{public(B) : public(B) \mid B \in Ag\} \cup \{shared(A, B) : shared(A, B) \mid B \neq A\}.$$

We need to define when send and receive actions are enabled, and the state updates that happen as a result of the communications. This is on standard lines, but some points need to be highlighted. A term being sent should be *constructible* by the sender: that is, $t : p$ should be derivable by the agent, but she may choose to communicate a weaker pattern p.

The notions of an action **enabled** at a state, and $update(s, a)$, the **update** of a state s on an action a, are defined as follows:

- A send action a of the form $A!B : [\![(M)t : p]\!]$ is **enabled** at any state s iff
    1. $t : t \in \overline{s_A \cup M}$ or $(p = \square$ and $t : \square \in \overline{s_A \cup M})$,
    2. and for all $m : m \in M$, $m : m \notin \overline{s_C}$ for every C (including A).
- A receive action $a = A?B : [\![t : p]\!]$ is enabled at s iff $t : t \in \overline{s_I}$ or $t : p \in \overline{s_I}$.
- $update(s, A!B : [\![(M)t : p]\!]) = s'$ where $s'_A = s_A \cup M$, $s'_I = s_I \cup \{t : p\}$, and $s'_C = s_C$ for $C \notin \{A, I\}$.
- $update(s, A?B : [\![t : p]\!]) = s'$ where $s'_B = s_B \cup \{t : p\}$, and $s'_C = s_C$ for $C \neq B$.

$update(s, \eta)$ for a state s and a sequence of actions η is defined in the obvious manner. Given a protocol Pr and a sequence of its events ξ, $infstate(\xi)$ is defined to be $update(initstate(Pr), act(\xi))$.

Given a protocol Pr, a sequence $e_1 \cdots e_k$ of events of Pr is said to be an **run** of Pr iff the following conditions hold:

for all $i, j \leq k$ such that $i \neq j$, $e_i \neq e_j$,
for all $i \leq k$ and for all $e \prec e_i$, there exists $j < i$ such that $e_j = e$, and
for all $i \leq k$, $act(e_i)$ is enabled at $infstate(e_1 \cdots e_{i-1})$.

A run $\xi = e_1 \cdots e_k$ of Pr (with $e_i = (\eta_i, \sigma_i, lp_i)$ for each $i \leq k$) is a b-bounded run (for b a natural number) if $|\{(\eta_i, \sigma_i) \mid i \leq k\}| \leq b$, i.e. there are at most b sessions in ξ.

4   The Decidability of the Proof System

We follow[2] the standard approach of reducing every derivation in our system to a normal derivation, and then proving a **subterm property** for normal proofs. This bounds the size of normal proofs for a given sequent $X \vdash t{:}p$. Thus we only need to search over a bounded set of proofs to check whether $t{:}p \in \overline{X}$.

The normalisation rules are quite standard. We basically avoid an application of an introduction rule (the *pair* rule, for example) whose conclusion is the major premise of an application of the corresponding elimination rule (the *split* rule, in this case). We also permute the application of rules so that no major premise of any rule is the conclusion of a disjunction elimination or a contradiction rule. We say that π is a **normal proof** if no further normalisation rules can be applied to it.

Theorem 2. *Every proof can be converted to a normal proof.*

Theorem 3. *Let π be a normal proof of $X \vdash t : p$ and let $u : q$ be a typed term occurring in π. Then $u \in st(X \cup \{t\})$ (where by $st(X)$ we mean the set $\{t' \in st(t) \mid t{:}p \in X$ for some $p\}$).*

The theorem places a bound on the set of terms that can occur in a proof of $X \vdash t{:}p$, but what about the set of *typed terms*? We show below that this is also bounded. More specifically, given a set of typed terms X, and a term t, we show that the number of patterns p such that $X \vdash t{:}p$ is bounded.

Given a set of typed terms X, we define $closure_1(X)$ to be the least set Y such that:

- $X \subseteq Y$;
- if $(t, t'){:}(p, p') \in Y$, then $t{:}p, t'{:}p' \in Y$;
- if $(t, t'){:}\Box \in Y$, then $t{:}\Box, t'{:}\Box \in Y$;
- if $\{t\}_{t'}{:}\{p\}_{p'} \in Y$, then $t{:}p, t'{:}p' \in Y$;

---

[2] Full proofs are found in the technical report [BRS09].

- if $\{t\}_{t'} : \Box \in Y$, then $t : \Box, t' : \Box \in Y$; and
- if $t : p + p' \in Y$, then $t : p, t : p' \in Y$.

Given a set of typed terms X and a term t, we define $closure_2(X, t)$ to be the least set Y such that:

- $closure_1(X) \subseteq Y$,
- if $(r, r') \in st(X \cup \{t\})$ and if $r : p, r' : p' \in Y$, then $(r, r') : (p, p') \in Y$, and
- if $\{r\}_{r'} \in st(X \cup \{t\})$ and if $r : p, r' : p' \in Y$, then $\{r\}_{r'} : \{p\}_{p'} \in Y$.

Lemma 1.

1. $closure_1(closure_2(X, t)) \subseteq closure_2(X, t)$,
2. $closure_2(closure_2(X, t), t) \subseteq closure_2(X, t)$.

Lemma 2.

1. $|closure_1(X)| \leq m \cdot |X|$ for some constant m.
2. $|closure_2(X, t)| \leq (|X \cup \{t\}|)^d$ where d is the maximum depth of any term in $st(X \cup \{t\})$.

Theorem 4. Let X be a set of typed terms and t be a term. Let π be a normal proof of $X \vdash t : p$ for some p and i. Then for any typed term $u : q$ occurring in π, $u : q \in closure_2(X, t)$.

Theorem 1 is an immediate consequence of the above theorem. There is a standard deterministic algorithm that checks, given X and $t : p$, whether the term is derivable from X in time polynomial in the size of $closure_2(X, t)$.

Application to the Information Leakage Problem

We describe the **information leakage problem** below. But for that we need a definition of when one pattern p is stronger than another pattern q. We shall formally define it below, but the idea is that for all terms t, if t is compatible with p, it is also compatible with q, but there is at least one term t' that is compatible with q but incompatible with p.

We first define when p and q are **equally strong** (in symbols: $p \sim q$). $\sim$ is the smallest congruence on patterns such that

$$\Box \sim \Box + p; \; p \sim p + p; \; (p + p', q) \sim (p, q) + (p', q);$$
$$(q, p + p') \sim (q, p) + (q, p'); \; \{p + p'\}_q \sim \{p\}_q + \{p'\}_q; \; \{q\}_{p+p'} \sim \{q\}_p + \{q\}_{p'}.$$

We now define when p is **as strong as** q (in symbols: $p \succsim q$). $\succsim$ is the least binary relation over the set of patterns that is reflexive, transitive, and such that:

$$p \sim q \Rightarrow p \succsim q; \; p \succsim \Box; \; p \succsim p + q; \text{ and}$$
$$p \succsim q, p' \succsim q' \Rightarrow (p, p') \succsim (q, q'), \{p\}_{p'} \succsim \{q\}_{q'}.$$

We say that p is **stronger than** q (in symbols: $p \succ q$) if $p \succsim q$ and $\neg(p \sim q)$.

The information leakage problem asks, given $Pr = (const, c_1 \cdots c_\ell, P, N)$, and a bound $b > 0$, whether the following holds:

1. for every $(A, t:p) \in P$, there exists a b-bounded run $\xi = e_1 \cdots e_k$ of Pr (with $e_k = (\eta, \sigma, lp)$) and $i \in \{0, 1\}$ such that $\sigma(t):\sigma(p) \in \overline{infstate_{\sigma(A)}(\xi)}$, and
2. for every $(A, t:p) \in N$, there **does not exist** any b-bounded run $\xi = e_1 \cdots e_k$ of Pr such that (letting $e_k = (\eta, \sigma, lp)$), and a **stronger pattern** $p' \succ \sigma(p)$ such that $\sigma(t):p' \in \overline{infstate_{\sigma(A)}(\xi)}$.

Theorem 5. *The information leakage problem is decidable.*

We first notice that for any given protocol Pr, the set of b-bounded runs of Pr. The only non-trivial part here is to check the enabledness of certain events, which reduce to tests of the form $t : p \in \overline{X}$ for an appropriate X. Theorem 1 guarantees that we can effectively perform this test.

Once we compute the set of b-bounded runs, we need to check the knowledge requirements. For a positive specification $(A, t:p)$, search for a b-bounded run $\xi = e_1 \cdots e_k$ of Pr (with $e_k = (\eta, \sigma, lp)$) such that $\sigma(t):\sigma(p) \in \overline{infstate_{\sigma(A)}(\xi)}$. Theorem 1 once again ensures that we can do this test effectively.

For a negative specification $(A, t : p)$, we need to check all b-bounded runs $\xi = e_1 \cdots e_k$ of Pr (letting $e_k = (\eta, \sigma, lp)$), to ensure that there is no **stronger pattern** $p' \succ \sigma(p)$ such that $\sigma(t):p' \in \overline{infstate_{\sigma(A)}(\xi)}$. Once we fix a run ξ and $X = infstate_A(\xi)$, we need to verify that there is no pattern p' stronger than $\sigma(p)$ is derivable for t from X. In general, there is no bound on the set of stronger patterns than a given pattern p. But we only need to check for patterns derived from X. Theorem 4 assures us that there are only boundedly many patterns for t derivable from X. Now we just need to check if any one them is stronger than $\sigma(p)$. Thus one can effectively verify the negative knowledge requirements as well, and hence the information leakage problem is decidable.

References

[AR02]   Abadi, M., Rogaway, P.: Reconciling two views of cryptography (the computational soundness of formal encryption). Journal of Cryptology 15(2), 103–127 (2002)

[Bau05]   Baudet, M.: Deciding security of protocols against off-line guessing attacks. In: CCS 2005: Proceedings of the 12th ACM conference on Computer and communications security, pp. 16–25. ACM Press, New York (2005)

[BHM08]   Backes, M., Hritcu, C., Maffei, M.: Type-checking zero-knowledge. In: ACM Conference on Computer and Communications Security, pp. 357–370 (2008)

[BMU08]   Backes, M., Maffei, M., Unruh, D.: Zero-Knowledge in the Applied Pi-calculus and Automated Verification of the Direct Anonymous Attestation Protocol. In: IEEE Symposium on Security and Privacy, pp. 202–215 (2008)

[BRS09]   Baskar, A., Ramanujam, R., Suresh, S.P.: A Dolev-Yao model for Zero Knowledge. CMI Technical Report (2009),
           http://www.cmi.ac.in/~spsuresh/content/pdffiles/
           zero-know-jun09.pdf

[BU08]   Backes, M., Unruh, D.: Computational Soundness of Symbolic Zero-Knowledge Proofs Against Active Attackers. In: Proceedings of the 21st IEEE Computer Security Foundations Symposium, pp. 255–269 (2008)

[CDL06]   Cortier, V., Delaune, S., Lafourcade, P.: A survey of algebraic properties used in cryptographic protocols. Journal of Computer Security 14(1), 1–43 (2006)

[CKKW06]   Cortier, V., Kremer, S., Küsters, R., Warinschi, B.: Computationally sound symbolic secrecy in the presence of hash functions. In: Arun-Kumar, S., Garg, N. (eds.) FSTTCS 2006. LNCS, vol. 4337, pp. 176–187. Springer, Heidelberg (2006)

[Cla]   Clausen, A.: Logical composition of zero-knowledge proofs, http://www.cis.upenn.edu/~mkearns/teaching/Crypto/zkp-disj.pdf

[CLS03]   Comon-Lundh, H., Shmatikov, V.: Intruder Deductions, Constraint Solving and Insecurity Decisions in Presence of Exclusive or. In: Proceedings of the 18th IEEE Synposium on Logic in Computer Science (LICS), June 2003, pp. 271–280 (2003)

[Cre08]   Cremers, C.J.F.: The Scyther Tool: Verification, falsification, and analysis of security protocols. In: Gupta, A., Malik, S. (eds.) CAV 2008. LNCS, vol. 5123, pp. 414–418. Springer, Heidelberg (2008)

[DKR09]   Delaune, S., Kremer, S., Ryan, M.D.: Verifying privacy-type properties of electronic voting protocols. Journal of Computer Security 17(4), 435–487 (2009)

[GLT89]   Girard, J.-Y., Lafont, Y., Taylor, P.: Proofs and Types. Cambridge Tracts in Theoretical Computer Science, vol. 7. Cambridge University Press, Cambridge (1989)

[GMR89]   Goldwasser, S., Micali, S., Rackoff, C.: The knowledge complexity of interactive proof systems. SIAM Journal of Computing 18(1), 186–208 (1989)

[Her05]   Herzog, J.: A computational interpretation of dolev-yao adversaries. Theoretical Computer Science 340(1), 57–81 (2005)

[Low96]   Lowe, G.: Breaking and fixing the Needham-Schroeder public key protocol using FDR. In: Margaria, T., Steffen, B. (eds.) TACAS 1996. LNCS, vol. 1055, pp. 147–166. Springer, Heidelberg (1996)

[MS01]   Millen, J.K., Shmatikov, V.: Constraint solving for bounded-process cryptographic protocol analysis. In: ACM Conference on Computer and Communications Security, pp. 166–175 (2001)

[RS05]   Ramanujam, R., Suresh, S.P.: Decidability of context-explicit security protocols. Journal of Computer Security 13(1), 135–165 (2005)

[RS06]   Ramanujam, R., Suresh, S.P.: A (restricted) quantifier elimination for security protocols. Theoretical Computer Science 367, 228–256 (2006)

[RT03]   Rusinowitch, M., Turuani, M.: Protocol Insecurity with Finite Number of Sessions and Composed Keys is NP-complete. Theoretical Computer Science 299, 451–475 (2003)

A Special Proxy Signature Scheme with Multi-warrant

Jianhong Zhang[1,2], Hua Chen[1], Shengnan Gao[1], and Yixian Yang[2]

[1] College of sciences, North China University of Technology,
Beijing 100144, China
jhzhang@ncut.edu.cn
[2] School of Information Engineering, Beijing University of Posts and
Telecommunications, Beijing 100876, China
yxyang@bupt.edu.cn

Abstract. Proxy signature is an important delegation technology. In this paper, we proposed a novel proxy signature scheme with multi-warrant by extending proxy signature. This extension is not a trivial extension, it makes that the size of extended proxy signature is approximate one of original proxy signature. And the size of the extended proxy signature is constant and is independent of warrant's number. The scheme is proven secure in the standard model and the security of the scheme is related to the Computational Diffie-Hellman Assumption. Comparison with Huang *et.al* scheme, our scheme has an advantage over Huang *et.al*'s scheme in terms of the size of proxy signature.

Keywords: proxy signature, multiwarrant, security proof, proxy signature with multi-warrant, the CDH problem.

1 Introduction

The notion of proxy signature scheme introduced by Mambo *et. al* in 1996 [1]. It allows an original signer to delegate his signing capability to proxy signer in a proxy signature. Since it is proposed, proxy signature schemes have been suggested for use in many applications [2,3,4,5], particularly in distributed systems, Grid computing, mobile agent applications, distributed shared object systems, global distribution networks, and mobile communications. And to adapt different situations, many proxy signature variants are produced, such as one-time proxy signature, proxy blind signature, multi-proxy signature, and so on. Based on the delegation type, proxy signature schemes are divided into *full delegation, partial delegation* and *delegation* by warrant. According whether the original signer know the proxy secret key, proxy signatures can also be classified as *proxy-unprotected* and *proxy-protected* schemes. In a proxy-protected scheme the original signer cannot forge the proxy signer to produce proxy signature. It means that the proxy signature can be produced only by the proxy signer. Thus we can clearly distinguish the rights and responsibilities between the original signer and the proxy signer.

A. Datta (Ed.): ASIAN 2009, LNCS 5913, pp. 147–157, 2009.

Obviously, we can easily extend a general based-warrant proxy signature into a proxy signature with multi-warrant. Namely, the original signer can regard several warrants as a new warrant to realize the delegation of right by concatenating them. It means that all the concatenated warrants are a part of proxy signature. Such way makes size of proxy signature longer, thus it is inefficient . Usually, a signed message only belongs to the admission range of some warrant, other warrants are unnecessary to this message in the phase of signature's verification. Sometimes, proxy signer hopes to make the verifier only know the warrant which the signed message belongs to. While he keeps other warrants secret for a verifier. Such as a big company manufactures many salable productions. And the company needs to delegate sale rights of several productions to n agents. The number of dealership is a private information of agent and has relation to his wealth. In general, the agent is not willing to reveal his number of dealership. When a user buys a production, it is sufficient for the user that the agent possesses the dealership of the sold production.

Being inspired with the delegation problem above, in this paper, we propose a proxy signature scheme with multi-warrant, and formalize a notion of security for proxy signature scheme with warrant. At the same time, we also show that the security of our scheme is tightly related to the computational Deffie-Hellman assumption in the standard model. Compared with Huang $et.al$ proxy signature schemes, our scheme has an advantage over Huang $et.al$'s scheme in terms of the size of proxy signature. In our scheme, the size of proxy signature is constant and is independent of the number of warrant.

2   Preliminaries

Let $\mathbb{G}_1$ and $\mathbb{G}_2$ be two cyclic groups of order q, P is a generator of $\mathbb{G}_1$. We assume that the discrete logarithm problem (DLP) in both $\mathbb{G}_1$ and $\mathbb{G}_2$ are hard. An admissible pairing $e : \mathbb{G}_1 \times \mathbb{G}_1 \longrightarrow \mathbb{G}_2$, which satisfies the following three properties:

- Bilinear: If $P, Q \in \mathbb{G}_1$ and $a, b \in Z_q^*$, then $e(aP, bQ) = e(P, Q)^{ab}$;
- Non-degenerate: There exists a $P \in \mathbb{G}_1$ such that $e(P, P) \neq 1$;
- Computable: If $P, Q \in \mathbb{G}_1$, one can compute $e(P, Q) \in \mathbb{G}_2$ in polynomial time.

We note the modified Weil and Tate pairings associated with supersingular elliptic curves are examples of such admissible pairings.

Definition 1. *Given two group $\mathbb{G}_1$ and $\mathbb{G}_2$ of the same prime order q, the Decisional Bilinear Diffie-Hellman problem (DBDHP) in $(\mathbb{G}_1, \mathbb{G}_2, e)$ is to decide whether $h = e(P, P)^{abc}$ given (P, aP, bP, cP) and an element $h \in \mathbb{G}_2$. We define the advantage of a distinguisher against the DBDHP as follows:*

$$AdvD = \mid P_{a,b,c \in_R Z_q, h \in_R \mathbb{G}_2}[1 \leftarrow D(aP, bP, cP, h)]$$
$$-P_{a,b,c \in_R Z_q}[1 \leftarrow D(aP, bP, cP, e(P, P)^{abc})] \mid$$

Definition 2 (Computational Diffie-Hellman (CDH) Assumption). .
Let $\mathcal{G}$ be a CDH parameter generator. We say an algorithm $\mathcal{A}$ has advantage $\epsilon(k)$ in solving the CDH problem in group $\mathbb{G}_1$ if for a sufficiently large k,

$$Adv_{\mathcal{G},\mathcal{A}}(t) = Pr[\mathcal{A}(q, \mathbb{G}_1, xP, yP) = xyP \mid (q, \mathbb{G}_1) \leftarrow \mathcal{G}^k, P \leftarrow \mathbb{G}_1, xP, yP \leftarrow \mathbb{G}_1]$$

We say that $\mathcal{G}$ satisfies the CDH assumption if for any randomized polynomial time in t algorithm $\mathcal{A}$ we have the $Adv_{\mathcal{G},\mathcal{A}}(t)$ is negligible function.

Proxy signature scheme with Multi-warrant: A proxy signature scheme with multi-warrant consists of three entities: original signer, proxy signer and verifier.

Definition 3. *An proxy signature scheme with multi-warrant consists of the following polynomial-time algorithms*

- Setup: It is a deterministic algorithm that takes as input a security parameter l, and outputs system parameters: **param**. The original signer and proxy signer produces their secret-public key pair (sk_o, pk_o) and (sk_p, pk_p), respectively.
- Delegation algorithm $\mathcal{DL}$: the algorithm takes as the input the secret key sk_o of an original signer and a warrant list $W = (A_1, \cdots, A_n)$, outputs a signature $\bar{\delta}$ on this warrant list W, where the warrant list W contains the identity (ID) of proxy signer and, possibly, restrictions on the message the proxy signer is allowed to sign.
- Delegation Generation Algorithm $\mathcal{DG}$: takes as an input a original signature's public key pk_o, the signature $\bar{\delta}$ of warrant list W and a proxy signer secret key sk_p, and output the proxy signing key s_p .
- Proxy Signing Algorithm $\mathcal{PS}$: the algorithm takes input the proxy signer's proxy signing key s_p, the proxy signer's public key pk_p and the message M, and outputs the proxy signature δ_p of the message M.
- Proxy signature Verification $\mathcal{PV}$: a deterministic algorithm $\mathcal{PV}$ takes input $(pk_s, pk_p, M, A_i, \delta_p)$, and output a bit, where A_i is a warrant of warrant-list W, other warrants A_j $(j \neq i)$ are secret to a verifier in the warrant list W. We say that δ_p is a valid signature for M if $\mathcal{PV}(pk_s, pk_p, M, \delta_p, A_i)=1$, otherwise outputs the $\perp$ symbol.

Security requirements of proxy signature with multi-warrant: Unforgeability is the most important property in a proxy signature. It denote that only proxy signer can generate a valid proxy signature. In fact, unforgeability includes the undeniability and prevention of misuse.

According to the model defined in [7,8], we divide the potential adversary into three attack types:

1. Type I: In this attack type, an adversary $\mathcal{A}_I$ only has the public keys of original signer and proxy signer.
2. Type II: In this attack type, an adversary $\mathcal{A}_{II}$ has the public keys of original signer and proxy signer, and it also has the secret key of the proxy signer.

3. Type III: In this attack type, an adversary $\mathcal{A}_{III}$ has the public keys of original signer and proxy signer, it also has the secret key of original signer.

Obviously, we know that if a proxy signature scheme with multi-warrant is secure against Type II (or Type III) adversary, the scheme is also secure against Type I adversary. In the security model defined later, we only consider Type II adversary and Type III adversary.

Existential unforgeability against adaptive $\mathcal{A}_{II}$ adversary: Roughly speaking, the existential unforgeability of a proxy signature scheme with multi-warrant under adaptive $\mathcal{A}_{II}$ attacker requires that it is difficult for a user to forge a valid proxy signature under a warrant A_i of warrant-list W by the following game between a challenger $\mathcal{C}$ and the adversary $\mathcal{A}_{II}$;

1. $\mathcal{C}$ runs **Setup** algorithms, and produces proxy signer's secret-public (sk_p, pk_p) and original signer's public pk_o. then its resulting system parameters and the secret key sk_p of proxy signer are given to $\mathcal{A}_{II}$.
2. $\mathcal{A}_{II}$ can issue the following queries:

    (a) Delegation queries: Proceeding adaptively, when $\mathcal{A}_{II}$ requests the delegation, $\mathcal{C}$ randomly produces a warrant list $W = (A_1, \cdots, A_n)$ and runs the Delegation algorithm $\mathcal{DG}$ to obtain proxy signing key s_p
    (b) ProxySign queries: Proceeding adaptively, $\mathcal{A}_{II}$ can request the proxy signature on the message M. In response, $\mathcal{C}$ runs Delegation algorithm $\mathcal{DG}$ to generate the delegation on the produced warrant-list W, where M must belong to the admission range of some warrant A_i in warrant-list W. Then $\mathcal{C}$ runs the ProxySign algorithm to obtain the proxy signature δ on message M and returns (A_i, δ) to the adversary $\mathcal{A}_{II}$.

3. **Outputs:** Finally, $\mathcal{A}_{II}$ outputs a signature δ^* with a warrant A_i^* and the message M^* such that

    (a) a warrant-list W which includes A_i^* has never been returned as one of the delegation queries.
    (b) δ^* is a valid signature on message M^* and M^* belongs to the admission of A_i^*.

Compared with the model defined in [6,2], an important refinement is $\mathcal{A}_{II}$ can adaptively request the ProxySign queries with message M^* under the warrant-list W which does not include A_i. The success probability of an algorithm $\mathcal{A}_{II}$ wins the above game is defined as $Succ\mathcal{A}_{II}$.

Definition 4. *We say a type II adversary $\mathcal{A}_{II}$ can $(t, q_d, q_s, \varepsilon)$ break a proxy signature scheme with multi-warrant if $\mathcal{A}_{II}$ runs in time at most t, $\mathcal{A}_{II}$ makes at most q_d delegation queries and at most q_s ProxySign queries and $Succ$ $\mathcal{A}_{II}$ is at least ε*

Existential unforgeability against adaptive $\mathcal{A}_{III}$ adversary: Roughly speaking, the attack shows that a proxy signature is only produced by proxy signer, even if original signer can not also produce it. The existential unforgeability of a proxy signature scheme with multi-warrant under a type III attacker requires that it is difficult for original signer to output a valid proxy signature by the following game between the challenger $\mathcal{C}$ and the adversary $\mathcal{A}_{III}$.

1. $\mathcal{C}$ runs **Setup** algorithms, and produces original signer's secret-public (sk_o, pk_o) and proxy signer's public pk_p. then its resulting system parameters and the secret key sk_s of original signer are given to $\mathcal{A}_{III}$.

2. $\mathcal{A}_{III}$ can issue **ProxySign queries**: It is the same as the above ProxySign queries.

3. **Outputs**: Finally, $\mathcal{A}_{III}$ outputs a signature δ^* with a warrant A_i^* and the message M^* such that

   (a) M^* has never been requested as one of Proxysign queries.
   (b) δ^* is a valid signature on message M^*

The success probability of an algorithm $\mathcal{A}_{III}$ wins the above game is defined as $Succ\mathcal{A}_{III}$

Definition 5. *We say a type III adversary $\mathcal{A}_{III}$ can (t, q_s, ε) break a proxy signature scheme with multi-warrant if $\mathcal{A}_{III}$ runs in time at most t, $\mathcal{A}_{III}$ makes at most q_s ProxySign queries and Succ $\mathcal{A}_{III}$ is at least ε*

3   The Scheme

In this section, we will describe the proposed proxy signature scheme with multi-warrant. The idea of our scheme is based on Waters's signature scheme and mutative identity-based signature. The scheme consists of the following steps:

ParaGen: Let $\mathbb{G}_1, \mathbb{G}_2$ be two cyclic groups of order p which is a prime number and g is the generator of $\mathbb{G}_1$. e denotes the bilinear pairing $\mathbb{G}_1 \times \mathbb{G}_1 \to \mathbb{G}_2$. Choose a vector $\mathbf{u} = (u_i)$ of length n_u and a vector $\mathbf{m} = (m_i)$ of length n_m, where $u_i, m_i \in \mathbb{G}$. Randomly choose $\beta \in Z_p$ to compute $K_i = g^{\beta^i}$ for $i = 1, 2, \cdots, n$. $H : \{0,1\}^* \to \{0,1\}^{n_u}$ is a collision-resistant hash function and H_1 is a one-way function which satisfies $H_1 : \{0,1\}^n \times \mathbb{G}_1^4 \to Z_p$. g_2, u_0, m_0 are randomly from $\mathbb{G}_1$. The master public *params* are

$$(g, g_2, \mathbb{G}_1, \mathbb{G}_2, K_1, \cdots, K_n, \mathbf{u}, \mathbf{m}, u_0, m_0, H, H_1)$$

KeyGen: The original signer Alice randomly chooses $s_a \in Z_p$ to compute the corresponding public key $y_a = g^{s_a}$. Similarly, for the proxy signer Bob, he also randomly selects $s_b \in Z_p$ to produce the corresponding public key $y_b = g^{s_b}$.

Delegation: Let $A_1, A_2, \cdots, A_n$ denote the different delegated warrants. To produce a delegation of these warrants, the original signer Alice computes as follows:

- compute $A_U = g^{(A_1+\beta)(A_2+\beta)\cdots(A_n+\beta)} \in \mathbb{G}_1$; Note that we can compute A_U by the public $params$ $K_1, \cdots, K_n$.
- compute the hash function $h_U = H(y_b, A_U) \in \{0,1\}^{n_u}$;
- Let $h_U[i]$ denote the i-th bit of hash value h_U and $\mathcal{U} \in \{1, 2, \cdots, n_u\}$ be the set of all i for $h_U[i] = 1$. The delegation is generated as follows: pick a random $r \in Z_p$ and compute d_U, where

$$d_U = (d_1, d_2) = (g_2^{s_a}(u_0 \prod_{i \in \mathcal{U}} u_i)^r, g^r)$$

ProxySign: Let M be an $n - bit$ message in the admission range of warrant A_i. To generate a signature δ on the message M, the proxy signer computes as follows:

1. According to the above parameters $K_1, \cdots, K_n$, the proxy signer computes δ_1 and δ_2 where
   $\delta_1 = g^{(A_1+\beta)\cdots(A_{i-1}+\beta)(A_{i+1}+\beta)\cdots(A_n+\beta)}$ and
   $\delta_2 = g^{\beta(A_1+\beta)\cdots(A_{i-1}+\beta)(A_{i+1}+\beta)\cdots(A_n+\beta)}$
2. Let $M[j]$ be the $j-$th bit of M, $\mathcal{M} \subset \{1, 2, \cdots, n\}$ be the set of all j for $M[j] = 1$.
3. randomly choose $\alpha \in Z_p$ to compute

$$\delta_3 = g_2^{s_b} \cdot d_1(m_0 \prod_{j \in \mathcal{M}} m_j)^{\alpha \cdot h_1}, \delta_4 = d_2, \delta_5 = g^\alpha$$

   where $h_1 = H_1(M, \delta_1, \delta_2, \delta_4, \delta_5)$
4. the resultant proxy signature on message M is $\delta = (A_i, \delta_1, \delta_2, \delta_3, \delta_4, \delta_5)$

Verify: given a proxy signature δ on message M, a verifier first checks whether M belongs to the admission ranger of A_i. If it is valid, then it verifies as follows:

1. check $e(\delta_1, K_1) = e(\delta_2, g)$
2. compute $A_U = \delta_1^{A_i}\delta_2$ and $h_U = H(y_s, A_U)$
3. compute $h_1 = H_1(M, \delta_1, \delta_2, \delta_4, \delta_5)$
4. check $e(\delta_3, g) = e(g_2, y_a y_b) \cdot e(u_0 \prod_{i \in \mathcal{U}} u_i, \delta_4) \cdot e(m_0 \prod_{j \in \mathcal{M}} m_j, \delta_5)^{h_1}$

If all equalities hold the result returns **True**; otherwise, the result returns **False**.

4   Security Analysis

In the following, we will provide security analysis of the proxy signature scheme with multi-warrant and show that the scheme is secure.

Theorem 1. *If there exists an adversary $\mathcal{A}_{II}$ can $(t, q_d, q_s, \tau, \epsilon)$ break the proposed proxy signature scheme with multi-warrant, then there exists another algorithm $\mathcal{B}$ who can make use of the adversary $\mathcal{A}_{II}$ to solve the CDH problem of group $\mathbb{G}_1$ with the probability $\epsilon' \geq \frac{\epsilon}{l_u \cdot (n_u+1)}(1 - \frac{q_s+q_d}{l_u \cdot n_u})$ where q_s denotes at most times of asking proxy signing queries, q_d be at most times of asking delegation queries.*

Proof. Assume there is a (ϵ, t, q_e, q_s)–adversary $\mathcal{A}_{II}$ exists. We are going to construct another PPT $\mathcal{B}$ that makes use of $\mathcal{A}$ to solve the CDH problem with probability at least ϵ' and in time at most t'.

Let us recall the CDH problem, given a CDH problem instance $(g, g^a, g^b) \in \mathbb{G}_1^3$, its goal is to compute $g^{ab} \in \mathbb{G}_1$. In order to use $\mathcal{A}_{II}$ to solve this problem, $\mathcal{B}$ need to simulates a challenger and the oracles (Delegation oracle and proxy signing oracle) for the adversary $\mathcal{A}$. The detail steps are as follows:

Setup: To simulate the game, $\mathcal{B}$ chooses two integers l_u, l_m which satisfy $0 \leq l_u, l_m \leq p$, meanwhile it also chooses $0 \leq k_u \leq n_u$ and $0 \leq k_m \leq n_m$, such that $l_u(n_u + 1) < p$ and $l_m(n_m + 1) < p$. For an n−bit V, we let $\mathfrak{V}$ be the set of all i for which $V_i = 1$.

Then it randomly selects the following parameters:

- $x' \in_R Z_{l_u}, y', z' \in_R Z_p$.
- for $i = 1, \cdots, n_u$, $x_i \in_R Z_{l_u}$ and set $\hat{X} = (x_1, \cdots, x_{n_u})$.
- for $i = 1, \cdots, n_u$, $y_i \in_R Z_p$ and set $\hat{Y} = (y_1, \cdots, y_{n_u})$.
- for $i = 1, \cdots, n_m$, $z_i \in_R Z_p$ and set $\hat{Z} = (z_1, \cdots, z_{n_m})$.
- choose $\beta \in_R Z_p$ for $i = 1, \cdots, n$, and set $K_i = g^{\beta^i}$.

For easier description, we define the following functions as follows:

$$F(H) = x' + \sum_{i \in \mathfrak{U}} x_i - l_u \cdot k_u \quad \text{and} \quad J(H) = y' + \sum_{i \in \mathfrak{U}} y_i$$

$\mathcal{B}$ constructs a set of public parameters as follows:

$$g_2 = g^b, u' = g_2^{-l_u k_u + x'} g^{y'}, m_0 = g^{z'}$$

For $1 \leq i \leq n_u, u_i = g_2^{x_i} g^{y_i}$, **For** $1 \leq j \leq n_m, m_j = g^{z_j}$

Then $\mathcal{B}$ chooses $sk_p \in Z_p$ to compute $y_p = g^{sk_p} \in \mathbb{G}_1$ as the public key of the proxy signer, and sets the public key of original signer as $y_o = g^a \cdot y_p^{-1}$. Finally, all public parameters, the public key $(y_p, y_o = g^a \cdot y_p^{-1})$ and the proxy signer's secret key sk_p are passed to the adversary $\mathcal{A}_{II}$.

Delegation Oracle: When $\mathcal{A}_{II}$ issues a delegation query, $\mathcal{B}$ chooses a warrant list $W_i = (A_{i_1}, \cdots, A_{i_n})$ to response as follows:

1. compute $A_{U_i} = g^{(A_{i_1}+\beta)(A_{i_2}+\beta)\cdots(A_{i_n}+\beta)}$.
2. compute the hash value $h_{U_i} = H(y_b, A_{U_i})$
3. compute $F(h_{U_i})$ function with h_{U_i}.
   (a) if $F(h_{U_i}) \neq 0 \bmod p$, $\mathcal{B}$ randomly chooses $r_u \in_R Z_p$ to compute the private key as $d_{U_i} = (d_{1_{U_i}}, d_{2_{U_i}})$, where $d_{1_{U_i}} = y_o^{-\frac{J(h_{U_i})}{F(h_{U_i})}} (g_2^{F(h_{U_i})} g^{J(h_{U_i})})^{r_u}$
   and $d_{2_{h_{U_i}}} = y_o^{-\frac{1}{F(h_{U_i})}} g^{r_u}$
   (b) If $F(h_{U_i}) = 0 \bmod p$, since the above computation cannot be performed (division by 0), the simulator aborts.

ProxySign Oracle: When $\mathcal{A}_{II}$ issues a ProxySign query with message M, $\mathcal{B}$ responses as follows:

1. First, it produces a warrant list $W_i = (A_{i_1}, A_{i_2}, \cdots, A_{i_n})$ and makes M to belong to some warrant's admission range of the warrant list W_i.
2. compute $A_{U_i} = g^{(A_{i_1}+\beta)(A_{i_2}+\beta)\cdots(A_n+\beta)}$ and $h_{U_i} = H(y_b, A_{U_i})$.
3. Then, $\mathcal{B}$ uses β to compute $\delta_{i_1} = g^{(A_{i_1}+\beta)\cdots(A_{i-1}+\beta)\cdot(A_{i+1}+\beta)\cdots(A_n+\beta)}$ and $\delta_{i_2} = g^{\beta(A_{i_1}+\beta)\cdots(A_{i-1}+\beta)\cdot(A_{i+1}+\beta)\cdots(A_n+\beta)}$
4. if $F(h_{U_i}) = 0 \bmod p$, then the simulator aborts; if $F(h_{U_i}) \neq 0$, the $\mathcal{B}$ randomly chooses $r_i, l_i \in_R Z_p$ to compute

$$\hat{\delta}_3 = (g^a)^{-\frac{J(h_{U_i})}{F(h_{U_i})}}(g_2^{F(h_{U_i})}g^{J(h_{U_i})})^{r_i}, \delta_4 = (g^a)^{-\frac{1}{F(h_{U_i})}}g^{r_i}, \delta_5 = g^{l_i}$$

5. Then, $\mathcal{B}$ sets $\delta_3 = \hat{\delta}_3 \cdot (\delta_5)^{h_1(z'+\sum_{i \in \mathcal{M}} z_i)}$, where $\mathcal{M}$ denotes the set of all i for which $M_i = 1$, and $h_1 = H_1(M, \delta_4, \delta_5)$.

Output: Finally, the adversary $\mathcal{A}_{II}$ outputs a valid forgery signature $\delta^* = (\delta_1^*, \delta_2^*, \delta_3^*, \delta_4^*, \delta_5^*)$ on (A_i^*, M^*) such that

1. M^* belongs to the admission range of A_i^*;
2. a warrant-list W which includes A_i^* has not been returned as one of the delegation queries.
3. δ^* is a valid signature which satisfies the verifying equation.

if $F(h_U^*) \neq 0$, $\mathcal{B}$ will abort it. Otherwise, when $F(h_U^*) = 0$, we obtain the following case

$$\delta_3 = (g_2)^{sk_o+sk_p}(u'\sum_{i \in \mathcal{U}^*} u_i)^{\bar{r}} \cdot (m'\sum_{i \in \mathcal{M}} m_i)^{l_i h_1}$$
$$= (g^{sk_o+sk_p})^b(\delta_3^*)^{J(h_U^*)} \cdot (\delta_5^*)^{h_1^*(z'+\sum_{i \in \mathcal{M}} z_i)}$$

Thus, we have

$$g^{ab} = \frac{\delta_3^*}{(\delta_3^*)^{J(h_U^*)} \cdot (\delta_5^*)^{h_1^*(z'+\sum_{i \in \mathcal{M}} z_i)}}$$

where $h_1^* = H_1(M_1, \delta_1^*, \delta_2^*, \delta_4^*, \delta_5^*)$. Note that $g^{sk_o} \cdot g^{sk_p} = y_p^{-1} \cdot g^a y_p = g^a$.

It denotes that given a CDH problem instance (g, g^a, g^b), $\mathcal{B}$ can compute $g^{ab} = \frac{\delta_3^*}{(\delta_3^*)^{J(h_U^*)} \cdot (\delta_5^*)^{h_1^*(z'+\sum_{i \in \mathcal{M}} z_i)}}$ in a non-negligible probability.

Now, we have to assess $\mathcal{B}$'s probability of success. For the simulation to complete without aborting, we require the following cases fulfilled.

- Delegation queries on h_{U_i} must satisfy $F(h_{U_i}) \neq 0 \bmod p$, for all $i \in [1, q_d]$.
- ProxySigning queries on M must satisfy $F(h_{U_j}) \neq 0 \bmod p$, for all $j \in [1, q_s]$.
- $F(h_{U^*}) = 0 \bmod p$

To clearly explain, we define the events A_i, B^* as follows:

$$\mathbf{A}_i : F(h_{U_i}) \neq 0 \bmod p, \ , \mathbf{B}^* : F(h_{U^*}) = 0 \bmod p$$

Then, the probability of $\mathcal{B}$ not aborting is

$$\Pr[\text{not abort}] \geq \Pr[(\textstyle\bigwedge_{i=1}^{q_s+q_d} A_i) \bigwedge B^*]$$

Note that the evens $(\bigwedge_{i=1}^{q_s+q_d} A_i)$ and B^* are independent. The assumption $l_u \cdot (n_u + 1) < p$ implies if $F(h_{U_i}) = 0 \bmod p$ then $F(h_{U_i}) = 0 \bmod l_u$. Since k_u, x' and $x_1, \cdots, x_{n_u}$ are randomly chosen.

$$Pr[A_i] = 1 - Pr[\neg A_i] = 1 - (Pr[F(h_{U_i}) = 0 \bmod p \wedge F(h_{U_i}) = 0 \bmod l_u])$$
$$= 1 - Pr[F(h_{U_i}) = 0 \bmod l_u] Pr[F(h_{U_i}) = 0 \bmod p | F(h_{U_i}) \bmod l_u]$$
$$= 1 - \frac{1}{l_u \cdot (n_u + 1)}$$

In the same way, we can obtain $Pr[B^*] = \frac{1}{l_u} \frac{1}{n_u+1}$

Since the evens A_i and B^* are independent for any i, we have

$$Pr[\bigwedge_{i=1}^{q_s+q_d} A_i \bigwedge B^*] = Pr[B^*] Pr[\bigwedge_{i=1}^{q_s+q_d} A_i | B^*] = Pr[B^*] Pr[1 - \bigvee_{i=1}^{q_s+q_d} \overline{A_i} | B^*]$$

$$\geq Pr[B^*] Pr[1 - \sum_{i=1}^{q_s+q_d} Pr[\overline{A_i} | B^*] = \frac{1}{l_u \cdot (n_u + 1)} (1 - \frac{q_s + q_d}{l_u \cdot n_u})$$

Thus, we can obtain

$$Pr[\text{not aborting}] \geq (\frac{1}{l_u \cdot (n_u + 1)})(1 - \frac{q_s + q_d}{l_u \cdot n_u})$$

If the simulation does not abort, $\mathcal{A}_{II}$ will produce a forged signature with probability at least ϵ. Thus, $\mathcal{B}$ can solve for the CDH problem instance with probability $\epsilon' \geq \frac{\epsilon}{l_u \cdot (n_u+1)}(1 - \frac{q_s+q_d}{l_u \cdot n_u})$.

Theorem 2. *If there exists a type III adversary $\mathcal{A}_{III}$ can (t, q_s, ε) breaks the proposed proxy signature scheme with multi-warrant, then there exists an algorithm $\mathcal{B}$ which is able to use $\mathcal{A}_{III}$ to solve an instance of the CDH problem in $\mathcal{G}_1$ with a non-negligible probability.*

Proof. It is similar to the proof of Theorem 1. Due to the limited space, we omit it here.

Efficiency Analysis: Here, we compare our scheme with Huang *et.al*'s scheme [7] in terms of signature size and operation cost of verification. Because Huang *et.al*'s scheme is not a proxy signature with multi-warrant. To fairly compare, we replace warrant with a warrant-list $W = (A_1, \cdots, A_n)$ in the Huang *et.al*'s scheme. In the following table, the notion $|\mathbb{G}_1|$ denotes the bit length of an element in $\mathbb{G}_1$, Let P_m be scalar multiplication on the curve, e be pairings computation. According to the above table, proxy signature in our scheme has the advantages over ones of *Huang et.al*'s scheme in terms of the sizes of public key of original signer and proxy signer, and the size of proxy signature.

Table 1. Comparison of our proposed scheme with Huang $et.al$ scheme

Scheme	R.O	Size	Verification	Generations	Size of PK
Huang $et.al$'s scheme	NO	$3|\mathbb{G}_1| + n|p|$	$5e + nP_m$	$(n+5)P_m$	$2|\mathbb{G}_1|$
Our scheme	NO	$5|\mathbb{G}_1| + |p|$	$6e + nP_m$	$(n/2+5)P_m$	$|\mathbb{G}_1|$

5 Conclusion

In this paper, we extend the general proxy signature notion into proxy signature scheme with multi-warrant. This extension is not a trivial extension, it makes that the size of extended proxy signature is approximate one of original proxy signature. And the size of the extended proxy signature is constant and is independent of warrant's number. The scheme is proven secure in the standard model and the security of the scheme is related to the computational Diffie-Hellman Assumption.

Acknowledgement

This work is supported by Natural Science Foundation of China (NO:60703044), the New Star Plan Project of Beijing Science and Technology (NO:2007B001), the PHR, Program for New Century Excellent Talents in University(NCET-06-188), The Beijing Natural Science Foundation Programm and Scientific Research Key Program of Beijing Municipal Commission of Education (NO:KZ2008 10009005) and 973 Program (No:2007CB310700).

References

1. Mambo, M., Usuda, K., Okamot, E.: Proxy signature: delegation of the power to sign messages. IEICE Trans. Fundamentals E79-A(9), 1338–1353 (1996)
2. Xu, J., Zhang, Z., Feng, D.: ID-Based Proxy Signature Using Bilinear Pairings. In: COLT 2005. LNCS, vol. 3559, pp. 359–367. Springer, Heidelberg (2005)
3. Zhang, F., Kim, K.: Efficient ID-based blind signature and proxy signature from pairings. In: Safavi-Naini, R., Seberry, J. (eds.) ACISP 2003. LNCS, vol. 2727, pp. 312–323. Springer, Heidelberg (2003)
4. Zhang, F., Safavi-Naini, R., Susilo, W.: An efficient signature scheme from bilinear pairings and its application. In: Bao, F., Deng, R., Zhou, J. (eds.) PKC 2004. LNCS, vol. 2947, pp. 277–290. Springer, Heidelberg (2004)
5. Shim, K.-A.: An Identity-based Proxy Signature Scheme from Pairings. In: Ning, P., Qing, S., Li, N. (eds.) ICICS 2006. LNCS, vol. 4307, pp. 60–71. Springer, Heidelberg (2006)
6. Boldyreva, A., Palacio, A., Warinschi, B.: Secure proxy signature scheme for delegation of signing rights. IACR ePrint Archive, http://eprint.iacr.org/2003/096
7. Huang, X., Susilo, W., Mu, Y., Wu, W.: Proxy Signature without Random Oracles. In: Cao, J., Stojmenovic, I., Jia, X., Das, S.K. (eds.) MSN 2006. LNCS, vol. 4325, pp. 473–484. Springer, Heidelberg (2006)

8. Wu, W., Mu, Y., Susilo, W., Seberry, J., Huang, X.: Identity-based Proxy Signature from Pairings. In: Xiao, B., Yang, L.T., Ma, J., Muller-Schloer, C., Hua, Y. (eds.) ATC 2007. LNCS, vol. 4610, pp. 22–31. Springer, Heidelberg (2007)
9. Goldwasser, S., Micali, S., Rivest, R.: A digital signature scheme secure against adaptively chosen message attacks. SIAM Journal on Computing 17(2), 281–308
10. Park, H.-U., Lee, I.-Y.: A Digital nominative proxy signature scheme for mobile communications. In: Qing, S., Okamoto, T., Zhou, J. (eds.) ICICS 2001. LNCS, vol. 2229, pp. 451–455. Springer, Heidelberg (2001)

Author Index